Chem-Free Sobriety

101 Trailblazers share wisdom and insight about their natural recovery from substance use disorders

Suzanne L. Thistle, MA, MLADC

DEDICATION

This book is dedicated to those who lost their lives from a substance use disorder and to those who still struggle.

In their honor, five percent of all net sales will go to abstinence-based recovery in New Hampshire.

CONTENTS

ACKNOWLEDGMENTS

First and foremost, I have to give the honor and the glory to God for planting the seed in me to write and continually nudging me to bring this book to fruition.

My heart is filled with gratitude for the participants in this book. They have shared their innermost thoughts and have agreed to let the world hear about their journey. I know their experience will help you and others.

I also believe no dream is complete without the help of others: family, friends, and professional associates. I am blessed to have wonderful people in my life who teach and guide me in the right direction. Without you, I would never have been able to reach the peaks I have and could not share this wisdom.

A special thanks to my partner and best friend, Phil Rollins, for your support throughout this project and for always patiently listening.

Preface

My professional team and I spent many nights emotionally exhausted as we worked to get people into residential care, and sometimes we just couldn't. At the end of their use, clients were couch-surfing and using whatever they could to keep the high going, even if it meant using a dirty needle. If they left our agency and were unable to get into a treatment center, they could die. The deficiency in financial assistance profoundly affected our team as well as others in the profession. I remember sitting with a funding source one day and starting to cry over the lack of resources. I apologized for my emotions, and the woman said, "Don't apologize. The last person I spoke to cried, too." Everyone deserves addiction treatment, regardless of their ability to pay.

As time progresses, the rise in clients addicted to prescribed medications increases. Medication is now the "gold standard" of care for treating opiate addiction. Fewer and fewer people talk about abstinence-based recovery. They talk about recovery now as something you can have even if you are using addictive drugs. Medication-assisted treatment facilities are popping up everywhere, and some keep people hooked on medicine.

A few years ago, a medical doctor said, "Because drug addiction is a chronic illness, clients need to be on medication for life." I feel as if I'm in the twilight zone. Are people not supposed to think and feel like humans anymore? What is happening? Doctors proclaim the use of opiates after abstinence to be associated with a high overdose death rate because of a loss of tolerance or misjudgment of safe amounts. Does this infer you have to stay on an opiate medication to avoid overdose?

Was I alone in thinking medication was not the "gold standard" others may have people believe? I felt driven to prove that the response to the addiction crisis wouldn't be found solely in medicine or the medical profession. After all, the medical and pharmaceutical businesses are part of what caused the addiction crisis in the first place. It is important to note that I don't believe all doctors, medication, or those who work in the pharmaceutical industry are unethical, and my opinions are mine, not those of the participants in this book. Their stories speak for themselves.

Medicine isn't the answer to this crisis. Though it may be needed for some, it is not for most. People struggling with a substance use disorder (SUD) need to know there is another way to recover. They need support in their decision to accept abstinence-based treatment and all the tools necessary to achieve continuous recovery without medication.

There are folks all over the world who have spent decades not using any medication to solve their SUD. Their voices have remained silent until now. My quest to validate abstinence-based recovery started by interviewing over one hundred people in New Hampshire. This book reveals what people behind the scenes want you to know. Their reasons for staying quiet are not limited to stigma, although this is a reason for many. Some people face the reality of their boss finding out they have a SUD and being looked at differently. Some remain anonymous because they want to live a humble life without standing at a podium and telling their story. However, they were all willing to share their stories in the hope that they will help others with a SUD.

Requirements for participants in these interviews included not partaking in addictive medications. The ones that are often abused and lead people back to active drug use include benzodiazepines, opiates, stimulants, or the like. Addictive medications can be a slippery slope back to active drug use. Many people in recovery relapse after taking them, even if for a short time.

Participants' ages range from their early 20s to their late 80s. They live in all parts of New Hampshire on a full or part-time basis. They all responded to the same interview questions, and their sobriety dates range from one year to over 40 years. They are from diverse socioeconomic and career backgrounds. Those included were business owners, general citizens, authors, government officials, medical professionals, educators, spiritual leaders, military personnel, artists and others from all walks of life. The stories are listed in the book alphabetically by first name and not by any other means.

The passion behind bringing you a glimpse of why abstinence-based recovery is the real "Gold Standard" began in 1987 when I stopped using all addictive drugs. The need to understand my obsession with using drugs and free myself from its grip became paramount in my life. I switched from a preoccupation with using drugs to a fixation on educating myself about addiction. Reading extensively about addiction and holistic healing ensued. I began to write papers about addiction and presented facts about it at wellness fairs and other community forums, all the while experiencing an inner desire to write a book about this topic.

The authors who wrote all the books I read about in the addiction profession had a master's or a doctorate. I figured I should have a degree, too, so I went to graduate school and obtained a master's degree in psychology with a substance abuse concentration. While in graduate school, I participated in internships and worked one-on-one with addiction clients. The human connection fascinated me, and it led me to work in the addiction profession for many years. I worked as a therapist and moved up to become a manager, then clinical director, and eventually the executive director at two different facilities. Although I found this work rewarding, that still small voice inside kept telling me to write this book. When the opportunity to write it became a reality, I jumped at the chance. I know it will help people struggling with addiction understand that abstinence is a viable choice and the real "Gold Standard."

Suzanne L. Thistle MA, MLADC

PART 1

Introduction

Medication may not be the answer to your addiction. An abstinence-based recovery could be the right path to take. Recovery is simple: it involves a connection to others, support from people who care, as well as understanding and working through your underlying issues. After I have spent 33 years studying addiction, living a drug-free life, and spending many years working in the SUD profession, it is such a gift to finally share this knowledge with you. Abstinence-based recovery, without the use of addictive medication, needs to be "The Gold Standard."

People who suffer from alcohol or other drug addiction attest to the fact that once they take a sip of alcohol or use an addictive drug, all bets are off. They are not able to guarantee they can stop after just one sip, one toke, or one small line of whatever, so it's best not to drink or use addictive drugs at all. The ability to stop, even though you know you may get hurt in the process, seems insurmountable when you're using chemicals. Alcohol and other drugs make you feel as if everything's okay and create a euphoria, and then you chase that feeling. The need to get and use drugs to support this feeling can be stronger than the love for a family member and even our children.

The disease of addiction is powerful. If you want to live a drug-free life, this book emphasizes getting the help you need. You no longer have to feel as if you are lost in the woods without the ability to find your way out. If 101 people from a tiny state like New Hampshire tell you they stopped using alcohol or other drugs and haven't found it necessary to pick up a drink or a drug since they made this decision, you can do it too. This type of recovery is not easy in the beginning, but it gets easier over time.

This book is a compilation of knowledge gained from my experience as a clinician, middle manager, senior administrator and a person in abstinence-based recovery, combined with the experience of over 101 people who are also in abstinence-based recovery. If you have medical complications, please check with your primary care doctor before making a change in your mental or physical health. Bring this book to your next appointment and share it with your provider. It will benefit your doctor to understand the path you are on in your recovery.

In the first section, you will read about how to use this book. The middle section provides 101 stories of hope, and the last section is a collection of advocacy points noted by the participants. You'll read how each participant's addiction progressed, their path to recovery, how they don't drink or use daily, their thoughts about medication-assisted treatment, what they want you to know, and their information for decision-makers. Please read the information for decision-makers at the end of the book. Lawmakers and other decision-makers need to hear from people in recovery. Offer this book to anyone you think can make a difference.

Take charge of your sobriety and plan to help others achieve it as well. If you like what you read, purchase at least one copy of this book for someone. If you can afford it, buy a case of books for a jail, treatment center, or community resource center. Help this message reach those in other parts of the world by sending a copy to someone who lives in another country and tell them to pay it forward. Let's spread the word internationally. We are a tribe that helps each other live naturally and without addictive drugs.

If you've picked up this book, you've made progress. If you decided not to drink or use today, this is significant. You may have wanted to stop in the past and didn't think you could. You may find a new path if you follow some of the suggestions in this book. Don't hesitate to get started in your sobriety. Read at least one participant's story daily and go to a support meeting every day for the next 90 days, and the chances of living a drug-free life can increase substantially. Each participant's story offers you a little nugget of wisdom and hope.

Entering the Trailhead

Have you ever drunk so much you blacked out or stuck a needle in your arm to get high even after you told yourself you would never stoop that low? Does it always seem as if you are trying to climb to the top of a steep mountain and there is a massive mountain lion chasing you back down? Do you feel that, if you don't turn around and run, you'll be devoured? It's time to stop the madness. You can climb many mountains. Your future is spotless. You design your destiny with the help of others. There are factors you need to know about, which are provided in this book.

In today's world, recovery does not mean the same thing as it did before we had an addiction crisis. In the past, recovery meant you were not using any addictive medication or drugs, including alcohol. This is because it is so hard for someone in recovery to take an addictive medication and not get hooked on it, get hooked on another drug, or go back to their drug of choice.

Some doctors are now saying, if after some time of abstinence, you go back to drug use, you can die. They report that you don't realize your tolerance level goes down, so you use more than your body can manage and overdose. I know it seems as if all odds are against you when you hear you will relapse and die if you don't take medication to manage your addiction. If you follow this logic, you infer you must be on medication for life. However, in this book you will find out how others manage their addiction recovery without medication.

Many people suffering with a SUD will go to a medical doctor and get diagnosed with attention deficit hyperactivity disorder (ADHD), post-traumatic stress disorder (PTSD), depression, anxiety, panic disorder, insomnia, borderline personality disorder, anti-social personality disorder, and the like. These disorders can and do get treated in natural ways without addictive medication. Some naturopathic doctors accept insurance and can assist you. Also, try seeking addiction treatment with a therapist who specializes in SUD's. SUD treatment is NOT the same as general therapy.

Controlling addiction and living a healthy life can be challenging. For many, it is best to leave addictive drugs alone. I don't know if we will ever have a fool-proof solution to alcohol or other drug addiction, but we already have one that works: abstinence. You will find how to obtain abstinence-based recovery in the contents of this book.

Each participant represents countless others in their community who live without addictive medications or alcohol. Healing from addiction is an inside job. Experience the hope you glean from the stories in this book, from those who have blazed the trail for you. Let their stories help you through the good and the tough times.

You are not alone.

Relying on a Compass for Direction

It is important to bring a compass and read about the trail whenever you head up one of New Hampshire's 48 4,000-foot mountains. Climbing can be tricky, and there are some dangers to climbing without the direction of a compass or the knowledge of how to scale the mountain. Hikers may fall while traversing treacherous grounds on their pursuit. Although blazed trails provide you with guidance, having a compass and knowledge of what is ahead is the safest policy.

As I thought about how to write about addiction recovery, I thought about how similar it is to the much-loved activity of hiking mountain trails. Recovery can also be tricky, even dangerous. The good news is thousands of people have already blazed the trail for you. They have hit rocky situations, fallen, and gotten back up.

Achieving lasting sobriety can resemble a strenuous hike up a 4,000-foot mountain. You need to take great care where you place your feet. Sometimes it seems as if you will never reach the summit, and you will want to give up. Those of us who have climbed a 4,000-foot mountain can honestly say we feel a sense of accomplishment upon reaching the summit. Basking in the amazing views, once you are at the top, you don't regret the intense exertion it took to get there.

Some of you will get and stay sober, and it will seem flawless. However, a smooth transition is not the norm. Detoxing from opiates or other drugs can be excruciating. The good news is that the old news is right. You don't need to go it alone or take a different path. Use this as your recovery handbook, your trail guide. It doesn't matter how old you are, what type of job you have, or whether you are financially secure. People can and do recover naturally.

When planning to hike a 4,000-foot mountain, you need to prepare. Plenty of hikers get lost in the woods, some are helicoptered out, and some perish. Read about the mountain you want to climb, figure out the best route, and prepare your pack correctly before you head up. Like preparing for an ascent, sobriety takes preparation, planning, and time. You need to plan each day around what you are going to do for your sobriety. You are worth it.

Work your recovery program diligently. Prioritize it over anything else. The first 90 days of recovery is when you are most vulnerable to relapse. This is why you will hear people say, "You need to go to 90 meetings in 90 days," when you first get sober. Your brain is learning to function without toxins and to survive without a chemical to soothe it.

Packing for a hike is tricky, and it's easy to overpack. You can fill your pack with things for the walk up, stuff to do at the top, tools for descending, and all the "what ifs." An overweight pack can slow you down and cause you to stumble. Your early recovery is comparable. You can fill your days with overworking, over-scheduling activities, and forget that you need time for your recovery. Put yourself first and give yourself time and space. If you don't have you, you don't have anything.

Set up a time to meet with an addiction counselor now or meet with someone currently in recovery to discuss becoming substance-free. There are many levels of treatment. It will help to find out what level of care you need: detoxification, residential, intensive outpatient, partial hospitalization, or another. Find a therapist trained to evaluate you and give you the proper assessment.

Start following some of the simple suggestions in this book. This book does not provide medical advice. The folks who offer their advice have gone through many trials before giving up their drug of choice to find peace. Use their stories as a compass to help you find the freedom you seek.

PART 2

Meet the Trailblazers

Date of interview: 6/10/19
Sobriety date: 3/29/87, 32 years
Hometown: Undisclosed

When did you start drinking or using drugs, and how did it progress?

My parents were both 16 when they married. They were young and innocent, with little knowledge of what they were beginning to embark on. They had my brother and sister immediately, within a year and a half of each other. Then they had me and my other siblings, my brother and a set of twins. All of us are two years apart. Although we were a large family, we were happy.

However, my father's drinking slowly progressed throughout my early childhood. My mother rarely drank but endured a lot as a result of my father's drinking. When I was six, they divorced. My father moved out, and my mother was left with all six kids. Little by little, most of us moved in with him. Just as my alcoholism took off, he got sober.

While I was living with my mother and 10 years old, I had my first drink of alcohol. A neighbor took a beer from his parents' refrigerator, and a few of us drank it together. We all drank out of curiosity more than needing to drink. However, when I was 12, I started drinking and getting drunk. I experienced a traumatic event at that age, mostly out of my parents' naïveté and lack of supervision. The alcohol took away all the negative feelings associated with the trauma. I started to drink regularly, got into trouble, and eventually was sent to live in New Hampshire with my father. In New Hampshire, the kids did not drink and do drugs the way that I did. I went to a small rural school and was able to stop, but when I reached high school, I took it up again.

By the time I was 16, I was a full-blown alcoholic, smoking pot, and taking other drugs. I controlled it well for some time. I made it through high school, but barely. When my grades would slide, I would work hard and pull them up. I wanted to graduate from high school; my father, mother, older sister and brother never had. I felt an internal need to carry the banner for the family.

I left New Hampshire and graduated from high school, a technical school majoring in business. After high school, I went to a community college, again majoring in business, and was achieving good grades. However, my first class was at eight o'clock in the morning. Having a class this early in the morning got in the way of my drinking and drug use, so I quit.

My need to party was more important than anything else. I had numerous odd jobs and vacillated from living in New Hampshire to living in other states, not even having an address anywhere. I don't remember receiving mail. The 10 years I partied excessively were painful. Bad things happened because I wasn't present. I did not know that alcohol and drugs were the reason for what was happening. I didn't think I could stop, or how.

And then one day, I met a man at a bar, got pregnant that night, and married him a few months later. I had always wanted a child, and when she was born, I fell in love with her. I remember thinking after I saw her, "This is what love truly is." I couldn't drink the same way again because I felt a tremendous amount of guilt when I did. Then one day, after an awful night of using cocaine so much that my nose was bleeding and I kept using anyway, I was sitting in the common in Plymouth, New Hampshire contemplating suicide. I didn't want to live but didn't want to die and not be with my daughter. It was such a horrible feeling.

A friend came up to me and told me she was going to Narcotics Anonymous (NA), and asked me if I wanted to go with her. At first, I couldn't believe she was admitting to going, as if I were the example of good behavior. She asked me if I wanted to go, and I went the following Wednesday. Shortly after that, I realized I also couldn't drink or take any other addictive drugs. Knowing this is why I decided to stop all drugs.

To say I was full of anxiety would be an understatement. I couldn't even go into a restaurant with friends because I was so full of fear and would have a panic attack every time, so I would have to leave. I went to the hospital a few times with panic attack episodes, only to be released with advice. I did not want to be on medication. I knew my way of dealing with medication was "more is better."

The first few years of sobriety consisted of me learning how not to be angry, depressed, or anxious. I read a lot of books, talked to my sponsor daily, and practiced the 12 Steps of Alcoholics Anonymous (AA). I decided to go to AA instead of NA because I saw more people in AA with many years of sobriety. I wanted what they had. They were living incredible lives and were happy.

Life has been an incredible sober journey. I sought out counseling for my trauma in early sobriety and went for many years. I went back to school and graduated with a bachelor's degree, on the Dean's list. Then I went on to get a master's degree and achieved high grades. I was married for 20 years to my second child's father and went through a painful divorce. I've had people close to me die, experienced major medical problems where I almost died a couple of times, and many other life events. Through all of this, the 12 Steps and the fellowship of AA helped me not pick up a drink or drug to deal with the emotions.

My life today is better than I could have ever imagined.

Looking back, when do you think it was mostly out of control?

It started in high school. I was lost, and it got a lot worse after that. The last night of my drug use was the worst time ever.

How are you able to not drink or use daily?

I pray and meditate almost every day. I read the *Bible*, *Twenty-Four Hours a Day* book from Hazelden, and *The Utmost for His Highest* by Oswald Chambers. I also have read extensively about spirituality, quantum physics, and aligning with my soul's purpose.

What is your thought about medication-assisted treatment?

I genuinely believe addictive medication is not needed to achieve sobriety. I know hundreds of people who never had to use addictive medication to achieve sobriety or improve their mental health. I do not condemn anyone who does and only wish them the best life can offer.

Is there anything you want those struggling with addiction to know?

Having been to the depths of hell and back can teach people a lot about life. Know that when you reach out and talk with someone who has been there, they have your back. We help you not use. You can only guess what life will be like when you are no longer held in bondage by your substance. Sobriety is better than you can imagine. Having others in your life is essential. Reach out.

Anonymous II

Date of interview: 6/8 & 6/12/19
Sobriety date: 4/3/18, 1 year
Hometown: Undisclosed

When did you start drinking or using drugs, and how did it progress?

The first time I tried alcohol, I was 17. I took it from my parents' liquor cabinet. I drank a few sips and wound up passing out for three hours. I only drank a few more times in high school. My upbringing was pretty normal. My parents are still together and are extremely high functioning. I was a good athlete and excelled in school. In my house, we did not acknowledge emotion. We were taught to suppress our feelings. By age eight, I was running compulsively for exercise, before school. Looking back, I realize I exercised obsessively to avoid feeling negative emotions. Exercise was the first "addictive" behavior I used to cope with my growing internal turmoil.

I applied to a variety of schools and was accepted by Ivy League universities, which offered me athletic scholarships, but I chose to go to a large public college instead. I joined a fraternity in my first quarter and became an EMT, working on a 911 ambulance. I partied a little bit but never really bought into it. I was only drunk a few times. My passion for emergency medicine, coupled with my desire to continue my education, led me to apply to medical school.

The first year of medical school was rough. I was anxious and obsessive. I started to go on and off my depression medication. I drank some, but soon, women became my drug of choice. Now that I look back, using women, exercise, and substances excessively were 100 percent because of a lack of coping mechanisms, an inability to process negative emotions. By my fourth year of medical school, I was a binge drinker. I got into one of the best medical residencies in the US and trained as an emergency room doctor. I was living with two other doctors; one of them introduced me to "hard drugs" such as cocaine and Ecstasy.

It was around this time that I met my wife, and we had our daughter. We were not ready to be parents. I believed I would quit drinking and doing drugs if I got married. I thought having a child would fill the void inside of me. We stopped using for a while and ate healthy food. But my obsession with drugs and alcohol resurfaced. I was so excited the night our daughter was born that I got drunk. That is sickening for me to say.

By age 31, I was addicted to opiates. It started with a medical emergency with my brain. My doctor prescribed me an insane number of opiates for my chronic headaches. It wasn't long before I knew I had a problem. I went to my parents' house to sweat out the withdrawals and see a world-renowned addiction doctor. He had a "solution" to my opiate abuse: Suboxone. I became addicted to Suboxone. He mentioned 12-step recovery to me, but I never attended a meeting. I thought Suboxone was a reasonable "treatment" for my addiction to opiates. I spent the next three years of my life using and abusing this drug. I still drank alcohol and took benzodiazepines for my anxiety.

After graduating from residency, I had a few more location and job changes, and eventually wound up working in my hometown. My wife and I were separated, and I started dating many of my female coworkers. Women became a problem again. Drinking was already a problem, and drug use not far behind. I was giving my wife extra money to take care of our daughter because I rarely saw her. I was too self-absorbed to see the pain I was causing this beautiful little girl.

By 2014, I was off the Suboxone, but my perceived "sobriety" was short-lived. I found a local drug dealer that kept me in a good supply of opiates and also periodically brought me cocaine. I was still on eight other prescription medications for all my other "symptoms." I abused them all. Whenever I wasn't working, I was using. My house was a mess, and I hadn't opened my mail for months.

One night, I made phone calls to my brother in a blackout. That night I overdosed on all my medications, hoping to die. I woke up in my first rehab and was put on Suboxone again as well as a variety of other medications. I finished the program, relapsed a few days later, and wound up heading to rehab in Southeast Asia. I brought all my medications with me on the plane. I was a master manipulator. I don't remember the flight, thanks to the benzodiazepines, and only stayed a month, leaving with a girl I met there.

Over the next four weeks, I lost 35 pounds. I was a shadow of a man, and my family thought I was dead. I was using a wide variety of drugs. I lost my passport and my belongings, and I wound up homeless on the streets for a few days, living outside a Buddhist monastery. Eventually, I was back in rehab for six months. When I got back home, I relapsed on alcohol with my brother the first day I saw my daughter. Disgusting. I went to a few 12-step meetings but did not get properly introduced to the steps.

In 2015, I took a job on the East Coast. I was using benzodiazepines for my back pain. I found Kratom too, an opiate-like herb you can purchase over the counter. I was struggling and suffering in silence. The obsession with using drugs and the phenomenon of craving was very active in me, so I went to see a psychiatrist. I manipulated her into prescribing me Ritalin; it's like doing cocaine. I would use a 30-day supply in five days. This went on for almost a year. I had started drinking alcohol again and got a DUI.

In the spring of 2018, I went to the Bahamas for a vacation, started drinking on the flight, and woke up in the ICU. I was in a blackout for almost the entire seven-day trip and made some blackout calls to my boss. I could have died. I had suffered for years and nobody knew. From the Bahamas, I went straight to a renowned medical institution, with a lot of support from the Physician Monitoring Program.

Next, I went to a world-famous rehab in the Midwest, which detoxed me off of everything. April 3rd, 2018, at 11 a.m., I took my last mind-altering substance. When I got back home, I went to a 12-step residential retreat center for three weeks and then on to sober living. Because of the work I did in rehab, I became willing to do anything not to use substances. I gave up the fight. I finally felt relieved of this burden.

Today, I am recovered from all addictions, and have chosen not to take my will back. I can be present with my daughter. Her mother is not in the picture, so I am raising her with the help of a fantastic family that has been there for me along the way. I have an opportunity to show her how to deal with unsettling emotions, the same emotions that led me to over-exercise, use women, and eventually become a full-blown drug addict and alcoholic. My daughter gets to have a father that she can count on to show up for her. I am also thriving in my medical practice and have renewed my passion for the art of medicine. Recovery is a phenomenal process. I have expanded my emotional capacity and no longer feel the need to suppress emotions anymore. I am free!

Looking back, when do you think it was mostly out of control?

March 2014, right before my suicide attempt. When I wasn't working, I was abusing Oxycodone, benzodiazepines, cocaine, and drinking moderately. Life was completely unmanageable, and I didn't want to live anymore. March 2018 is a close second.

How are you able to not drink or use daily?

My day starts by getting on my knees and praying, "God, please help me be the most beneficial to your people today." If it is before work, I ask to have the knowledge, thoughts, and action to serve God's patients today. I choose to be selfless. I use guided meditations, breathing exercises, and meditation music every day. It allows me a reprieve from my cluttered brain. I accept that I cannot control others and can only control my actions. I call my sponsor, do inventory, and talk to friends in recovery. We go to meetings, hike, and eat breakfast together on a routine basis. I plan sober activities with friends. We talk about actionable things that will keep us sober.

In addition to the 12 Steps, I engage in a variety of cognitive programs in search of a better understanding of what makes me, me. By doing this type of "mind" work, I have become more self-aware, and this awareness allows me to walk through emotional distress and not have any desire to use a substance. I truly have recovered from the desire to drink or take drugs.

What is your thought about medication-assisted treatment?

There is no prescription medication for someone to recover from addiction that will compare to the spiritual part of the 12-step program. The same goes for Suboxone, Vivitrol, or methadone. I was on Suboxone for three years, and I work with addiction every day in the emergency room. Suboxone is a crutch. You can't treat opiate addiction with an opiate. Medication-Assisted Treatment (MAT) therapy is harm reduction. If it is used to keep a person alive until they find an abstinence-based solution, then I am for it. That being said, all MAT programs should have constant and direct exposure to abstinence-based recovery and not pretend that MAT in itself is "recovery."

Is there anything you want those struggling with addiction to know?

Do the work on the front end to transform your future. Relapse is founded in complacency. Living an honest and selfless life will keep you sober. The 12 Steps are the prescription pill. However, it doesn't come in a pill form. It comes as a gut-wrenching, soul-searching, rigorous inventory that all human beings should have the opportunity to do.

Anonymous III

Date of interview: 3/22/19
Sobriety date: 3/20/98, 21 years
Hometown: Northfield

When did you start drinking or using drugs, and how did it progress?

At age 12, I made a mixed drink for me and my best friend. We got the alcohol from my father's liquor cabinet, and I blacked out that night. I began seeking opportunities to drink. I had three older siblings get married in the same year, so there were many celebrations and a lot of alcohol.

At 15, I began smoking pot and using cocaine. I was attracted to cocaine and did not seek out pot. I also began using speed: 20/20s and black beauties. By the age of 16, I left home and moved in with an older sister and began going to bars and drinking more. My father made wine in the basement of our home, there was always alcohol. We also had a refrigerator with a half keg of beer in the basement, so drinking was easy.

When I was 15, I started seeing a man who later became my husband. We went to a very large high school and were both popular. We got married right after high school and had two children together. We were married for five years and legally separated three out of those five. I was a single mother of two by the age of 25.

Sadly, I stayed with my ex-husband off and on for the next five years. It was a very violent relationship, and I didn't fight back until after we were divorced. He broke my finger when I was 17. The violence and control progressed from there. Before having children, we went to keg parties all the time and went to New York to drink because the bars stayed open later. One night, he beat me in front of our two children; they were seven and nine. He was on top of me, punching me in the face. I was able to get away from him by breaking his glasses. After this last fight, I reached out to my oldest brother and he offered to bring me and my children to New Hampshire. I knew if I had stayed near my ex-husband, he would have killed me.

We were in New Hampshire for three months when I had a stroke. My son called the ambulance, and I was taken to Concord Hospital. I was put on nine different medications, 23 pills a day. The doctors informed me the stroke was caused from the fight with my ex. I left the hospital against medical advice because I felt I needed to take care of my children. I went home, lit up a cigarette and had a glass of wine.

People from our town offered to pick things up from the store for me. On every shopping list was cigarettes and wine. I was not able to read, write, or walk for some time. I wasn't able to help my children with their schoolwork. I'd repeat myself constantly. I couldn't work for eight months, and my ex was not paying child support or providing medical insurance for our children. He was, however, making good money.

Six months into my medical recovery, a friend contacted me and asked if I wanted to go to the Cape for the weekend as a birthday gift. I had known this person for 20 years and trusted him with my life, until that weekend. He raped me. This is when everything changed. I no longer waited for my children to go to bed at night to drink. I didn't take pills as prescribed. I wasn't sure what pills I was taking and when. I would just take some after drinking and go to bed.

Eventually, I got involved with a married man and he ended the relationship abruptly. The night he ended the relationship, my children were at their friend's house and I was home alone drinking. I dumped all my meds on the table, mixed them up, took a handful, swallowed them, and then laid down to die. I woke a couple of days later in the hospital and was told I had died and had had to be resuscitated. I had been in a coma. My family came, took my children, and brought them to their father's. I was in the hospital for two weeks. While at the hospital, someone came and talked to me about Fresh Start, a program to help people with alcohol or drug problems. I politely told them, "I do not have a problem, but thank you anyway." I did not know what I did not know.

When I left the hospital, I was evicted from my apartment. I moved to Franklin, alone. A couple of months later, my children came back to live with me. One night, I got a sitter and went to a party at a friend's house. I walked in with a bottle of tequila, a four pack of B-52's, and a case of beer. The last thing I remember that night was drinking out of the bottle of tequila.

The next day I woke up in my apartment in Franklin with my children and asked them how we got there. My son said, "You picked us up at the babysitter's last night. Don't you remember?" At that moment, I walked into my bedroom, fell to the floor, and said to myself, "Oh my God, I'm an alcoholic." I called the AA hotline and found out there was an AA meeting that day, but that was too soon. I went a couple of days later.

I went to a Living Sober meeting and sat in the seat closest to the door. I followed along with what they were doing even though I knew nothing about AA. The woman speaking that night had three months of sobriety, and I was in shock that anyone could go that length of time without a substance. There were three other women there. The rest were men, old enough to be my father. I met a man named Larry. One of the things he said to me was, "You never have to feel this way again." I got a 24-hour chip and didn't know what it was. Larry told me to come to 90 meetings in 90 days. He also pointed his finger at my chest and said, "But I don't think you can do it."

Great, another guy telling me what I could and couldn't do. I had to prove him wrong, so I did. In this meeting, they told me only one out of every 30 people make it. It's jails, institutions, death, or sobriety. I thought to myself, "I'm staying." Out of the three women at that first meeting, one died, one went back to drinking, and one went to prison for selling drugs to someone who died. I was six months sober before I met my sponsor. Up until this point, I hung around Larry and another old timer named Al. They truly saved my life.

I hope my story helps at least one person. I am forever grateful for finding the halls of Alcoholics Anonymous.

Looking back, when do you think it was mostly out of control?

After I was raped, without a doubt. Hands down. I was always able to take care of my children and my husband. After being raped, I just drank.

How are you able to not drink or use daily?

Coming into AA and changing my life. I don't have the desire to drink anymore. I just don't have that obsession. I go to three meetings a week. I stay connected to AA and have an everyday connection with my higher power.

What is your thought about medication-assisted treatment?

When I first got sober, I was on all kinds of medications. I told my doctor everything, but he did not know I was an alcoholic. I take one medication today because of the stroke. If programs will help people reduce the medication instead of increasing them, I'm all for it. I hope these programs work with others to help people recover.

Is there anything you want those struggling with addiction to know?

Don't give up on yourself! I am grateful every day that I did not die in my attempt to kill myself. When I tell my story today, I feel as if I am talking about someone I knew, not me. My life is nothing like it was. Recovery is possible and living well is too.

Abraham S.

Date of interview: 6/10/19
Sobriety date: 9/18/17, 1 years
Hometown: Derry

When did you start drinking or using drugs, and how did it progress?

I was 11 years old and drank hard cider, a couple of cans. I walked into the store and bought them. At the time, I lived in Cypress, which is an island in the Mediterranean. There was no regulation on alcohol then. I never got turned down for buying cigarettes or alcohol after age 11. The first time I felt intoxicated, I drank 22 ounces of Woodchuck and loved it. I got sick and threw up but loved the way it made me feel. I drank whenever I would see my friends.

My dad was a pastor, and both of my parents were missionaries on the island; they had started a church there. Not homeschooled, like a lot of the missionary kids were, I made friends outside the tightly-knit church community. The church my parents started had 50 people in it, with only one or two kids my age.

When I turned 14, the year we came back to the States, I started smoking pot and fell in love. It was different than alcohol and had a much stronger intoxication by smoking a little. I smoked daily during my junior year in high school, not all day long though. I almost got kicked out. I went to a Christian school that my parents had also started. They caught me smoking pot at a nursing home, which is where we would go on Fridays to visit older adults as part of an outreach.

I often got in trouble for using drugs. At this point my parents had a clue, but I was very independent. It made monitoring me difficult. They had some personal things going on, so I wasn't their number one priority. Once I got my driver's license, I started becoming more involved in the drug-using lifestyle. As a young sophomore in high school I started using cocaine. I got involved with older people who introduced me to the business of drugs, selling drugs, and committing petty crimes. I adapted to the environment quickly.

By the time I was 16, I was using cocaine four times a week, smoking pot, and drinking. At 17, I was using daily and got arrested for aggravated burglary. I went downhill quickly from there. My parents kicked me out, and I went to live with my brother, paid rent, and lived my own life.

After high school, I decided to go to a Christian college in Pennsylvania and wound up getting in trouble there because of drugs. I made trips back and forth to Kansas to bring the pot to Pennsylvania and dropped out after one semester. I didn't go to class and didn't do much of anything anyway. I smoked weed, laid around, and used drugs.

In 2007, I switched from cocaine to methamphetamine. I moved to Houston, Texas, and worked as a pest control guy. I had success even though I was using meth. For the first 10 years, I was pretty functional. I held down a job and got promotions, but all the while, I was engaged in criminal activity. Eventually, I started using meth intravenously.

I moved back to Kansas in 2014 and started my own pest control business, which was successful for a short time. I gave the company up for drugs and the lifestyle. I stopped answering the phone when customers called and was in a dark place emotionally. I had a bad breakup from a girlfriend and just pressed the "f-it" button.

For years, my IV drug use caused me to have psychosis. Everything didn't fall apart right away. It would have been better if it had because then I wouldn't have been able to go on using as long as I had. There were times when I was an absolute lunatic wandering around on the streets with no shoes. I got arrested more times in two years than I had ever been detained throughout my whole life. I got locked up, was in and out of jail, violating my probation, and getting sanctions.

My parents decided to bring me up to His Mansion, a Christian alcohol and drug treatment center in New Hampshire. My uncle worked there, and they wanted me to get help. Mostly out of fear, as I was going to have to do a sentence, I agreed to come. The court fought me coming because it was out of state, but at the last second, they allowed me to come. I got in the car with my dad, drove up here, and he dropped me off.

I would love to say life immediately got better, but part of the reason I kept using drugs is because of the mess I made. It was challenging to face up to my past. I have a long way to go, but my life has been redeemed in ways I never thought possible. I'm still dealing with the impact addiction has had on my mind, and the desire to do drugs has not entirely left. I still battle that every day, but I've found reward in a lot of places that I didn't expect. For instance, when I was about four or five months in, somebody was speaking, and I found a lot of hope in what they were saying. I first looked at going to rehab to take a break, get my legal issues in order, get my financial situation in order, and go back to living the way I wanted.

After four or five months, I realized that wasn't an option. For the first time, I saw things clearly, saw the damage I had done to my family and how much they loved me. I saw how unhappy I was and didn't think I would ever be happy again. Now I find myself being filled by the Spirit through a relationship with God. I have always considered myself a Christian, but for the first time, I believe God is happy with the way I'm living. This acceptance means a lot to me. I got too old for the cheap thrills–they're just not worth it.

I'm not on any meds now and don't have psychosis. I took Seroquel for the first six months because I had severe meth psychosis, delusional thinking, as well as auditory and visual hallucinations.

Looking back, when do you think it was mostly out of control?

In 2015, when I was IV Meth using, in and out of jail, selling drugs, psychotic, and living a dark life.

How are you able to not drink or use daily?

I serve the Lord and serve at His Mansion. I know idle hands are the devil's playground. I'm where God wants me to be, and doing His work is keeping me sober. I start the day with a quiet time. Ideally, I read the *Bible*, pray, and reflect on the Word. I pray a lot, worship, and view my interactions as prayer. I invite God into all my situations, interactions, and problems. I keep the line of communication open to Him in every situation and remind myself always to acknowledge His presence. I read science fiction to blow off steam and be entertained. I've also read books by C.S. Lewis and Tim Keller.

What is your thought about medication-assisted treatment?

I don't think opiate medication is a valid treatment. I know people who know which over-the-counter medications help kick their methadone into high gear. They know how to use alcohol in combination with drugs; they know how to sell their Suboxone on the street to buy a gram of coke. It's a bunch of baloney.

Is there anything you want those struggling with addiction to know?

Give sobriety a chance. You might be shocked at what the world has out there for you to experience besides drugs. I was a hippie and thought drugs opened the world to me in a way that nobody else experienced. I thought I had a unique perspective on the world and experienced the world in a more pleasurable way than anybody who wasn't using drugs. This idea brainwashed me. I've come to discover this world is a significant and fantastic place. There are far more wondrous things to experience than drugs and that lifestyle. If you think sobriety is bullcrap after a year and you want to go back to using, what have you lost?

Adam S.

Date of interview: 5/15/19
Sobriety date: 11/25/17, 1 year
Hometown: Manchester

When did you start drinking or using drugs, and how did it progress?

I started drinking when I was 14 years old. My friends and I drank and smoked pot. I came from a very intense and successful family. My parents weren't around much; they worked a ton and traveled a lot. Even when they were gone, there was a lot of pressure from them to succeed. My life was mapped out from the moment I was born.

When I went to college at NYU, I was in a fraternity and felt right at home. I excelled at school and did very well socially, but my drinking was pretty crazy. The day I graduated from college, I enlisted in the US military. I went into the infantry and then special forces. Eventually, I was deployed to Afghanistan and did four tours, two in Iraq and two in Afghanistan. I led my battalion and made the rank of Captain. One day I was hit with an AK-47 on my right shoulder. It ricocheted off a marble column behind me and came out on my left side. It collapsed both my lungs and tore my liver pretty badly. I woke up in a German hospital six weeks later. I was furious when I came to and pulled all the tubes and IVs out. I was mad because I didn't die an honorable death in combat and got sent home. I didn't want to go back home. The military was life for me.

My girlfriend was by my side when I came to, and she was with me when I came home, but what she didn't tell me was she was very sick herself. She had Hodgkin's Lymphoma, and she died six weeks after I came back. I came home a mess and had to watch her go through illness and pass away. I was a train wreck. The Veterans Administration gave me a little green pill that not only would solve all my pain but solve all my mental anguish. It was called OxyContin. They gave me 90 pills a month.

I came home not only to have PTSD from being in combat but also depression from not being in the Army anymore. When my girlfriend died, she was the only person I had, and now she was gone. I spiraled out of control pretty quickly. I went on a tear for a long time. I self-destructed and alienated myself from my family. I didn't speak to them, not one word, for 10 years. For a good chunk of this time, I was a very high functioning addict. I worked for a private firm in Boston and traveled a lot. I was very good at my job but miserable.

The only outlet I had was drugs. It started with pills. Eventually, I discovered heroin and realized it was a lot easier to get. It was also so much more potent, so I started shooting up. I would do it as much as I could, all day long. I stopped working. I turned from this very functioning addict to this absolute train wreck of an addict. Once the job was gone, I had all this time on my hands. I was 30 at this time and came back up here to Manchester.

Things got worse quickly here. I was an absolute train wreck junkie. I was hanging out with people I would have never hung out with if I weren't using drugs. I started getting arrested for possession and stupid things like that. I was living out of a crappy hotel and did every drug under the sun. The police found me outside a hotel, face down at three a.m., and I didn't remember anything. I went to jail and didn't know what had happened for the past four days.

Since I had a bench warrant for missing court, they arrested me. They allowed me to go through Drug Court because I wanted to do something to change my life. I knew I couldn't be this way anymore. I went to Drug Court, graduated last week, and never looked back. Where I am today would not have come about without Drug Court giving me a chance. They provided me with immediate consequences and accountability for my actions.

Looking back, when do you think it was mostly out of control?

The end there, for sure.

How are you able to not drink or use daily?

I'm involved in a program of recovery. I work in the recovery field and help others. I also stay busy, attend meetings, and spend time with family.

What is your thought about medication-assisted treatment?

If it works for someone, who am I to tell them not to try it? I tried methadone and Suboxone, and it didn't work for me. On a fundamental level, it's a mind-altering substance, and I had no growth. I wasn't developing. I was clouded, and it almost stunted me mentally. I have seen it work for others, though.

Is there anything you want those struggling with addiction to know?

Get involved in recovery. Take that step and walk through the door.

Albert L.

Date of interview: 5/30/2019
Sobriety date: 12/4/78, 40 years
Hometown: New Boston

When did you start drinking or using drugs, and how did it progress?

At age nine, I took my first drink with my father. I was brought up in an alcoholic home; both my parents were alcoholics. My father was the designated alcoholic, and my mother would take speed all day and drink at night to come down. Alcohol was always present in my environment.

When my father lost his relationship with his brothers, I became his drinking partner. After a night of drinking with him, I would climb into several beds before I found my own. He made me ginger ale and wine and called it wine coolers. I didn't like being drunk. I didn't like beer at all. He and my mother split up for several years. I would spend Saturday nights with him and drink. Eventually, they got back together again.

I became an altar boy and started drinking wine with a buddy behind the altar. The priest couldn't see us; he was drunk too. Then my oldest sister got married in the late '50s, and I was helping her husband steam the wallpaper at night. I got so thirsty. There was a six-pack of Black Label on the porch. It was the only thing there to drink. I opened one and guzzled it. It was just wonderful. It was the first time I enjoyed alcohol.

At age 15, I was going to Catholic schools. My mother was a fundamentalist Catholic and, at the same time, very violent. She would beat us breathless, sometimes bloody, and even semi-conscious. She was crazy. She hit my sisters in front of me and I developed PTSD from seeing this. I'm still recovering.

From the fourth to the eighth grade, I was a student of Brothers of the Sacred Heart. I suffered significant abuse at their hands. My sisters weren't abused in Catholic schools, but I certainly was. On one occasion, I was kicked across the floor and hit with wooden instruments. After the eighth grade, which was a complete blackout–not due to alcohol, but the loss of my soul–I went to another Catholic high school. By age 17, I started bulking up and thought about hitting back.

Off I went into the '60s with all this trauma in my background. I drank, got stoned, tripped on acid, and did speed. I went from school to school. I ended up having to drop my majors in college, which were literature and history, because I was too stoned to read. I graduated with a degree in art history in 1971. By the time I graduated, I had been through a couple of mad relationships with women.

Our whole generation seemed crazy, although everything seems crazy when you're a drunk. You don't notice the people who aren't doing things the way you are. I was now poly-drug addicted. I was drunk all the time, snorting meth, eating pills, and doing speed. I was down to 130 pounds; my pants were falling off my hips, I was malnourished, teeth rotting, and hair falling out. I staggered through the 1970s.

One of the drinking episodes that stands out to me was at age 25; I tore apart my apartment in a blackout. I broke everything, stabbed pictures, and urinated on the two most important books of my life, *Tao Te Ching* and *Collective Poems* by T. S. Eliot. When I finally sobered up, I realized that when I drink, I piss on the very best part of myself. It may have been a moment of clarity about my addiction because, within a year, I got sober for a month. However, the artist I lived with brought home a 70-dollar bottle of wine for my birthday. I drank it and found out I couldn't stop even though I wanted to. I was dependent on the cellular level. I didn't get sober again for another five years.

My last drink was on December 3,1978. I had nine 12-ounce bottles of Miller High Life, which didn't usually count as a night of drinking for me. That night I drove to Manchester, New Hampshire to a Tuesday night meeting and have not drunk or taken a drug since. I wanted a clear mind to continue my studies. My desire to study and understand poetry became more important than drinking.

Looking back, when do you think it was mostly out of control?

During my undergraduate studies at the University of Minnesota, 1966-1968. I was drunk and doing other drugs seven days a week.

How are you able to not drink or use daily?

For the first several hours of the day, I study philosophy and theology. I work the 12 Steps. Every single morning, I go on this path to open myself up. I read a lot. I also have a very supportive wife. She decided to never drink again for me.

What is your thought about medication-assisted treatment?

Any kind of drugged approach to sobriety can only be valid in the short term. You should be in a residential facility and taper off before you leave. For that to happen, there should be a minimum of six months of residential treatment, not 28 days.
Antidepressants may be helpful in the beginning but are not necessary for the rest of your life. Sleep right, eat right, live right, and the brain will find homeostasis.

Is there anything you want those struggling with addiction to know?

Avoid anyone who's telling you there's anything more important than getting sober. Go to as many meetings as you can and take it very seriously. Don't argue with spirituality; it works. Whatever the addiction, the only lasting answer is spirituality.

As soon as the chemicals are gone, then suddenly, the portal opens to the soul. This connection with the soul is where healing starts.

31

God is present as us and in us. We are in the presence of the Sacred. If we allow the brain to run on its natural chemistries and don't inject interruptions, such as drugs or alcohol, the brain begins to serve the soul. As a result, the soul heals us.

As soon as you put drugs or alcohol in your body, the neuropathways that lead to the soul close off, and we can no longer feel like we're fully alive. Let the brain function the way it's supposed to, and you recover.

Allen P.

Date of interview: 5/22/2019
Sobriety date: 6/22/12, 6 years
Hometown: Hancock

When did you start drinking or using drugs, and how did it progress?

The first time was in my early 20s. I had one or two bottles of beer. I was very closely supervised by my parents, not in an aggressive way, so I didn't drink much while they were around. They were both children of alcoholic parents and were aware of the genetic predisposition. My drinking didn't progress until my mid-20s. It was frequent and, at times, daily. I very quickly stopped drinking beer and started drinking distilled liquors. I drank enough to feel a strong effect and was drinking three to five ounces a day.

There was a brief period of sobriety in my late 20s and early 30s for about three years. I was attending a graduate school that focused on consciousness-based education in Iowa. This experience taught me that the basis of my life is the correct functioning of my nervous system, so this became important to me. I returned to drinking after starting to travel and was living a life of great success.

I created an information system for running colleges and universities and was wildly successful. A company formed around me, so I traveled all around North America, going to colleges and universities installing and tailoring this information system. I didn't like to eat alone, so I ate in bars and, of course, what else do you do in bars but drink. I became addicted to alcohol by doing this until my 50s.

By the end of it, I was drinking every day, and drinking as much as was available. I would drink until it was gone, or I was gone. It was 10 years of that kind of drinking, from my 40s until my 50s. I was also using whatever drug I could get my hands on throughout this whole period too. I used heroin, cocaine, and methamphetamines. The only class of drugs I stayed away from was benzodiazepines and never injected. On two occasions, I got arrested, convicted, and jailed for a month each time. One was from my fifth DWI.

During this series of events, my life partner, who I had been with since I was 21, told me that she couldn't live this lifestyle. She had named my addict persona Al, and she said she loved Allen, but she couldn't live with persona Al. As I was being carted off to jail, I was aware I didn't have anywhere to go once released. I asked her about it, and she told me she didn't know where I was going either. I finally realized if I got rid of persona Al, then I could be Allen. This change in thought was the beginning of my sobriety.

Since I spent my life dwelling on consciousness as a science, it was a natural move to apply the science of consciousness to this behavior. I went back to school and got my second master's degree in mental health counseling at New England College. I then became a Master Licensed Alcohol and Drug Counselor and applied models of western psychology and Vedic Science to my recovery and helped others with theirs.

Addiction is a response to dissatisfaction with our experience in life. Every single cell in our body has a blueprint for the perfect us. This perfect us doesn't make mistakes, doesn't fall sick, lives in a continuous state of enjoyment, and accomplishes anything we can think. When the experience of life doesn't add up, you've got to do something to fix it. You take some chemical, and it appears to work, at first. This glimpse at life while using a chemical becomes mistaken for the real thing. Some of the damage it does makes you less able to function the way you want. You become less able to function, desperate, and dissatisfied.

The human body is like a vehicle, and there are two significant features. One is the steering mechanism, and the other is the engine. The steering mechanism is what we have in terms of all the methods and techniques we have in the addiction science world. The problem is that addiction science doesn't have an engine. There isn't anything that propels you forward. That's where the technology from Veda comes in. It provides you with tools such as Transcendental Meditation. Tools like Veda, coupled with ideas to change your actions, give you different results. The combination of the two is pretty compelling.

Using things like Veda and what I have learned in life have made my abstinence from chemicals quite effortless. I stopped remaining abstinent to avoid negative consequences and started continuing sobriety because I wanted to avoid the negative experience of using the chemical. The chemical experience is less enjoyable than my normal state of mind.

Looking back, when do you think it was mostly out of control?

Around the years 2000-2006, it reached a peak. It was the centerpiece of my life.

How are you able to not drink or use daily?

I meditate twice a day, in the morning and the evening. There is no routine I need to follow that is helpful to avoid what I don't want. Drugs and alcohol are in the category of the things I don't want in the same way that poison ivy is. It just doesn't feel right.

What is your thought about medication-assisted treatment?

It helps get people from a place of complete chaos to a situation where they can think. When you think clearly and systematically, you can begin to recover. As long as you are in turmoil, you will not have much success, including recovery. Using medication long-term is not a good idea. The human nervous system is ideal without medication.

Medical and psychology professionals have been studying pathology. We don't have medicine for health; we have medication for pathology. We know a bit about darkness; we know almost nothing about the light. What we keep on finding out when we study high-end human beings is that human beings are the most glorious creatures there are in the universe. We know medicating them is not going to bring them to their potential.

Is there anything you want those struggling with addiction to know?

Addiction is a mistaken expression of the deepest laws of nature. It's a misguided expression of the law of evolution, the desire for more. What's mistaken is the ability for more. This need is built in. The technique to unlocking it had been forgotten for some time. Learning Transcendental Meditation will give you the technology you need to open this. You should learn to meditate with someone who knows how to apply the skill of living. Scientific evidence shows Transcendental Meditation is the easiest to learn and practice. It also shows this practice to be much more useful than others that sound similar.

Amanda B.

Date of interview: 4/18/19
Sobriety date: 6/19/77, 41 years
Hometown: Sanbornville

When did you start drinking or using drugs, and how did it progress?

I was stealing whiskey from underneath the kitchen counter when I was very young. As kids, we were allowed to drink a glass of wine on Thanksgiving and Christmas. Things started to change when I got my driver's license and got into a relationship with a man who later became my husband. He was a mason. We worked together for a year, until 1974, when we started fighting.

We both liked to party. We hung out at gin mills and were the life of the party until we got into a fight, and then people didn't want us around. We always ended up in trouble. He was physically abusive, and I was never very good at being abused. I would grab the biggest weapon I could find and come after him with it.

One day in 1975, we had a fight. My head was all smashed up, and I could barely see. I had to call someone to take me to the hospital. A state trooper asked who hit me, and I told him it was my husband. It took three state troopers and one cop to take him to the police station. They took me to the hospital. The police told me he was pretty beat up. I guess I beat him with a breadboard to protect myself. After the hospital, they took me to my mother's house and him to a locked ward in Concord. The doctors said I had a concussion.

My doctor came to our house on horseback to check on me. I saw bugs on the wall and white lights coming out of the corner of my eye. The doctor thought it was because of the concussion. It wasn't until I got into the program of Alcoholics Anonymous that I realized withdrawals have similar symptoms to a concussion. The doctor didn't know the difference. After I got through my concussion, I went to see my husband. He didn't remember much of anything. They had him all strapped down on a bed.

He had just gotten back from Vietnam a few years before and had a mental flashback. He thought he was there again. After he straightened out, he started going to Alcoholics Anonymous on the hospital campus. The hospital staff told me I should go to Al-Anon. I played the dutiful wife and wanted to fix this poor man, so I went. Al-Anon meetings didn't go very well. I told them, "If you had my husband, you would drink too." I didn't identify with them. However, when I went to an Alcoholics Anonymous meeting with my husband, I liked it. I thought, "These people are just like the people in the gin mill." I fit right in and felt comfortable. It took a while before I realized that I might have a drinking problem too.

One time, I went to a meeting, and I heard a woman speak. I swore to God that my husband, his sponsor, and his sponsor's wife had all gotten together and told her my story so that she would tell it, so I would know I had a problem. Talk about self-centered ego. I bopped around for a couple of years in AA. I was telling everyone what to do and how to do it. The problem was, I never understood the program. I read all the books, so I was a walking, talking genius. I never really believed I was an alcoholic. I was just on a horrible dry drunk. They kept telling me, "Keep coming back." I was obnoxious. I don't know how they put up with me.

After a couple of years, my husband disappeared and ended up in the hospital with a heart attack. I didn't know what to do. On the way home from visiting him, I stopped at the American Legion to tell everyone. I never got out of the American Legion that day. By now, I had a son and didn't know where he was that day because I was drunk. I did what drunks do without a 12-step program: I drank.

After sobering up, I called a woman in the program, and she said, "We can get through this." Her saying this and me being ready was my moment of reality. I realized that I wasn't running the show. I wasn't in charge. I couldn't put alcohol or other drugs in my body. I started doing the 12 Steps and reaching out to help other people struggling with addiction. I've been doing it ever since.

If I'd known that I would live to be 70, I would have taken better care of my body. I have done incredible things since I got sober. I went back to school, got a teaching degree, and taught math for 30 years in a New Hampshire high school. I used to pass this beautiful lake every morning, and I would ask my higher power what He wanted me to be when I grew up.

After seven years of asking Him, I told my sponsor what I was doing, and she said, "Maybe He wants you to be a high school teacher." I was a high school teacher for much more than just teaching math. Many of my students were with me for learning life lessons. When they became adults, I helped them get sober.

Today, I live three miles in the woods. I have my higher power and nature all around me. My higher power is a more natural and nature-oriented God. I have to attribute 99 percent of my sobriety to a belief in a higher power running the show, and if I try to do the next right thing, things come along pretty well.

Someone told me I drank because of not having a higher power. Before I started to go to AA, I had no belief in a higher power. I was raised to believe you can do anything you want if you just set your mind to it. When I started working the 12 Steps and could have a higher power any way I wanted, I was spoiled and wanted a higher power that would take care of me, watch over me. I was very arrogant and knew I had to learn some lessons.

Looking back, when do you think it was mostly out of

control?

It was out of control in college. I would wake up in all kinds of places and with all sorts of people.

How are you able to not drink or use daily?

Every morning, I ask my higher power to keep me away from a drink, a drug, or a cigarette. I help other people that have alcohol or other drug problems. Some people know they can call me anytime, day or night. I may not have the answers, but I can certainly listen. AA Steps 10, 11, and 12 keep me on the right path. I still go to AA meetings almost every day.

What is your thought about medication-assisted treatment?

I'm a little prejudiced because I got sober by just abstinence. I see people taking these medications, and they get high. Even when it's prescription and supposed to help them sleep, reduce anxiety, or help with other things. They can't seem to get sober or grasp the 12-step program. They're not in control.

I'm very fortunate. I don't use any drugs whatsoever. If I need a pain killer, I take an aspirin. If you can get your mind clear through abstinence and not using drugs, it's easier to continue not using them. I've seen a lot of people on Suboxone or methadone, and they can't seem to get off it. The few I have talked to said it was worse getting off it than it was coming off their drug of choice.

Is there anything you want those struggling with addiction to know?

You only have today. Make today the best. Then you can have a good yesterday, and tomorrow will look bright. It's today that matters. Don't put a mind-altering substance in your body right now, and it will be all right.

Angela J.

Date of interview: 6/6/19
Sobriety date: 1987, 32 years
Hometown: Bethlehem

When did you start drinking or using drugs, and how did it progress?

It was the summer of seventh grade. My best friend and I were bored and looking for something to do. We got into her parents' liquor cabinet and took some whiskey. I loved the smell and taste. My best friend wasn't too keen about drinking because both her parents were heavy drinkers and her older siblings had troubles with alcohol. Neither of my parents drank much at all. I've never seen either of my parents under the influence. I had heard stories about my dad's father's heavy drinking but hadn't witnessed it firsthand.

Rather than alcohol or drug use problems, there was violence in my family. One particular incident marked the beginning of an irrational belief that led to my problematic use of alcohol and cannabis. On that day, I crawled out of the living room in our home and into the hallway, where we had a rotary telephone. I was in the third grade and trying to be invisible during one of the violent episodes; 911 didn't exist then. Cellphones didn't exist. I dialed seven very loud digits to call the police. I was afraid for my life and for my sister's life. I thought, finally, somebody is going to help us.

I'll never forget looking through the white sheer curtains on our front door. I watched the police car slowly drive by. I thought, "Maybe they're going to turn around and come into our driveway." They didn't turn around; they never put their lights on, didn't stop. At that moment, when I realized the police were going to do nothing, I decided I was alone and that asking for help was worthless. From that point forward, my motto was if I wanted anything done, I would do it myself. Changing that thinking has been more difficult than letting go of getting high from alcohol or weed.

From the very beginning, when I discovered alcohol during the summer of seventh grade, it became a release. It gave me a place that felt all my own, where no one or anything could bother me. I would come home under the influence. My body was there, but my mind and spirit were somewhere else. Alcohol and smoking marijuana served this purpose.

By high school, I was drinking every weekend. My tolerance was high by the time I got my driver's license. I'd end up being the designated driver because even though I was under the influence, I was what my friends considered the "safest" driver. Several of my high school friends were killed while driving under the influence.

I earned an athletic scholarship for undergraduate college. I didn't continue my involvement with organized sports because it interfered with my desire to continue "partying." I was fortunate to maintain a place on the honor roll, which kept my academic scholarship intact, and I was employed. Although several close friends tried to talk with me about their concerns about my drinking, I was defensive about it and believed I was "okay" because I hadn't gotten into any trouble and appeared "successful."

The man who is now my husband is the first person able to get that message of concern over to me. He is a teetotaler–someone who has never consumed alcohol or any illicit drugs. His immediate family was torn apart by alcoholism. It was through his eyes I began to understand the destruction it can cause.

Looking back, when do you think it was mostly out of control?

My junior and senior years in high school is when it was the most out of control.

How are you able to not drink or use daily?

Drinking was a temporary solution for a problem I had no control over. It served a purpose that helped me survive a difficult period in my life. Once I began to understand that much of my thinking during that time was a survival mode, it became easy to let go of "getting high" from drinking or smoking weed. I've translated those highs into passions for being in the forest and mountains, working in the earth with my gardens, raising my children, working with my dogs, and working alongside others at various stages of recovery.

What is your thought about medication-assisted treatment?

I'm concerned about how pharmaceutical and advertising companies make dealing with life's ups and downs and pain, whether it be physical, emotional, or spiritual, look easy by taking a pill. Our bodies are designed to keep itself in balance–you know, that's homeostasis. Modern medicine can work miracles when things go awry–but that's only one piece of the puzzle.

Is there anything you want those struggling with addiction to know?

There's no quick fix. Trust your gut. Give yourself plenty of compassion. Drink lots of water. Get outside. Walk barefooted in the grass. Smell the roses. Let yourself ask for help, and then accept the help that is offered. Be grateful. Laugh when you can.

Dr. Anne Wilson Schaef is an author who made a difference in my thinking around behavior, drugs, alcohol, sugar, and caffeine. In her book, *When Society Becomes an Addict*, published in the 1980s, she predicted what we are experiencing now. We don't have to become a statistic. Each of us has a choice. All the prophets we read about tell us in one way or the other that our mind is a powerful tool.

Arvid D.

Date of interview: 5/29/19
Sobriety date: 11/11/15, 3 years
Hometown: Nashua

When did you start drinking or using drugs, and how did it progress?

I was eight years old. I was at a wedding with my parents, and when it came time for the toast, my dad replaced my wine with water. Then my mom returned it to wine, so I drank the wine. The next thing I knew, I was on the table drinking out of the bottles. I fell in love with it and loved the feeling. I got very sick that night, very ill. I didn't drink again until years later when I was about 12. My mom was an alcoholic, and she encouraged drinking. She didn't care if I drank and would give me alcohol at family events. I always liked the feeling.

My parents got divorced when I was 13. My mom was a pretty bad alcoholic, so I lived with my dad in Auburn. It had gotten crazy one night, so my dad took me. We left her, went to a hotel and lived there for six months. It was costly, so we moved. He had his businesses, five pet stores. We ended up living in his office and sleeping on couches for a year. He was trying to make it work with my mom, but she wouldn't stop drinking.

My mom made up a lie and got custody of me, so I ran away. My sister, who is eight years older, had already moved to California. My mom's drinking escalated. She tried to win me over because she wanted custody of me. She wanted the house and the businesses. My dad wasn't drinking at the time and was doing well. He did everything he could to protect me, but I would still go to my mom's, and she'd give me alcohol and weed. I started regularly drinking at 13. When I'd go to my mom's, my dad would stay outside in the car, and my mom would give me alcohol.

While I was in high school, my dad had his business to run, and my mom wasn't around. I went to school in Manchester and started hanging out with the kids who used drugs. I was selling weed and started doing cocaine, pills, and OxyContin. I got carried away by selling heroin and methamphetamine. I was making good money and still managed to get through high school. Eventually, my dad got the house, and we moved back in. My mom was off somewhere. I didn't talk to her for three years.

I went to college at Hesser for business, and in my second year, I got arrested. This was the third or fourth time being arrested for possession with intent to sell. It was on the front page of the newspaper. The newspaper mentioned the college I was attending, so the school asked me not to return. It was all downhill from there.

Things got worse and worse. I was using OxyContin for a while and eventually shot up. When they stopped making OxyContin, I had no choice but to go to heroin. I was selling it and using it for six years. I was in and out of jail, trouble after trouble. I got arrested and put on probation. I was facing 7 ½ to 15 years in prison—no drug court. My record was so bad they wanted to put me away for a long while. I kept violating probation because I couldn't stay sober. I got arrested again, and my probation officer said, "Go to treatment or go to prison." I decided to go to treatment.

I had tried treatment before and failed my drug tests—this time, I did long-term treatment, 14 months at GateHouse. First, I went through detox at the Farnum Center and then residential treatment at GateHouse. The GateHouse is where they introduced me to the

12-step program. I was on Suboxone during detox, and GateHouse got me off it. You couldn't take Suboxone in the residential unit. I was in the residential program for 30 days and then went to sober living.

I also did the GateHouse intensive outpatient program and immersed myself in counseling. The owner would come by and read the *Alcoholics Anonymous* Big Book every day, and then they'd bring us to meetings. They showed me how to stay sober. They told me the truth and helped me see my truth. I got a service position, a home group, a sponsor, and went through the 12 Steps. It was the best thing that ever happened to me.

They spent a lot of time with me, and I did everything they asked. They helped me change my old ways. I didn't know how to live because I'd been a criminal for such a long time. I stayed in sober living as long as I could, since I was doing well for the first time in my life. Today, life is hectic. I work full time, go to meetings, and sponsor guys. I'm in school again and working on my business degree. God works in mysterious ways.

Looking back, when do you think it was mostly out of control?

When I was 23, the progression of my disease got worse. A girl I knew for a very long time got in some trouble and sobered up. She was on methadone and was determined to save me. We started dating, and she tried to get me out of that drug-dealing life. She had a lot of money and was paying for my drug habit so that I wouldn't sell drugs. One night, we got in a fight, and she ended up relapsing and died. After that, I was on a suicide mission. I didn't want to live, so I tried to overdose on heroin and ended up just going crazy. I was using heroin, methamphetamines, and taking Xanax. The next thing I knew, I was wrapped up in this bullshit case.

How are you able to not drink or use daily?

I pray, go to meetings, ask for help, and work a program of recovery. Sometimes I meditate, not as often as I should. Working with others helps me. I've been through the 12 Steps twice and have a service position. I'm in connection with others in recovery, show up, and have a purpose. God is in my life today.

What is your thought about medication-assisted treatment?

If medication-assisted treatment is done appropriately, it can be useful. With that said, I was on Suboxone for a year. I stopped taking it after three months and started selling it. It is for the short term. If people can take it and get off it in a short time, then yes. When I was on it, I wasn't happy and wasn't working a program either. That's the thing about Suboxone: you have to go to counseling once a week, and it's just a check-in, how's your week going, whatever.

Reality is, I wasn't doing anything to make myself happy; I didn't know how. I was existing. Long-term MAT is not appropriate or helpful in any way. People are taking advantage of it because it's a moneymaker. Methadone is the same issue. They keep people on it for five, six years, whatever. They'll keep them on it for 20 years, if the person wants it. That's crazy. You're just a fucking zombie. That's just ridiculous. It's no way to live, it's not. It's liquid handcuffs.

Is there anything you want those struggling with addiction to know?

There is a better way. There's a way out of suffering. Pain is inevitable, but suffering is optional. Whenever you're ready, there's a way out. There's a solution. You can live a good life without alcohol or other drugs.

I go to shows, concerts and sky diving. I like thrill-seeking and an adrenaline rush. I went on vacation in Bermuda last year. I can enjoy things and remember them. I don't wake up the next day and look at the pictures and think, "Oh, I must have had fun because I was so fucked up the night before." I have found happiness. All I ever wanted was to be happy, and I am.

Barry T.

Date of interview: 4/24/2019
Sobriety date: 9/18/ 82, 36 Years
Hometown: Newmarket

When did you start drinking or using drugs, and how did it progress?

I was 15 years old and in boarding school in Rindge, New Hampshire. I was one of six students to do an off-campus experimental education program, living on a farm. We had tutors residing with us, and when they had their night off, we got into the liquor cabinet.

One night, three of us took a bunch of hard liquor, mixed it all, and drank it. I enjoyed the experience. When my tutor came back that night, he found me up, being silly, and slurring my words. He confronted me in a friendly way. He told me that lots of kids try it, but I needed to be careful, and he wasn't going to get me in trouble this time.

When I was 17, it was the end of the 1960s, and I was heavily into music. I was in a band and grew my hair long. Up until that point, I hadn't smoked pot, but when I went to a Janice Joplin concert, I did. My friends had marijuana, so we went out into the woods and smoked it. I didn't get high. A day later, I smoked it and loved it. I loved everything about it and embarked on smoking marijuana regularly.

I returned home from a boarding school in June of 1969. I spent the whole summer hanging out at the beach with kids my age and older ones who were using a variety of drugs. I drank a lot of beer and wine and smoked a lot of pot. Amphetamines and black beauties were available, so I used those and loved them. I was using pretty heavily, basically the whole summer. I was living with my mom or my sister when my mom and I weren't getting along.

I started attending Gloucester High School and lasted a month. I could not handle a mainstream school, so I dropped out. I couldn't stand living at home anymore, so I called up the people I had stayed with on the farm, and they hired me to work. One of the kids I went there with was having trouble at home, and he lived on the farm too. The two of us got into some pretty significant using, mostly smoking pot and drinking.

I stayed there for a year but then decided to go back to high school and moved in with my stepfather in Bedford, Massachusetts. On September 18, 1970, I dropped my first hit of acid and loved it. I tripped hundreds of times over the next bunch of years, and my drinking continued. I was in the music business, playing in and out of clubs all over New England. As a result, my using picked up. Liquor was always available in the clubs. I was also doing amphetamines because it kept me awake. That pattern went on for quite a while. I lived with a variety of people who were in bands. There was always using going on. At one point, I got into barbiturates and almost overdosed. Somehow, I survived that.

I hooked up with a band from Littleton, Massachusetts, and became their road manager. For five years, we played almost every single night. That was pretty intense. I did a lot of drinking, a lot of speed, and had a lot of late nights out. Then I got involved in a relationship with somebody, and we bought a home. We had a common-law marriage. During my time with her, my drinking increased even more. I had a love affair with brandy and drank a quart to a quart and a half a day. Eventually, I backed out of the band thing.

I worked locally and continued to drink excessively. At the 10 o'clock break, I'd go to the pub and have a pitcher of beer, spend my whole lunch break drinking, and three o'clock break back to the bar for another pitcher of beer. I'd get out of work, drive to the package store, and get a half a quart of brandy and drink it on the 25-minute ride home. I'd stop at the package store in town, buy another liter of brandy, and bring it back and drink. I drank like this for years.

Finally, I started a wood business in 1981, but my business partner got sober, and I was still heavily drinking. He tried to 12-Step me, and I didn't know it. Another friend of mine's alcoholism progressed. Six months later, he was having blackouts. The court sentenced him to five AA meetings a week for an entire year. A lot of people that I used to drink with started to disappear, and I didn't know where they were.

My girlfriend was much older than me and eventually had an affair. I moved out that summer and drank every single day, all day, generic vodka. My routine was to go to work, come home, and drink a fifth of vodka, pass out, wake up, and do the same thing the next day. One morning there was blood all over my pillow. I had passed out and smashed my head on the radiator. I started to have violent thoughts and was very depressed. I thought about killing myself or somebody else.

My now-ex-girlfriend's sister was sober and in AA. She sent me a copy of the Big Book of AA and took me to an AA meeting in Rockland, Maine, to help me stop drinking. I lasted two days. My alcoholism brought me to a place where I couldn't get drunk, and I couldn't get sober. It was terrible. While I was with her in Maine, I read the Big Book cover to cover.

I was very interested in spirituality. I came home and decided to try to stop drinking with the help of AA. I had my last drink that Sunday afternoon. I drank four 16-ounce Miller beers before going to the AA meeting. Then a friend asked me to go to an AA meeting that Tuesday night. I remember having an argument with myself about going. Then, there was this inner voice that said, "If I don't go now then I won't go," so I went. I have been sober and drug-free since.

Looking back, when do you think it was mostly out of control?

The very end of my drinking.

How are you able to not drink or use daily?

I'm responsible for the choices I make. I flipped a switch and told myself that it is unacceptable for me ever to pick up a drink or a drug. It doesn't matter how bad it gets or what happens in my life; I can't drink. I also recognized that I needed to be a part of a support network to remain vigilant. For me to stay abstinent, I need to practice vigilance. I can't ever get complacent about this. I also meditate daily.

What is your thought about medication-assisted treatment?

I have been a SUD professional for 32 years and have seen many people maintain abstinence, in light of the opioid crisis. Medication-assisted treatment can be beneficial for some people on a short-term basis until they find confidence and stability, but not everybody. People should give their best effort to abstinence, but if all else fails, medication is an option. I have concerns about the long-term, but I don't know enough.

Is there anything you want those struggling with addiction to know?

People have to find their path to recovery. It takes a lot of effort, regardless of which way you choose. It's worth it. You'll get your life back and find direction.

Bonnie B.

Date of interview: 5/14/ 2019
Sobriety date: 6/4/83, 35 years
Hometown: Littleton

When did you start drinking or using drugs, and how did it progress?

When I was 17, the summer of my junior year in high school, I drank a 16-ounce bottle of Budweiser. It was supposed to be good, and I was told that I'd like it, so I guzzled it right down. I blacked out immediately.

The next time I drank was a week later. I gradually increased my drinking throughout that summer. When I started my senior year of high school, I planned to shape up and be a good girl. I got through, but only with the help of the guidance counselor and the principal. I graduated in 1968, got a job working from 6 a.m. to 1 p.m. as a waitress, still living with my parents. Five nights a week I would go home after work, sleep a little bit, and go out drinking at night. I'd get drunk and black out almost every time. My parents didn't know.

I met my first husband while I was working at that restaurant. By 1969, I was pregnant, got married, and had my first child. I was abstinent from alcohol for the nine months I was pregnant, but I gained 100 pounds. When he was born, it put a cramp in my drinking abilities. His grandmother, on his father's side, was more than willing to babysit on weekends. I controlled my drinking during that time. However, it got boring for me. I began to hate my husband and found reasons I shouldn't be married. Eventually, we got divorced after four years of marriage.

I got married again and had my second child in 1974. I couldn't afford to drink or take care of my child on my own. My husband was very involved in taking psychedelics. We used to do crystal meth and speed together. We did this every weekend, all weekend long, for four years. We hung out with his band a lot too.

It didn't take long until we were divorced. Shortly after that, I went to a doctor, and she prescribed me Valium. It was so easy to get. I knew she would give me the prescription. I took it, went to the bar that night, and drank. The Valium didn't last more than a month. I'd always take it at night with alcohol. I took it to enhance my drinking. At this point, I was living in low-income housing and gave my son to his father. He was eight years old. I dropped him off with his father for the summer and never came back to pick him up. From 1978-1983, my drinking increased drastically. I went to bars more often. I smoked pot, snorted cocaine, used psychedelics, black beauties, and continued to drink.

In 1983, my brother committed suicide. I went into some sort of mental state. I isolated and pulled the shades. I put a sign on the door, asking people to leave me alone. Someone recommended I go to counseling, so I went for four months. I was talking about what life was like growing up in an alcoholic household, being the youngest child and the only girl. The counselor told me she had heard all about my childhood, and it was terrible. She then asked me why I was there, and I said, "I don't want to die with a drink in my hand."

Then she said, "Well then, why don't you stop drinking?" I was taken aback. It hit home, and I thought I could stop. I went through a few more disturbing things while drinking and realized I couldn't stop. Eventually, I asked her how people stop drinking, and she gave me a list of ways people stop. Alcoholics Anonymous was the only one on the list that didn't cost money, so I went. I've been sober in AA ever since. I've learned to live a sober, peaceful life free of fear, doubt, and insecurities.

Looking back, when do you think it was mostly out of control?

After my brother committed suicide.

How are you able to not drink or use daily?

I thank God each morning for another day of living clean and sober. I go on about my day, which only includes AA people and living the maintenance steps in AA. I take my inventory, keep a conscious contact with God at all times, and help others.

What is your thought about medication-assisted treatment?

I think it's necessary if a doctor is prescribing the drug, and the professionals in a treatment center are distributing the medicine according to guidelines. Before people leave the facility, they need someone to talk to about recovery. People in recovery need help in their decision-making regarding other drugs. Alcoholics who have been sober for a long time need to live a clean and sober life. There is a big long list of opioids that cannot be used in recovery, unless during surgery.

Is there anything you want those struggling with addiction to know?

Some people will help you, and a 12-step program will teach you how to live without alcohol or other drugs. Your job is to show up at meetings and give it enough time. You will learn another way to live that will keep you happy, joyous, and free.

Bonnie T.

Date of interview: 3/25/19
Sobriety date: 1994, 24 years
Hometown: Bristol

When did you start drinking or using drugs, and how did it progress?

At age 12 I drank Heffenreffers with my friend, who is now dead from alcoholism. I think we each had two. We both had older sisters and brothers, so it was easily accessible. I wanted to belong. I wanted to do what everyone else was doing. I wanted to be the cool kid. We grew up in Lynn, Massachusetts. You could stand outside a package store and ask someone to buy alcohol.

I drank every weekend and couldn't walk home from a party without falling over. By age 15, I got introduced to drugs: mescaline, acid, mushrooms, cocaine, lots of marijuana, and speed. I'd party all night and take speed to get me going during the day. I started keeping a bottle of hard alcohol in my school locker so that I could drink during the day. I changed the friends I hung out with and preferred to be with people who drank and drugged like me.

At 17, I got pregnant and, shortly after that, had another child. No father around and no job. I tried to maintain my drinking and drugging lifestyle while raising two kids. Eventually, my father showed up and dragged me to Seminole Point rehab in New Hampshire. After I got out, I stayed sober for six months. I had met my husband at rehab, and we sold marijuana and cocaine together. I had another child, and then DCYF started to get involved. They had me fill out a questionnaire which asked about my drinking. I said I drank one drink a night. The DCYF worker knew I was lying about my drinking and told me to see a counselor.

My husband got busted and was no longer around. By age 25, my world started falling apart. I was tired of living a lifestyle where I would wake up every morning trying to figure out how I was going to use drugs. The police were watching me because I was still selling drugs. I moved nine times in one year because they were watching me.

I got busted with two pounds of marijuana, and they took my kids. For two months, I went on a binge, took a lot of acid, did a lot of drinking, and had a lot of blackouts. New Year's Eve was my last binge. I was living in Hampton Beach and woke up in a place I didn't know. It scared me that I didn't even know what had happened. I was tired, very tired. Reality set in, and I thought of my kids. My father was always in recovery. He got sober when I was three. He hadn't spoken to me in two years. I called Derby Lodge (a seven-day detox) in New Hampshire, and then called my dad. I said, really quick, so he wouldn't hang up, "I need a ride. I want help." He came, bought me lunch—apparently, I hadn't eaten in five days—and drove me to Derby Lodge.

They asked me if I was on any hallucinogens, and I lied. I said no, but I was coming off mushrooms and drinking. I thought there were squirrels in the ceiling. I didn't sleep well that night. From there, I went to Friendship House for a 28-day program but stayed for six months. They taught me how to live life without a crutch, no medication, and one day at a time. I was facing 15 years in prison. Through all the traumatic things that happened to me, divorce, facing prison time, and my best friend dying at 42, I was able to stay sober after I left.

Looking back, when do you think it was mostly out of control?

Right after high school, my drug use kept getting worse, and I felt as if I were always searching for myself but couldn't find me.

How are you able to not drink or use daily?

I have an awareness of where I came from and remember experiencing that bottomless pit. I know enough about how it felt to not want to go back. My friends, AA, and counseling helped me through it all.

What is your thought about medication-assisted treatment?

The medication would have stopped me from finding out who I am. It would have muffled me from experiencing the good in me and the places I can go. It would have put earmuffs on me, and I wouldn't have been able to hear adequately.

Is there anything you want those struggling with addiction to know?

You have a choice to say "no more." There is a way out. Learn to love yourself more than your addiction.

Bruce B.

Date of interview: 5/13/ 2019
Sobriety date: 4/23/80, 39 Years
Hometown: Campton

When did you start drinking or using drugs, and how did it progress?

I was 13 and drank a Budweiser in a can, partially frozen. A friend and I stole it and drank a few of them. It was terrible. The next time was a year later. I soaked grape gumballs in whiskey and brought them to school. I'd eat them and catch a buzz. I was restless in school; they couldn't contain me. I'd talk in class, interrupt, have the dunce cap put on me, and have to sit in the corner. I used to get slapped with a wooden pointer in the back of the neck by the teacher. I didn't learn from anything and kept repeating the same stuff. I wasn't teachable.

When I got into high school, my drinking took off. I tried pot and loved it. My first purchase was a pound. I preferred to smoke weed over drinking because I didn't puke. I'd smoke an ounce of marijuana a day. When we drank, we'd put mescaline or acid in it. We called it electrified wine. I doubled everything right from the beginning. We smoked coke, heroin, hash, all that stuff.

I was angry, the world sucked, and everything was against me. In 1978, I stopped doing all the drugs after my cousin died. I saw him after he got shot; there was blood everywhere. I decided to drink straight alcohol after that. It replaced the drugs. I drank whiskey, gin, grain alcohol, whatever was available, and whatever I could afford. I didn't draw a sober breath for a long time.

Then, I was beating people up, very violent. Consequences were starting to show up, but I was willing to accept them so I could drink. One night, I went to a party, and the only thing I remember is going to the party and the cops coming. I guess I got into a fight and took off in my car. I was on the wrong side of the road and crashed into the guardrail. I rolled the front end up into me.

A guy who had been sober for 15 years came up to me. He knew who I was. I was in and out of a blackout. He said, "I've got to call the ambulance. We don't want any trouble." I said "Okay," and the next thing I knew, I was being shipped off to the police station. Before the crash, I remember feeling the most at peace I had ever felt. Something had changed in me.

The cops brought me to the police station and put me in protective custody. They told me I could go, but I had to appear in court. I got freaked out about leaving because I was afraid of what I would do again if I drank. I told the police, "I need help; I'm crazy." A guy at the police station, who was 17 years sober, told me, "I know what you need." He and another man took me to Concord Hospital for detox.

A man who worked at the hospital comforted me. I told him what was going on and that I was crazy. He said, "You're not crazy; we don't dry crazy people out." I attended their Burbank Addiction Program, which was very powerful. I got educated and learned how to live without alcohol or other drugs. I committed myself because I thought I was crazy but found out it was the booze that made me crazy.

When I got out of the hospital, I had to go to court and face a DWI charge. I was nervous but was told to tell the truth. The judge said, "How do you plead?" He knew me and thought I would give him a bunch of bullshit. I said, "Your Honor, whatever you need me to do, I will do. I've had enough." The judge said, "Mr._____, I believe you." He said, "You're an alcoholic, and you have a built-in forgetter. You're going to forget all this, so you need to go to AA meetings." I started to go to meetings and knew this was my lifeline. I knew if I was willing to do the work, they were ready to help me.

I was unemployable and had burnt a lot of bridges. Eventually, I got my license back and got my GED. I was able to work on a farm for five dollars an hour doing chores and helping to raise calves. It took me five years to get out of debt with the court and everything else. Eventually, I got married and had two children. She stopped going to Al-Anon, and I continued to change. She asked me to leave.

I was scared, broke, embarrassed, and hurt. My sponsor and I opened the *Twelve Steps and 12 Traditions* book of AA, read Step 11, and I sought through prayer and meditation to improve my constant contact with God. I knew I was right where I was supposed to be. Drinking was not an option. My life has progressively gotten better over the years.

Looking back, when do you think it was mostly out of control?

It was always out of control. My mother told me that every time she answered the phone, she thought someone would tell her I was dead.

How are you able to not drink or use daily?

When I get up, the first thing I say is, "Thank you, God," and I ask Him for help to stay sober. I remain humble. The day I think I don't need help, I'm in trouble. I have to be honest in all my affairs. I go to meetings, store up all the information I learn about how people stay sober, and use it when I need it. At every meeting, I learn new things. When the man's okay, the world is okay.

What is your thought about medication-assisted treatment?

It's only a Band-Aid. Expose the wound and let it heal. Medication postpones life. It delays the gift of the Spirit. Take the beating now. Once you go through it, you will never want to go through it again.

Is there anything you want those struggling with addiction to know?

Surrender. Give up and tell the truth. You can get restored to sanity, and there is a God. If you go to meetings, you pick up the Spirit. You pick up the truth. Don't quit before the miracle happens. Whatever you are dealing with now, will pass. You don't have to drink or use drugs.

<u>C.S.</u>

Date of interview: 5/8/2019
Sobriety date: 2/29/87, 32 years
Hometown: Wentworth

When did you start drinking or using drugs, and how did it progress?

I was in sixth grade in Connecticut, where I grew up. The first thing I had to drink was Bacardi 151 and Coke. A friend brought it to school. We had walked to school because it was under a mile, snuck out around the back of the school, and drank it. It felt perfect.

I didn't have any friends and was picked on all the time. I didn't fit in, so when someone finally said, "Hey, come hang with us," I thought, okay, this is what you do. I was accepted because I could drink as they could. They were a little older than I was. I also have an older brother and would hang out with him and his friends, and we would drink. We drank at least three times a week right from the get-go, and we would drink till it was gone—Bacardi 151 and Coke. I stuck with it, too, because it was quick and easy. It got me drunk fast, and I liked it.

In eighth grade, I drank every day. It was tough to go to school. I almost didn't graduate. I smoked pot here and there in high school, but I liked alcohol more. I got into an all-girls Catholic school. I thought going to this school would help me stop drinking, but it didn't. I was good for two or three days, but then I'd come home from school and get drunk. I'd get up in the morning sick, and I'd still go to school. I did this for three years.

My parents just thought there wasn't anything they could do, maybe because my brother was worse than I was. He was in and out of rehab and family therapy. During my senior year of high school, I got kicked out for bringing drugs to school. I went crazy and was into everything. My brother and I would use Quaaludes, mescaline, and acid. Whatever was out there, we did it. If someone had drugs, we did them.

From 18 to 24, I worked at a topless massage parlor and an escort service. The drinking started interfering with my work. I had the same boyfriend from age 17 on, who is my kids' father. He was drinking as much as I was, so it got very tough to maintain the relationship and my job.

I went to work in a factory, and because I didn't get along or play well with others, they put me in my own little area. They left me alone all day. I'd go home, get drunk, and then go to work the next day. I made good money. I got sober at 24 and I am still sober today.

Looking back, when do you think it was mostly out of control?

From 18 to 23, I was the most out of control. At age 18, I was drinking and could legally get alcohol. By the time it changed to 21, I had turned 21 and was still able to get alcohol legally.

How are you able to not drink or use daily?

I wake up every morning and thank God I'm awake because I could be gone. I look around, see the things I have and say, "This is because I don't drink." I try to go to meetings every day. Sometimes I miss a day here and there, but it works for me. Once a month, I plan an hour or two drive and go somewhere else, pick a new meeting out, and meet new people. For the last three years, I've gone on recovery retreats. At the retreat, I would eat every meal at a different table to meet new people. Being uncomfortable is what keeps me from drinking now. Getting out of my comfort zone and finding out that life is still okay keeps me sober.

What is your thought about medication-assisted treatment?

I don't know much about it. I see people on it, and it works. I see people on it, and it doesn't work.

What do you want those struggling with addiction to know?

Just don't drink or use drugs. Complete abstinence is the only thing that worked for me. I had to come to grips with the fact that I can't have anything, no matter what. I can't do it, because it'll kill me. I know it will. I've seen people go out and use, and I've seen people not come back. I've seen people die from it, and I know that's what's out there for me. I have to look at drugs as if they were poison. I have to keep that in my head. I have to live life on life's terms.

It took a while to learn how to live. I was young, with kids, and trying to stay sober. I'd bring my kids to meetings. There's always somebody there who can remember that struggle. People want you to bring your kids because they don't want you not to go. Get as much help as you can.

Cheryl K.

Date of interview: 4/17/2019
Sobriety date: 12/30/90, 28 years
Hometown: Plymouth

When did you start drinking or using drugs, and how did it progress?

I was 12. My older sister gave me a sip of whiskey and ginger. One day, we were in our bedroom, and she told me to taste it. It was just a few sips. The next time wasn't until a year later. Some friends and I were babysitting, and we drank wine. I got sick. It was my first real experience with drinking. I gradually got into drinking a beer here and there with people. One or two would get me drunk. There was no regular drinking at that time.

When I was 14, we'd go out to a dance club on weekends. You were supposed to be 16, but we weren't. I would drink maybe three or four beers at most. I couldn't handle much. Then it turned into drinking whenever I could get it. I would be at school, and someone would say, "Hey, let's sneak out." I'd go to a friend's house and we'd skip a couple of classes. We drank beer or coffee brandy and milk. It was like this all through high school.

At 17, I got pregnant and finished high school at night. From 17 to 19, I drank heavily. My relationship with my son's father was messed up. From then on, I drank to get drunk. I smoked a little bit of pot, but I didn't like it. It made me sick. I tried a few other drugs but preferred to drink. I started to recognize I would do stupid things when I drank, like drinking and driving.

Near the end, I got two DUIs. I wasn't having fun anymore. I had to go to a weekend program to get my license back. In a room with a bunch of people, I remember someone saying that alcoholics aren't bad people, they're just people that can't drink. The idea of me not being a bad person, but a sick person, was a revelation: I'm not a bad person. I left that weekend and got the ball rolling. It was the right time to hear that. I was ready.

I started realizing I couldn't keep drinking the way I was. I remember the holidays that year because I felt like I had it together, but I didn't. A couple of nights after Christmas, we had a party at my boyfriend's house, and I got trashed. I got to the point where I'd rather sit and drink than spend time with people. This behavior is kind of crazy.

On December 30th, I went to a New Year's Eve party. Everyone I worked with drank. I got to the party, and they said, "We have your favorite wine." I said, "No, I'm all set." I stuck with the girl I came with, who wasn't drinking. Midnight came, and I hadn't drunk all night. Someone went to pass me a glass of champagne. I looked at it and thought, "I'll have the glass of champagne because everyone else is." I remembered saying to myself, "No, I'm not going to drink. I haven't drunk all night."

I woke up the next morning, lay in bed, and saw a blue sky outside. I said to myself, "Oh my God, it looks beautiful out. I'm never going to drink again." That was it. I went to an Alcoholics Anonymous meeting a week later and to the same two meetings twice a week for three years. I have not had a drink or drug since.

Looking back, when do you think it was mostly out of control?

It was the most out of control right before my last drink.

How are you able to not drink or use daily?

I went to AA meetings for eight years. I always use what I learned to help me move through situations in my life. I exercise daily and enjoy being outside in nature. I do yoga and meditation. I stay connected with people who are on the same path. I stay close to God and listen to what He's trying to tell me. I breathe and say my prayers every day.

What is your thought about medicated assisted treatment?

Medication treatment is beyond what I know.

Is there anything you want those struggling with addiction to know?

If you want help, call someone sober. Call the AA hotline. Don't use and call someone. Figure out why you're here. Be quiet and listen to stay on your path.

Dan L.

Date of interview: 3/28/19
Sobriety date: 3/21/94, 25 years
Hometown: North Conway

When did you start drinking or using drugs, and how did it progress?

At age eight, I started smoking pot and cigarettes. I progressed rapidly from there. At age 11, I started drinking and regularly using on the weekends, mostly pot. By age 12, I started dealing pot and using LSD. I was smoking at least an ounce of pot a week and using a couple of hits of acid on the weekends. I didn't like drinking that much because it made me sick, but I did it anyway. I would drink a six-pack of beer and Sun Country wine coolers on the weekends. I could drink two liters of wine cooler by myself, which was more than anyone else. This got me notoriety in school, and I liked that.

I made decent money selling drugs and didn't like school, so I dropped out of my freshman year. I started using an eight-ball of cocaine a weekend, smoking and snorting it. At age 17, I stopped using cocaine but was still using LSD regularly. We had friends that were making it and would give us sheets for free. I ate a lot of it, seven to eight hits on the weekend. I was still smoking pot regularly and drinking to intoxication.

I had two kids by age 18, stopped doing LSD, and just drank a lot and smoked an ounce a week. This persisted until I was 22. My ex-wife told me I had to stop drinking, or she was going to leave, so I said, "See ya." My ex-wife lost custody of my son, and I wanted to get him. I went to rehab and showed up obliterated, so they put me in detox for three days and then a 28-day program.

After treatment, I went to a halfway house. It was a year-long program, and I was there for 11 months. In December of 1992, I left. I remained sober the whole time. I put myself in dangerous situations where people were using, and by February 1993, I was doing lines of cocaine on the back of public toilets and drinking.

In 1993, my son was living with me, and I was using a lot of pot and alcohol. In March of 1994, I was out at a bar, and my roommate was watching my son. I blew $200 at the bar that night, even though I couldn't afford it. At this time, my son was three. I don't remember going home that night, but I do remember lying in bed that night and contemplating: should I kill myself or kill my son first, so he won't have to wake up to find me dead. It's interesting that I don't remember going home, I don't remember it being dark out or walking home, but I do remember that. I remember this thought very clearly.

The next day, when I woke up, I called my DHS worker for help. She got me into a family shelter in Sanford, Maine. It was called the Alfred Shelter Program, and it had a recovery program in it. I knew I was done. When I woke up the next morning and remembered what I'd thought the night before, it hurt really badly, and I never wanted to go back there. I embraced the programming. I could go to two to three AA and NA meetings a day because they had childcare. We had recovery groups and recovery education.

I was there for three months and then moved out on my own. I had a sponsor and knew I needed to be abstinent. I don't have self-control over any drug. There is no such thing as just this or just that; it's all or nothing. I do it till it's gone. I knew if I wanted a chance to give my son a life, I had to give recovery a chance. I started seeing a counselor, went to a men's group, and developed relationships with people outside the program.

I stayed in Sanford for a year and met my current wife, who is also in recovery. We incorporate our sponsors in our relationship. We work our recovery program individually and together. I began to spend more time going to support meetings than with my family. I switched my addiction to drugs for my addiction to meetings, so I decided to put balance in my life. I have stayed sober ever since and have an incredible life.

Looking back, when do you think it was mostly out of control?

From the get-go, I spent my childhood trying to gain acceptance from my family. My family was into smoking pot and drinking, so I became heavily into pot and drinking as well. It provided me with an opportunity to feel okay.

How are you able to not drink or use daily?

When I first got sober, I went to AA and NA meetings every day. Now, I get up in the morning and pray. Sometimes I do a devotional, and sometimes I don't. I'm there for my family today. When I experience stress, I remind myself drug use is not an option. I also have a huge support system.

What is your thought about medication-assisted treatment?

It has its applications. When I have the flu, my doctor prescribes me medication, and when the flu is gone, I stop taking it. Medication-Assisted Treatment was created to help people get past the cravings. It was made to be a temporary tool, not a permanent solution. There is no financial gain to people getting well, so they keep them sick. The easiest way to do this is to keep them doped up. People trust their doctors, so they take what they are prescribed. Some people abuse it. Suboxone and methadone are being used for maintenance and not harm reduction. Campral is an anti-craving medication for alcoholics and can help with cravings. Once they get through the cravings, they're taken off.

Is there anything you want those struggling with addiction to know?

You are valuable and have worth. If you can't see it now, some day you will. Understand that all the negative noise you create about who you are isn't true.

Dana P.

Date of interview: 3/23/19
Sobriety date: 2/14/09, 10 years
Hometown: Bridgewater

When did you start drinking or using drugs, and how did it progress?

I was 15. I walked up to a kid's house; his parents were gone, and we smoked pot. I thought it was the coolest thing. I didn't get high. A couple of days later, we smoked again, and I got a buzz. The third time we smoked, the room was full of smoke from the pot, and his father, a college professor, came in. I thought that was going to be it and he was going to rat me out to my father. But his father asked to smoke with us.

I gravitated to the drug scene. I used whatever else came down the pike: black beauties, white crosses, Dexedrine, LSD, THC, pills, etc... I would have done anything. At age 16, we took white crosses, broke them down with water in a spoon, and shot it.

I think I used drugs because my dad was a strict, under-educated (eighth-grade education), alcoholic. He beat up on my self-esteem. He used to say, "You couldn't go to bed without a beating, even if you tried." Doctors wanted to puff me up with Ritalin back then. My dad should have been in jail for what he did: beating us with a belt all the time. Everything I tried to do with him, I couldn't do well enough. I felt as if I didn't have any gifts to give the world.

My drug use was sporadic through high school. After high school, I went into the military and found out I did have some talents. I excelled at being an outstanding soldier. I still gravitated toward partying though. On the weekends, I would party and get blasted drunk. I made a good rank, E-5, in four years. When I was 24, I got out of the military and got married. I got busted for pot and honorably discharged.

I went to work at Dick Cheney's company, in the oil fields of Texas. We had three children between 1980 and 1985. I got busted again for having a pound of pot, so we moved to Connecticut. I went to my first rehab at Seminole Point in New Hampshire. I had been shooting cocaine and heroin regularly. Eventually, my wife took the kids and went back to Texas, and I went to Maine and lived with my mom.

I drove a tractor-trailer and couldn't go over the George

Washington Bridge without scoring drugs. In 1987, I was driving a tractor while overdosing on cocaine and went to the hospital for a week, with three days in a coma. The doctor said I had enough cocaine in me to kill a Shetland pony. My heart rate was 220 beats a minute. I don't know how I survived. Then I went to the VA for 28 days. I came out and drank and drugged again.

In 1990, I got a DUI in Maine and went into The Bottle Fund Rehab. After I got out, I went to a clean and sober club and met a girl who was four years sober. I stayed sober for seven years after that rehab. This girl moved to Florida, and I followed her down. Our relationship was good when we were lying down, but vertically we didn't get along. She took off for Maine, and this time I didn't follow her.

I met another woman in 1992 and married her. I bought my tractor-trailer, made a lot of money, and got my children back. I was clean, sober, and doing well. I came home one day, and she was gone. I found out later on that she had committed suicide at age 46, a direct result of her alcoholism.

I began working too much and stopped going to AA meetings; I was too busy. Within a few months, I threw everything away. I told them to come get the truck, sold everything, and the kids went back to their mom. I started using crack cocaine and ended up in two to three spin-dries (seven-day detoxes) in Florida. It got so bad with crack cocaine that I started living under a bridge in Fort Myers, Florida. I threw away $40,000. I don't have a whole lot of memory of what happened.

My mom was living in North Carolina by then, so I went to visit. During a drunk incident, I crashed into a car and put two people in the hospital. I went to prison for two years. Right out of prison in 1998, I moved to New Hampshire to chase my ex-wife and moved into the McKenna House in Concord. I met the owner of a restaurant in Plymouth, and he offered me a job. I moved into a ghetto apartment in Plymouth and started working at Plymouth State University. I am still here after 20 years. I drank for 10 of those years but have been sober for almost 10 years now. I met my current wife at PSU and have all my material stuff back.

Looking back, when do you think it was mostly out of control?

The first time I got severe with drugs in 1980 to 1990. In the end, I was drinking.

How are you able to not drink or use daily?

I go to Alcoholics Anonymous. I have a relationship with a higher power and get on my knees daily to connect with this power. I have relationships with people in AA and work the 12 Steps.

What is your thought about medication-assisted treatment?

Not everyone needs to be on medication; maybe some of them do. In 1997, they put me in a psych ward for a 72-hour evaluation after I threatened to commit suicide. They put me on Lithium and Klonopin. I did not want to be on psych meds. I had admitted to being on a lot of drugs and alcohol before coming in. They didn't give me anything for my drug use and didn't refer me to a rehab. I knew I needed time away from drugs. I knew I wasn't bipolar. I knew the reason I was going up and down was because of my drug use.

Is there anything you want those struggling with addiction to know?

It's not your fault that you're an alcoholic or a drug addict. It's just your fault if you don't do anything about it. There is a solution. God doesn't make junk. If I can get sober, anyone can.

Daniel L.

Date of interview: 3/28/19
Sobriety date: 6/2/75, 43 years
Hometown: Hopkinton

When did you start drinking or using drugs, and how did it progress?

We started out living in Cambridge, Massachusetts. Both my parents were alcoholics. When I was 14 years old, I had my first drink. I drank three Heffenreffers behind the dryer at the dry cleaners where I worked; I wasn't a falling-down drunk. However, it changed my perspective on what and who I cared about in my life.

From ages three to five, I was a very anxious, having lived in foster homes on and off. When I was five, my mother went to state prison. We had a huge family, so my siblings and I were split up. I went to live with my aunt in Massachusetts; others went into foster care, and some went to live with other family members. I made it through my senior year in high school, but when I was 17, I went out drinking, came home, and passed out on my bed. I woke up to my aunt screaming at me. I had gotten sick on the bed, so she made me strip the bed and bring the sheets down to the basement. I had to wash them the next day. She berated me for doing this.

After this incident, my aunt took me back to my father's and dropped me off at the doorstep. When my father answered the door, she said, "I brought your child back to you." He said, "What am I going to do with him?" My aunt said, "Put him in the military. They will make a man out of him." I stayed with my father for a week and brought him home from the bar every night. I knew this wasn't the life I wanted, so I went to the Boston Army Base and signed up. The day after I signed up, I was in Lackland Air Force Base in Texas for boot camp. My father was so hungover he didn't even get up to see me off. He only gave me three dollars to go.

I never graduated from high school, and after a short time in the military, I got thrown out for drinking. Life seemed bleak. I went back to Lynn, where I felt I had some roots. I got my old job back at the dry cleaners and went to live in a room at a friend's house while he was in the military. It didn't take long before they asked me to leave, too, because of my drinking. I didn't feel as if I belonged anywhere.

I started living in different apartments. I knew how to sing, so I joined a band and even got thrown out of that. However, I kept at it and joined another band. I had a girlfriend who had two brothers in the band and lived with them. Something told me not to get a driver's license while growing up. It wasn't until I was 20 years old that I finally got it.

Within a month of having my license, I crashed my girlfriend's father's car while I was drunk. They asked me to leave their house too. I got another apartment in Lynn, got pneumonia, and the mother of one of our band members came and took care of me. After healing from my illness, I went back to the band, got drunk, and made a pass at the drummer's wife. My girlfriend—who, at this time was my fiancé, told her father. He and I got in a fistfight that night. Someone called the police, and they told me I couldn't go back to the house.

I was in a couple of bands off and on after that. There were a series of apartments, drunken episodes, and hanging out with a lot of bad people. There were drugs, alcohol, and loose women, as well as a lot of jackpots. In one of the apartments I had, my cousin moved in with me, and I started using methamphetamines and continued to drink. It was at that time that I shot up methamphetamines and smoked opiates. I would go to parties where there were bowls full of drugs. My solution to getting away from the crowd I was hanging out with was to get married. I got married, and we had two kids.

Unfortunately, I continued to drink, use drugs, and hang out. My wife got fed up with my lifestyle and my physically and emotionally abusing her. She knew our marriage was rocky and was afraid of the instability; we would move every six months. Finally, she decided to move to Haverhill, Massachusetts, where she could stay on welfare; her mother lived just over the border in Plaistow, New Hampshire. This is around the time she began going to Al-Anon.

I never tried to get my license back after the car crash when I was 20. I just decided not to drive, instead of not drinking. However, I knew if we were going to live in Haverhill, I needed to get my license, so I went and got it. It had been 10 years; I had no problem getting it. In a matter of two months, I totaled two cars.

One day I told my wife I was going to do the laundry in New Hampshire on a Sunday. You couldn't buy alcohol in Massachusetts on Sundays back then. My wife knew I was going to get drunk, so she said she would do the laundry; this was her way of keeping me from going. I convinced her I would be able to. On the way back from doing the laundry and getting drunk, I hit a telephone pole. I just sat and waited for the cops to arrest me.

My brother-in-law picked me up and brought me home. My wife confronted me when I came in the door. She asked what I planned to do with the alcohol I had taken from the crashed car. Right then, I had a strange vision in my mind of me going down a big slide into a black hole. Out of nowhere, I said, "I think I'll go to AA."

I got hooked up with the Community Employment Training Agency (CETA) program, and they got me hooked up with Haverhill Alcohol Information Referral (HAIR) as a maintenance man. I went to AA meetings every day. In the evening, there was a van that I used to take to meetings. We also took active drunks to detox. After I had been sober for five years, my wife asked for a divorce. Two years later, I married again. I wound up working at HAIR and Lawrence Detox. Most were street drunks who came in just for a place to sleep.

I met my sponsor at HAIR. He had had 42 years of sobriety before he died in the year 2000. During my time with my sponsor, I followed him and worked with him at Hampstead Hospital. It was here I learned about a weekend school program. I got my bachelor's in psychology and went on to get my master's in counseling psychology in 1995. I started work at Lake Shore Hospital in Manchester, New Hampshire.

My second wife and I divorced a year later. Two to three years later, my current wife and I got married, and we have been married now for 30 years. I worked in the addiction profession for 30 years, and for the last 10 years, I ran SUD services for the state prison system. I am retired now and enjoying life.

Looking back, when do you think it was mostly out of control?

Between ages 20 and 30, it was the most out of control.

How are you able to not drink or use daily?

I just don't drink. I don't put myself in a situation that would jeopardize my sobriety. I don't have alcohol in the house or let people bring it to my home. If I go into a place where there is alcohol, I know when to leave. I realize when people ask me to stay, they will forget about wanting me there after I leave. I bring someone sober with me if I go to a place where people are drinking. I buried myself in a 12-step program. Those were the only people I knew who didn't drink.

What is your thought about medication-assisted treatment?

I don't know enough about this to comment.

Is there anything you want those struggling with addiction to know?

Long-term sobriety is a reality. You work at it; it doesn't just come. It means you change the way you think. There is no perfect way. I choose to believe in GOD: Good Orderly Direction.

David L.

Date of interview: 6/7/2019
Sobriety date: 8/13/14, 4 years
Hometown: Portsmouth

When did you start drinking or using drugs, and how did it progress?

In the first 16 years of life, I got off on people's approval. It was my drug of choice. I was always good at school and sports and had a great childhood. My parents separated when I was 11. I spent half my time with my mother and the other half with my father. I was an angry and controlling child. When I was six, my mother thought I would be in jail for a violent crime. At the same time, I was a top-performing student, and things were going very well. Raised in a household where drinking was readily available, I don't remember anyone ever getting drunk. We would go to family events, and everyone would drink. We were allowed to have sips of drinks but getting drunk wasn't a thing.

I was 15 years old when I had my first drink. We went to Florida. It was an excellent family adventure. We went out to a restaurant, and my mother was letting me and my younger brothers drink Mudslides and Lemon Drops. She was fueling a good time. Alcohol was never more than a good time in her mind. One time, I had a conversation with my stepfather about someone he knew who was an alcoholic. I remember saying that alcoholics were just weak-willed.

I dropped out of high school to pursue a modeling career. My mother and I flew down to Florida, and a hurricane started. It knocked out the power, and planes weren't leaving for a day or two. So, we went to Miami for dinner. I was with my mom, and she told the waitress it was my 16th birthday. The waitress then asked me how old I was. Without missing a beat, I said, "I'm 21." I ordered a Mojito and had two.

At 16, during driver's ed class, I went to my first Alcoholics Anonymous meeting. That's how I knew about AA. The main thing I remember is people were talking about how drunk driving was like a sport. I didn't drink with friends during high school, only when I was with my parents. When I was 18, though, the fall of my senior year, my friend and I bought mushrooms and took them. It was one of the most incredible and fun experiences of my life, so I thought. It was unlike anything I had ever experienced.

In the spring of my senior year on my brother's birthday, we celebrated at home. I drank a bottle of Mead. A friend picked me up, and we met up with other friends. I was drunk at the time, and she offered me weed. I smoked a bowl and felt like I'd been transported into this new sense of freedom. I didn't know where I was and didn't care. It felt incredible. I went home, listened to music, and thought, "This is what life should be." It was such a great experience, so why wouldn't I want to chase it?

Six weeks later, I started smoking pot every day. I was smoking weed every night and went to one class a day. I loved it. It was fun, and I was carefree. I also started growing mushrooms so that I could take them every week. I planned to take mushrooms every Friday and have the weekend to come down from it. I could never make it to Friday, so I'd end up doing them on Thursday. I was living between my mom's and my dad's, and tripping at both places. I would take acid sometimes, and my parents knew, but they just wanted me to be safe while I was doing it.

I finally ended up finishing high school. I started to realize the drug use was getting out of hand. When I went to St. Thomas to live with my dad's friend for seven weeks, I decided I wasn't going to drink or smoke pot. I was sober for the whole seven weeks, but it was a terrible experience. I cared only about myself and was miserable.

When I got home, I went to a festival with people I wouldn't usually hang around. We took LSD, smoked opium, and did other drugs. I was getting messed up all the time, which was one of the most significant changing points for me. I thought, "I don't ever have to work hard again, and I want to do drugs. Life will be easy."

The first time I was able to drink the way I wanted to was in college. I had the mentality of I'm not drinking during the week, but I'll smoke pot. I'll drink on Fridays and Saturdays. On Sundays, I'll do my homework. I continued this drinking pattern throughout my freshman and sophomore years of college. I began to hate everyone and everything. I would ride my motorcycle drunk, and once on heroin, I would swim in the third fastest current in the US, climb trees, houses, and buildings downtown, just for fun.

I decided to move to Florida and move in with my grandmother. I got drunk on the flight there, landed at 10 p.m., and drank a bottle of wine with my grandmother. She barely drank any. I had the rest and blacked out. I lived in Florida for 55 days, drank every night, and took my grandmother's Ambien. Then I moved to New Orleans. On my third night there, a stripper and her boyfriend showed up, and they invited me to go to their house to smoke weed. I ended up living there for three months. We didn't drink a ton but always smoked weed. We took Molly or whatever came our way.

By the time I was 24, my girlfriend and I were living at my mom's house and drinking all the time. I was also trying to quit drinking. One time, I drank five bottles of wine and wanted cigarettes, so I took my brother's car out and totaled it. I got arrested and charged with an aggravated DUI, but I continued to drink heavily up until three days before my court date.

I went to an AA meeting drunk, smelling like cigarettes, and heard about the 12 Steps for the first time. I found the answer for how to be a good human being there and cried. I ended up staying sober and getting a sponsor. He told me I needed to go to more meetings, which I did. I have been clean and sober ever since.

Looking back, when do you think it was mostly out of control?

I was the most out of control between 22 and 24. I had discovered bar drinking and finally had a sense of community!

How are you able to not drink or use daily?

I get on my knees and pray every morning. I used to pray and ask God to help me stay off drugs and alcohol. Now I ask him to remove my nasty, selfish, dishonest, and resentful thinking and help me be of service to others. I go to a meeting most days, pray every night, and talk to my sponsor. I get phone calls every single day from men I help not use alcohol or other drugs. Every weekend I try to organize an AA get together.

What is your thought about medication-assisted treatment?

I never used it. When it became time to stop, I just stopped. I stopped because I was afraid of going to jail. I am skeptical of pills of any sort, but that doesn't mean it doesn't work for other people. Everyone has a path. If you're going to use Suboxone in a controlled environment instead of heroin in a basement, then I think it's better. Anyone can get sober and stay alive. If this is going to help, by all means, use it.

However, I was in a meeting, and this person said, "Well, why can't I use weed? Every time I use weed; I don't smoke dope." What happens that one day when you don't have any weed, and you need it, but the only available thing is dope, so you take it? You overdose, and you die. That is why Suboxone would be hard for me.

Is there anything you want those struggling with addiction to know?

There is help. It is okay to ask for help. It isn't taking away from somebody else to ask for help. The greatest joy I have is helping other people. I ask for help from people when I'm struggling, and I give support to people when they ask for it. It's a mutual, symbiotic thing, and both people grow as a result. It is okay to be hurting. You can get through it and get to the other side.

David W.

Date of interview: 5/13/19
Sobriety date: 10/28/80, 38 years
Hometown: Concord

When did you start drinking or using drugs, and how did it progress?

I was 15. I drank for the first time in a cabin my father and I had built behind our house, so I could paint. I could have gone to greater heights with my art if I hadn't been an alcoholic. I didn't go to a cool art school; I went to a school that showed the connection between history, art, and spirituality. I'm self-taught. My father was a wonderful man, and I had a wonderful childhood. Although he was an alcoholic, he wasn't a typical one. He didn't drink often, but when he drank, he was a different person. He knew when he drank that everything changed. He loved his family, and he loved his profession.

I mowed lawns in the summer and had keys to the owners' houses. One time, I stole a bottle of Taylor Sherry and brought it back to my cabin. I drank it with my close friend. We went through all the euphoria. We were listening to Billie Holiday and Myles Davis on my little record player, and I threw a cherry bomb at him. It went off right by his head. I could have blinded or made him deaf. When I drank, I did stupid things. My friend went home and threw up; I didn't. The next day, I looked for that experience again. It was an important experience for me. I related it to a spiritual experience. There was nothing else, including my first sexual relationships, that came close to the euphoric experience of taking that drink.

After that, I drank every time I could. If I was in your house and you went into another room, I would drink your drink. I stole alcohol a lot because I was too young to buy it legally. Back then, the drinking age was 21. I'd go into stores and steal bottles of it. I wasn't a thief, but I became a thief to get alcohol.

I was a binge drinker. I tried very hard to deny myself and go for long periods without it but would inevitably drink again. I drank with nasty people. I would go on binges. I'd go to the city and drink in the worst bars in Boston. The worse they were, the better I liked them. My people were down the dark alleys, writing poetry or painting. You know, the elite, the artistic people. These were my people, and they were all drunks.

I met a young woman in London, and we created a beautiful child together. I did not want to be married but couldn't walk away from the relationship. I couldn't conceive of an abortion either. The next years were absolute hell. It was terrible between 1964 and 1980 because I was in three mental hospitals. I almost got electric shock treatment in a Brattleboro retreat. Lots of alcoholics received electric shock treatment. This was our medical profession. It was terrible.

My wife and I have an excellent relationship now. She has her life, and I have mine. We love each other and have three kids together. We've been married for 55 years, and I'm a good husband now. I wasn't for years. I can say without equivocation that we have a good marriage now. She helped me get sober. She'd had it with me when I was drinking and moved out in the middle of the winter. She didn't go to a lawyer as they do now. She went to a shelter. If she'd gone to a lawyer, we wouldn't still be married. When she went to the shelter, I realized how bad it was. She left with no money, didn't have a job, and took the kids. Immediately, I had someone tell her to go back to the house, and I'll never come there again unless invited. The house was hers. Our problem was drinking.

When I was at one of the mental hospitals in Concord, an old doctor looked me right in the face and said, "You're a classic alcoholic, and until you go to Alcoholics Anonymous, your life will be shit." He had no psychology background; he just knew. He was in AA. Unfortunately, I didn't stop at that point. I heard it though.

Eventually, I started going to AA, stopped drinking, and learned how to live without alcohol, but I used all the other unclean coping tools like cheating and sexual promiscuity, to name a few. I didn't change myself. I didn't do the spiritual part and just used the fellowship. People in AA told me I needed to do the steps, so I stopped going to AA. I didn't go back out drinking, but I was very depressed. I knew drinking wasn't going to change anything. I considered it though.

After 15 years of not drinking, I got a sponsor, and he took me through the 12 Steps. This is when I understood the vast difference between drinking and not drinking. I stayed sober without the steps, went to meetings, and everything was the same with me except for the booze and going to meetings. When I decided to get honest with another person and go through the steps, my life changed. My wife and I were almost completely broken up. She lived here in New Hampshire and I had a house on Nantucket. Little by little, I started to change. Little by little, our marriage began to change for the better. It didn't happen overnight.

Families and spouses can lead us into deeper hells because they put up with things they shouldn't. I never could draw the line with my daughter. I was always there for her, but it didn't work. She died of an overdose three years ago. I couldn't save her. She was 40 years old and a talented ballet dancer. She was very charismatic, and a lot like me. We were very, very close. Yes, I stayed sober.

Looking back, when do you think it was mostly out of control?

In my early marriage years, it was the most out of control. I was hauled out a couple of times and taken to mental hospitals by the police. Once when I almost burnt the house down while on LSD because I thought I had a mystical experience.

How are you able to not drink or use daily?

I remember my disease. It's a sickness, and all I have power over is the first drink. I have a choice today. I don't drink, because it doesn't work for me. I have a choice today and choose not to drink. I got that choice through AA and a power greater than myself. I go to meetings and work the 12 Steps.

What is your thought about medication-assisted treatment?

Medication doesn't work. It just deals with the physical side of the person. It's a physical, mental, and spiritual disease. Unless you deal with this disease on a physical, mental, and spiritual basis, you aren't going to beat the disease. You can't just beat it with physical and mental, either. It has to be all three.

Is there anything you want those struggling with addiction to know?

Give yourself a chance. Go to AA with other people in recovery. Most psychiatrists do not know about or have the best experience working with alcoholism. People who have the experience of being an alcoholic or an addict and have overcome it can help.

Donald M.

Date of interview: 3/27/19
Sobriety date: 3/11/17, 2 years
Hometown: Hebron

When did you start drinking or using drugs, and how did it progress?

When I was young and had colds, my father would give me a shot of brandy. It helped me go to sleep. When I was 11, my brother gave me vodka and orange juice. He was having a party at the house and thought it would be great to get his little brother drunk in front of all his friends. By the time I was 13, I could ask my parents for a 12-pack, and they would give it to me. I would drink and get buzzed. By 14, I drank to get a good buzz or drunk. In the summer, I would drink four to five days of the week. When I was 17, I worked for a landscape company and would drink every single day. I dropped out of school to work. In high school, I smoked pot and started to get into cocaine.

When I turned 20, I stopped doing cocaine and marijuana because I started going to night school. I worked for a landscaping company on weekdays and did side work on my own on weekends, while also going to school at night for an associate degree in law enforcement. In 1993, I started to work for the fire department part-time and continued to work full-time and run a landscape business on the side. I got married and had my first child.

By 1998, I had my associate's degree and later became a paramedic. I went on to get my bachelor's degree in fire science and drank every night to get a buzz. I deserved to drink because I busted my ass. I didn't drink while at work though. In 2005, I injured my back and was prescribed Percocet, my back never healed. I took the Percocet as needed.

After being promoted to Captain of the Fire Department in 2007, I controlled my drinking and called in when I needed to take Percocet. In my early 40s, PTSD symptoms were starting to creep in from an accumulation of having witnessed numerous traumatic events as a firefighter. I increased my drinking to medicate the symptoms. In 2013, I went to West Virginia for a week with our church and couldn't drink. I was jonesing for a drink. I needed it. When I came home, I couldn't wait to get a drink.

In December 2014, my life was threatened at an emergency incident, which brought out the full symptoms of PTSD. My drinking increased significantly, and I started to abuse the Percocet. I went from Percocet to OxyContin; I got them from my family and others. I used alcohol and drugs to numb my feelings. I did not want to feel anymore. Within a month of this emergency incident, and using all the drugs and alcohol, I didn't care if I lived or died. I thought about suicide at least two to three times a week.

In the spring of 2015, my life started to become unmanageable. My mental and physical health went down rapidly. I was losing weight and couldn't deal with my business. I wasn't doing my paperwork, my home life suffered, and I was isolating myself. I would come home from work, and my kids would ask me how my day was, and I would say, "It sucked. Everything sucks."

In February 2016, the union president of the fire department approached me. He asked if I had a medical problem because I had lost so much weight and my attitude was not right. The other firefighters thought I had cancer. I told them it was just stress. I started to see a therapist, and we had a plan of action to help me get better. There was no plan for me not to drink or use drugs. I lied to my counselor about my alcohol and drug use. I took a couple of weeks off to get myself together and wound up taking four weeks. Mentally, I started to feel better.

In the spring of 2016, I went down mentally again. In July, the deputy at the fire department, the police chief, and the union president did an intervention on me, and I voluntarily went to McLean Hospital for the first responders' program. I detoxed for five days and did the Leader Program for first responders who also have a SUD. I went from McLean to Brattleboro Retreat for their Uniform Services Program, a program for anyone in uniform that has a SUD and PTSD. Both McLean and Brattleboro introduced me to AA.

After I got out, I relapsed and went back to work. I attended a few AA meetings. I was around AA, but I wasn't involved in AA. In November 2016, my wife kicked me out of the house for drinking and using drugs. I started to live in hotel rooms. I didn't have to answer to anyone. I had an incident at the fire department and was relieved of duty that night.

On December 10, 2016, the Pembroke Police Department did an intervention on me. They brought me back to detox at McLean. From there, I went to High Watch Recovery Center in Connecticut, where the foundation of AA started, along with working on my head and heart. I was there for 45 days. From there, I went to On-Site in Westminster, Massachusetts, for first responders with PTSD, SUD, or both. I was still around AA. My first weekend home, I got into an argument with my wife and relapsed. I left and stayed in a hotel room and used that night.

On March 10, 2017, I was in court by a Section 35. The police and my family requested it, and I was sent to Bridgewater, Massachusetts, for the state-run alcohol and drug program. It was the worst place I ever lived, but a lot of positives came out of it. I gave my will over to God and read the Big Book. After 32 days, I went back to On-Site and became a peer support staff there for a few months. I am now retired from the fire department, divorced, and living in New Hampshire. I run my own business and life is the best it's ever been because I am involved in AA and live by God's will.

Looking back, when do you think it was mostly out of control?

It was the most out of control after the emergency incident.

How are you able to not drink or use daily?

Working and being involved in AA. I got the proper counseling for my PTSD symptoms. I keep an open mind and read self-help literature.

What is your thought about medication-assisted treatment?

I got offered Suboxone, and I didn't want it. I was trying to get off as much medication as possible. My wife had done the research, and she didn't like the statistics about Suboxone.

Is there anything you want those struggling with addiction to know?

You need to embrace a program of recovery and be of the right mindset—without a mind-altering medication. The 12 Steps are a program of action. Read self-help books, eat healthily, and get proper medical treatment for any psychiatric disorders.

Doug P.

Date of interview: 5/29/2019
Sobriety date: 8/28/75, 43 years
Hometown: Sanbornton

When did you start drinking or using drugs, and how did it progress?

I got drunk at 15 years old. I didn't drink after that for a while, but I liked it, and I liked what it did to me. It gave me great relief from the tremors I've had my whole life. It acted as a sort of self-medication.

I drank heavily at around 18 years old. I left home and went to Boston to go to school. I couldn't wait to drink. While there, I went to see a psychiatrist for my depression. Depression played a big part in my life for many years. I got married at age 20 and had two boys. That marriage lasted for about seven years. I was an alcoholic nightmare, so of course, the marriage didn't work.

I left the family and moved to New York City (NYC). My brother lived in Brooklyn. I started working in the city and doing well, but I began to realize the alcohol was having a significant effect on my life. I would get up in the morning, pour a fifth of vodka in a bowl, and sop it up. It was a real problem. My relationship with people went downhill. I didn't care to be around them unless they drank like I did.

In 1974, I left NYC and moved back in with my parents. I couldn't do anything because of alcohol; I was drinking all the time. I'd get out of bed and start drinking. Vodka was my drug of choice, but I drank beer too. I never got into drugs. I tried some, but I liked alcohol and drank all the time. I was very depressed from it and had multiple suicide attempts.

After one of my suicide attempts, I went to a clinic at a mental health center. I met a doctor there who asked me to stay in their rehab for six weeks. Six weeks was an extended stay in those days. Rehab introduced me to Alcoholics Anonymous. This is the first time I realized I was an alcoholic. The doctor pointed it out to me. In the fall of 1995, I went to another treatment center in Vermont, and we went to AA meetings twice a day. I started connecting with people in the AA program. I was there for three months. I had a terrible struggle with my anger in the first couple of years of sobriety. I would get angry and feel guilty. After the guilt passed, I felt tremendous anger again.

Eventually, I met a woman in Vermont, and got married. We had two girls, and we've been together for 31 years. I became a counselor and studied art. I was also a director of addictions at a medical center for five years, which burned me out, so I left. Taking care of yourself is so very important. I am retired and enjoying life today—so grateful to be sober.

Looking back, when do you think it was mostly out of control?

In the end, I was suicidal and had terrible depression due to alcohol.

How are you able to not drink or use daily?

I read a lot about recovery. I'm very involved with a spiritual path. I meditate every day and go to church on Sundays. Books play a big part in my sobriety; I read the AA Big Book and the step book from time to time. AA saved my life.

What is your thought about medication-assisted treatment?

Get a good sponsor, go to psychotherapy or see a psychiatrist if you need these things. I don't go along with medication in treatment, except if a person has an underlying medical condition. As far as narcotics or muscle relaxers go, forget about it. Real sobriety comes out of staying clean.

Is there anything you want those struggling with addiction to know?

There is hope. You don't have to live the way you are living. You may have to jump through some hoops to get to the other side. You have to go through them. There's no way around it. You have to go through it. Sponsorship is one of the greatest things going. It is priceless to have a mentor to help you. Quitting alcohol or other drugs may be the hardest thing you've ever done in your life, but there is so much help out there. It's crucial to take advantage of resources too.

Dustin H.

Date of interview: 6/10/2019
Sobriety date: 5/21/17, 2 years
Hometown: Deering

When did you start drinking or using drugs, and how did it progress?

I was 13 years old. I used marijuana with a kid in my neighborhood. I lived in Melbourne, Florida, and this kid was a little older. He asked if I wanted to smoke pot with him. I didn't want to, but he overpowered me in a threatening way to get me to smoke it. I gave in. I was scared by the whole thing. My parents had just split up, and I lived with my father. This kid meant a lot to me. I wanted to feel accepted. Most of the guys I hung around were older and forced me to smoke with them. Then it turned into drinking.

My first alcoholic drink was right after the first time I smoked pot. It was my dad's Russian vodka. I took a few shots out of it; it was very harsh. I drank sporadically after that. By the time I was 15, I would smoke a dime bag of pot every day and have someone buy me a fifth of liquor. This period is when I got hooked on alcohol. Alcohol became the main thing in my life. I was living with a friend and his sister; she was a dancer at a club. I had my first arrest for marijuana and was also experimenting with Ecstasy, LSD, and even cough medicines. The cough medicine wasn't really for the addiction, but the roller coaster ride and the thrill.

At 16, I stopped smoking weed, but that's when the drinking intensified. I went to my first detox at 17 and was there for three days. I didn't want to drink anymore and wanted to stop everyone from nagging me. After rehab, I started to feel regularly empty, like there was a hole, and I needed to fill it.

I met my wife. She was trying to get into the Navy because her mother wanted her in there, and we both decided to clean up our acts. At age 18, we got married, and she eventually joined the Navy. We both started drinking at the beginning of the marriage, so it was a little rough. We were living in DC at the time and eventually separated. I moved back to Florida before we found out we were expecting a baby. So, I moved back up with a whole new goal of making things right with her and getting ready for our son. Shortly after moving there, I drank a half-gallon of Jack Daniels and committed myself to a hospital at the air force base. After detox, I was able to quit and got an excellent job working for the Navy.

When our son was born, my wife had a case of pretty bad postpartum depression. She started drinking heavily. Now we were both drinking. A few months after our son was born, she got arrested for domestic violence. She lost her Navy career, and we moved to Florida. She got arrested again for domestic violence in

Florida. Our marriage was tough. I had my son for a while by myself and started drinking more. It became an everyday thing again.

My wife and I got into another argument, and she took my son out of the state without my knowledge. It destroyed me. It felt as if my soul had been ripped out of me. That was the beginning of my drinking to an extreme. I almost didn't care if I died; I drank over a fifth a day by myself. Those were some of the darkest years of my life, between ages 24 and 25.

I went into the hospital for pancreatitis, and when I got out of the hospital, I started taking pain killers. I had not only physical pain but mental pain. I was using anything I could to numb myself. It got to the point where I had injected over 300 mg of Oxycodone at one time. That was the last time. I tried getting off of it, so I went on Suboxone. I was on Suboxone and Valium for a little bit, which helped me get off everything and injecting. I had been smoking crack for six months. When I tried weaning off the Suboxone and Valium, the urges came back. I felt empty, there was nothing, and so the drinking started back up again.

When I was around age 26, there was a domestic violence incident with my son and my ex-wife. His mother and her new husband called me and asked me to help them. I went up there and moved in with my ex-mother-in-law to help with my son. At this time, I was on Suboxone and Valium and was able to keep everything at bay. I got a house in Kentucky, had my son about 80 percent of the time, and things were going okay, but then I had surgery for a hernia. I started drinking again and got pancreatitis twice. After this, everything started slipping. I couldn't maintain myself anymore, so I relocated and left my son there.

I moved to southern West Virginia with a dancer, the woman I had lived with when I was 15, and left my son in Kentucky. I drank a lot and ended up with pancreatitis a couple more times. After eight months of staying there, I moved back to Florida. I was drinking non-stop and lived with a lady for a couple of years. A year before I left Florida, she committed suicide in the house while I was sleeping. I was in bad shape, so I moved out of the house and ended up sleeping in my van. I almost had utterly given up.

My whole life felt traumatizing. It felt like 20 years of living in a war zone. The kids I grew up with were vicious; there was a lot of violence in my marriage, and the only person I had left took her life. I was at the end of my rope, feeling like an empty shell. Physically I was dying; my pancreas was shot, my liver was shutting down, and I stopped trying to drink six months before I came to New Hampshire, which put me into a seizure.

I went into the hospital, and they found me a halfway house before they released me. I went to a counselor and he told me about New Hampshire, and he pushed everything through for me to come up here. When I first got here, it was hard to break out of the old routines of smoking cigarettes or cracking open a beer, but the most beautiful part is that I don't have one craving for any of it now.

Looking back, when do you think it was mostly out of control?

Right before I stopped drinking and using, it was the most out of control.

How are you able to not drink or use daily?

I get up in the morning, get everything ready, make my bed, read a devotional book, pray, and connect with God. I prepare myself for the day and make sure everything is in order. I also spend a few moments in silence, going over everything and reflecting.

What is your thought about medication-assisted treatment?

My personal experience is that it's like putting a Band-Aid on a scar. You're not focusing on the source of the problem, and Suboxone puts a patch on your psychological pain. It only helps temporarily fill the void. It alters your perception and your natural way of thinking. You're relying on something to get you by. In the long run, it's still causing an addictive situation. Used in extreme circumstances while focusing on the underlying issues, it may be helpful. You have to get off of all of it, or you'll never find peace and freedom.

Is there anything you want those struggling with addiction to know?

Christ is the way. I've tried everything else, and my connection with Christ works. I am completely content.

Ed G.

Date of interview: 3/28/2019
Sobriety date: 5/5/02, 16 years
Hometown: Silver Lake

When did you start drinking or using drugs, and how did it progress?

At age 17, right after high school. I drank on the weekends and smoked weed. I grew up in an alcoholic family. I believe I have the gene, and it just took off. I didn't know when to stop after I started drinking.

My first drunk driving arrest came at 18. I was working at a body shop, and didn't have a vehicle, so I borrowed a customer's car. I picked up a six-pack of beer and thought I'd drink and drive. I planned to drink the six-pack by the time I got to where I was going. On the way back, I rolled the car and got arrested. Shortly after that, I got another DUI and ended up going to rehab for 14 days. I heard some good things there. Someone knew I was an alcoholic and thought I should stay an extra two weeks. I had my cousin pick me up and got out of detox. I didn't drink but went full speed ahead into drugs. I thought I couldn't drink anymore, so I smoked weed. The weed progressed into using all the drugs that were present in the 1980s. I didn't have a drink for 10 years, but I never gave up mind-altering substances.

Alcohol always brought me trouble, and the drugs never seemed to, so I thought I didn't have a problem with drugs. They just made me into a vegetable. I thought drugs eased my soul, so I continued doing them: cocaine, LSD, and other hallucinogens. As soon as pills came around, I swallowed all of them.

I met a woman and got married. I couldn't accept life on life's terms and picked up a drink again. Back then, I'd blame my drinking on jobs, situations, my wife, etc. There was nothing wrong with me, and there was always something wrong with everyone else. One day, I wound up at a noontime 12-step meeting in Gardener, Massachusetts, and because of that meeting, I was able to get and stay clean.

Looking back, when do you think it was mostly out of control?

It was the most out of control at the end of my drinking and using drugs.

How are you able to not drink or use daily?

I go to Narcotics Anonymous and Alcoholics Anonymous. These programs taught me about God. I believe there is something out there looking after me. I'm here, and I'm still not drinking or using drugs.

What is your thought about medication-assisted treatment?

When I went through withdrawals, it was painful, and it hurt, but I needed that. When I go to meetings, I see young kids come in. They're doing Suboxone or methadone, but they don't want to feel the pain, so I see them for a few months, and then they're gone again. If they need Suboxone and it helps them not do drugs, that's fine, but it doesn't. You need to feel the pain. If they don't need it, then don't prescribe it to them.

Is there anything you want those struggling with addiction to know?

Go to meetings. You might think that it's nonsense at first; I did. I heard the same things over and over again. My sponsor told me I needed to listen to this because I might forget it. The guy next to me may need to hear something I already understood. The newcomer is the most important person in the room. The program has given me the knowledge to know I was that person. I'm not that person anymore, so I'm not ashamed to let people know that I'm a recovering addict.

Ed M.

Date of interview: 6/5/2019
Sobriety date: 2/11/11, 8 Years
Hometown: Nashua

When did you start drinking or using drugs, and how did it progress?

The first time I drank, I was 10 or 11. A nurse and a cop raised me. I had a good upbringing and knew right from wrong. I do remember feeling anxious all the time though. I always felt as if I didn't fit in and was teased a bit. I never felt a part of anything. I didn't belong. I was a loner and enjoyed my own company.

At age 12 or 13, I got introduced to girls. It was a big thing for me because I went to an all-guys school. At a middle school dance, someone suggested that we drink some alcohol they had stolen from their parents. It was a bottle of vermouth. It didn't taste good. I don't remember a lot after that, but I do remember feeling as if I didn't have a care in the world, and my anxiety was gone.

The story the following Monday was that I was the most popular guy in school. I couldn't wait until the next opportunity where I could steal alcohol or someone else could get it. I drank that spring and then that summer at a concert where everybody was tailgating. We got dropped off with someone's older brother, got beers, and got drunk. I liked the way it made me feel.

I eventually wanted to play college hockey and was talking to college coaches. During my freshman year in high school, I made the varsity team. It was another instance where I felt as if I didn't fit in. Any time I felt like this, I would drink. I didn't crave it or think about it much. I just thought about how much fun drinking was and associated it with that. Then I got introduced to smoking marijuana. I loved the way it made me feel. It was the same feeling that brought me out of my anxiety and discomfort.

One day I hurt my back and was taken to the emergency room. My back was all spasmed up, and they could tell, so they gave me a shot of morphine and sent me home with three or four Percocets. I liked the way they made me feel. I felt no physical or emotional pain. Playing hockey, you're very rarely pain-free.

My family moved in with my grandparents because my grandfather was sick. They initially gave him six months to live, but he ended up living for another six years. I had to transfer high schools to a public school, and it was co-ed. I had always had to wear a uniform and now I didn't. This change brought on another form of anxiety. One day my mother ran an errand, and I was downstairs hanging out with my grandfather. He had three or four large bottles of pills, the same kind the doctor prescribed for me. I took one, and no one noticed. It made me feel great. I had a mental escape and started to take them in class. It wasn't every day, but it was frequent. I was also drinking at parties in the woods.

Around 2001, I got introduced to OxyContin. It felt 50 times more powerful than Percocet, so I tried them, Vicodin, and other pain pills. I didn't use them every day, but close to every day. At age 18, I started selling pills to people I knew. I had a bunch of friends who played physical contact sports and were already taking them. I didn't want anyone to know that I took them, just that I could get them. My goal was to go to college and be a police officer, so I didn't want anyone knowing that I was a drug addict.

For two years after high school, I would go to hockey practice, coach, and get high. I liked the pills. I could drive and talk to people without being anxious. I felt normal. No one knew I was under the influence. When I got to college, I got off pills for a brief period and then got hurt again. The doctors told me I couldn't play hockey for a couple of months. I smoked pot during the day when class was over and took pain pills. Eventually, I ended up getting arrested. I got pulled over and charged with possession. They dismissed the case because no one knew I was under the influence, and it ended up being an illegal stop.

I transferred colleges and started my sophomore year on the hockey team. I was still using OxyContin and Oxycodone. I was using them more than to mask a physical injury; I was also addicted at this point. I always kept up appearances with everything. During my senior year in college, my mother and stepfather divorced. I called him my dad because he came into my life when I was three. I didn't see that coming, so my drug use peaked. Everyone knew it was emotionally tough, but I just kept it in and self-medicated.

An average day that year looked something like, wake up, break into a house, go to a pawn shop, go to a drug dealer, and then off to hockey practice. I took night classes, sometimes was dealing drugs, used cocaine and dabbled in methamphetamines, acid, and Ecstasy. I would use anything, but my drugs of choice were opiates.

I was coaching hockey camp and got caught stealing money from the kids. I went into treatment at that time and blamed it all on depression. Then I did better for a little bit and relapsed. I tried Suboxone for six or seven months and didn't have a craving to want to get high. I still felt anxious, smoked weed, and drank every day though. There was no accountability, and I wasn't working on anything. Things just kept getting worse. I started using a needle for a couple of months and took benzodiazepines. Eventually, I got charged with armed robbery, which made a couple of local newspapers. I couldn't hide anymore. I walked into the courtroom that I had once worked in, and the parents of kids I'd coached were there.

The court appointed me a case manager. One day I met with her, and she pulled out a picture of herself in front of a house she had just bought. She said she bought this house and was five years sober. I was like, "Excellent, good for you." Then she pulled out another picture of a park bench with a playground in the background and told me she lived on that park bench for four to five years, smoking crack. I asked her how she got from that bench to where she is now. She told me she was in a house that kept her accountable, and she did the 12 Steps.

I had been in treatment enough times to know what the 12 Steps were. She called her friend in Nashua, and I went there to live in their sober house. I was required to go to a bunch of meetings and started to go through the 12 Steps. I held on to something I heard early on: you don't have to drink, even if you want to. You don't have to use drugs, even if you want to. I could sit there and not use drugs or drink for an hour, and that built up to a longer time.

Slowly, but surely, I started to feel good on the inside.

Looking back, when do you think it was mostly out of control?

It was the most out of control the last year and a half of my using. My disease took me to new lows. I was committing crimes to support my habit. I was a daily polysubstance user and was using more of everything. I went into treatment facilities multiple times in one year. I ruined multiple relationships and was charged with armed robbery as a direct result of my disease. This period also led me to my sobriety.

How are you able to not drink or use daily?

I ask a power greater than myself to keep me away from drinking and drugs. This spiritual connection has worked for a long time, so I don't gamble with it. I got sober enough to see a bunch of people I know die from this disease, so why would I mess with it? It's that serious.

There are a couple of us that met while working in a treatment center, and we have a 15-minute call every day. We read the Big Book, discuss it, and give our thoughts on it. I read the *Daily Reflections* book at some point during each day. Technology is great. I use the app called My Spiritual Tool Kit, and it gives me nightly review questions. I also meditate at night.

What is your thought about medication-assisted treatment?

If we're going to give someone Suboxone for opioid addiction, put them on a plan for a couple of months with therapy in a supervised program. Let's work to get them off. The goal should be abstinence-based. I don't think everyone needs medication-assisted treatment, but I guess some do. Let's figure out how to bridge the gap between needing medication-assisted treatment and abstinence. We need data. We need to measure outcomes. There tends to be a more holistic approach to abstinence-based sobriety. I have yet to see someone who's been on methadone for an extended period say that life is good and that they've made progress. However, I see people in abstinence-based recovery saying this all the time.

Is there anything you want those struggling with addiction to know?

There is hope. There is no right or wrong way to achieve long-term sobriety. Just give meetings a shot, even if you don't believe in a higher power yet. Just show up. Sobriety is possible. You can live a life without having to pick up a drink. You don't have to be good to get sober.

Ed P.

Date of interview: 5/31/19
Sobriety date: 6/17/93, 25 years
Hometown: Franklin

When did you start drinking or using drugs, and how did it progress?

When I was nine, I had my first taste of alcohol but didn't get drunk for many years after that. I watched my father and mother as they drank and smoked heavily. My father was a raging alcoholic. When he drank, he was violent. I saw his violence as a young child, so I didn't want anything to do with alcohol. We lived in a French Catholic community in northern Vermont. If you didn't say the right thing in confessional, you would get beaten by either the priests or the nuns.

During my high school years in the 1960s, all the kids were partying, but I never did. I worked a 40-hour week, went to school, and graduated. After high school, at age 17, I joined the Marines.

That was an eye-opener for this naive child. I thought when you went into the Corps that you were big, bad, and tough. They humbled me very quickly. In basic training, the drill sergeant beat you and screamed at you if you didn't follow directions. I got out of the service at age 19 and came home. I married my first wife, and we had two kids together. I drank at the reception, and off I went to the races. I drank more and more heavily. I'd get home every night and have a routine beer, but I didn't touch the hard liquor yet. Eventually, this marriage ended in divorce.

In the late 1970s and early 1980s, I just kept on drinking and drinking. I always had jobs and never got fired. I also never got a DWI, but that doesn't mean I shouldn't have had one. I was single for several years, and during those times, I drank heavily. Eventually, I moved toward the seacoast and got a job. I met a young lady, got her pregnant, and got married. While she was pregnant, I held off on a lot of heavy drinking. After my son was born, though, I took right back up with it.

There was a point when I drove a tractor-trailer. When I did that, I didn't drink. Believe it or not. I took this job seriously. I did that for a year and then decided I didn't want to be away from my family anymore, so I quit. I got a job in Burlington, Vermont, and the drinking took off again. I'm not sure why. I made my wife's and son's lives miserable, and she left.

What happened to me in the service was starting to bother me. I had never talked to anyone about it. The reasons I drank came from my military abuse and also the physical and verbal abuse by the church. At the end of my use, I would eat over-the-counter medicines that were supposed to help you sleep. I'd eat those like candy, take a shot of alcohol, and drink beer. I was working third shift, and it was hard to sleep. I'd come home, have a couple of beers, eat a lot of sleeping medication, and go to bed. In the end, I took a bunch of pills and attempted to end my life. I woke up the next morning with a terrible hangover, picked up the phone—couldn't tell you why—and called a human resource line. They told me I needed to get checked into a detox hospital.

I was there for 30 days and was introduced to Alcoholics Anonymous. I went to an early morning meeting in Burlington, Vermont, five times a week and on Saturday nights. Getting sober was, by far, the hardest thing I've ever had to go through in my life. Getting shot at was easier.

Looking back, when do you think it was mostly out of control?

Towards the end, when I was taking all those pills and drinking, it was the most out of control.

How are you able to not drink or use daily?

I wake up in the morning and say thank you to God for another day. I go through the day and focus on what I can do to be positive to myself. I read a little from the Big Book. Reading is difficult for me, but I still make sure I read recovery literature. I stay busy and positive in my thoughts. I talk to my sponsor regularly and make sure to attend AA meetings.

What is your thought about medication-assisted treatment?

It's just a Band-Aid. It starts another form of addiction. The body gets immune to it, and then it wants more and more. When the body doesn't have enough Suboxone, people go out and get heroin, cocaine, fentanyl, or meth, and eventually die.

Is there anything you want those struggling with addiction to know?

Alcoholics Anonymous is there for you. It's a very simple program for complicated people. It's not easy, but it's simple. Go to meetings, get a sponsor, and get involved. People who get involved, stay involved and volunteer to do things, stay sober.

Elizabeth R.

Date of interview: 3/26/19
Sobriety date: 1/16/12, 7 years
Hometown: Campton

When did you start drinking or using drugs, and how did it progress?

Age 16. I grew up in Plaistow. I was 85 pounds in the third grade, and my mother was morbidly obese, over 400 pounds. She would give me food to make me feel better. The sugar part of the food was my addiction. I was teased and bullied a lot in school. The first time I remember being involved with alcohol, I bought it for a party. I don't remember drinking it then, but I remember drinking in my 20s.

When I was 30 years old, they held my promotion because of my weight. Food and sugar helped me escape. When I was 37, I decided to have gastric bypass surgery. Six of us from where I worked had the surgery, and five of us became alcoholics. My drinking took off after the surgery. It wasn't until February of 2005 that I had a euphoric reaction to alcohol and thought to myself, "Hmmm, this could be good." By April, I was drinking daily. I was also blacking out at least twice a week. I was drinking mixed drinks, rum, whatever.

By August of that year, my husband was questioning what was going on with me. I had to start hiding my alcohol outside the house. I would have to leave work and drink. He thought I was into drugs and put a tracking device on my car. In June 2006, he filed for divorce. By August, the divorce was final, six months before our 20th anniversary.

I was doing very well financially and was the regional division cash manager in the finance department where I worked. I left our family home and got an apartment near my favorite bar. On February 28th, 2007, my 40th birthday, I walked into my first detox. At that time, I started calling out of work and had the shakes, terribly. I was physically sick. Because of my bypass surgery, I couldn't fit a lot in my stomach, so I stopped eating as much. I was barely eating enough to be alive. Because of a lack of nutrition, I wound up with a rash on my face called angler fasciitis. It started in the corner of my mouth and went up to my cheek; it was red, and it wept with a clear liquid. When I had the rash was the first time I took a leave of absence from work.

Over the next year and a half, I went to two more detoxes and saw an addiction counselor after the second one. This counselor referred me to AA, and I didn't want to go. I wanted a pill or surgery to fix me. I didn't want something that required a whole lot of my energy. In December 2008, after my third detox, I got my first DUI. I went through a red light and hit a car, and that car hit another vehicle. When the officer tested me, I blew a .27 blood alcohol level. They treated me as a multiple offender because my alcohol level was so high.

I wound up in emergency rooms often, during blackouts. One nurse said to me, "You know this is your seventh time here this summer?" I went to the police department many times and was put in protective custody. A week before the accident, my job wanted me to work out west. I turned down the offer because I thought I would die if I went out there. I didn't think anyone would be keeping an eye on me. I took their severance pay and left. A few days before the car accident, I found out my mother had breast cancer. She was living in Campton. She told me, if I moved up to live with her, she would help me get through my license requirements if I helped her with her cancer treatments.

My mother brought me to AA right away. I first had to go to jail for three days, a drunk school for seven days, see a licensed alcohol and drug counselor, and then I lost my license for a year. I didn't do very well the first six to seven months of going to AA. I just wanted to control my drinking. I wanted to go to AA and learn how to drink right. Somehow in July 2009, I learned this wasn't going to happen. I stayed sober for 20 months, and then in April 2011, I relapsed for four hours. I drank bottles of wine. I wanted to die because I hadn't found another solution.

I picked up a waitress job where they serve alcohol. I was white knuckling it and thought about drinking all the time. It was always on my mind, thinking should I drink or not drink. I had a sponsor and was working on the steps. I was too intellectual for a higher power. I stayed sober for nine months, drank again, and got another DUI. In 2012, I drank for another 4-hour stint, stopped, and have been sober since.

Looking back, when do you think it was mostly out of control?

In November and December 2008, because of being stuck in a vicious cycle of drinking and not wanting to, and then doing it again.

How are you able to not drink or use daily?

Once I became open to the idea of a higher power to help me, I have not had a drink since. I still didn't know what a higher power was or how it looked. Having one was the one thing I hadn't tried. I work with other alcoholics and bring them through the 12 Steps of recovery. Having a higher power and helping others are the two primary keys to my sobriety.

What is your thought about medication-assisted treatment?

I don't know enough about it.

Is there anything you want those struggling with addiction to know?

You are not alone. Surrendering is to win. Find someone in recovery who has what you want and do what that person does. The more you beat yourself up, the more it blocks you from hope. Go to recovery meetings, ask for help, and surround yourself with people who are just like you.

Eric M.

Date of interview: 4/26/19
Sobriety date: 7/11/13, 5 years
Hometown: Center Ossipee

When did you start drinking or using drugs, and how did it progress?

When I was seven years old, my mother was cleaning out this big walk-in closet where I kept all my stuffed animals. She said she found over one hundred empty bottles of stuffed peperino peppers hidden inside the stuffed animals. I share this because my behavior was compulsive right out of the gate.

The first time I remember drinking was when I was 10 years old. My buddies and I had a homeless man buy us our first six-pack. We also smoked cigarettes and drank. It was easy to have homeless people buy for us. We were drinking here and there, and it wasn't excessive by any means. I was introduced to marijuana around age 11. The pot was easy to get because we all had older siblings.

We moved to New Hampshire when I was 12. Having to move here pissed me off, but I was glad to introduce alcohol, cigarettes, and marijuana to all my new friends. Booze wasn't hard to get, so I drank every weekend and drank to get drunk. I started getting into trouble at home and skipping school.

By the time I was 17, my parents had gotten sick of calling the police to drag me home, and I was sick of being brought back, so I got emancipated. Having this freedom allowed my drinking to take off. Now that I was out of the house, I moved in with people who were five years older than me. They thought it was funny when I got drunk at first, but in a few months, they realized I wasn't drinking like everyone else. I had no off switch, and they did. They stopped getting me alcohol altogether. That's when I started selling marijuana.

I got a job at a factory when I was 18 and kept that same job for over 18 years. I would walk by employees, and they would comment that they were catching a buzz just from me walking by them. Management never said anything, maybe because I was a workaholic too. I was drinking Jim Beam and smoking over an ounce of weed a week. I don't even know how much cocaine I was doing, but I know it was a lot. I still showed up for work every day.

By the time I was 26, I was married and had a son. I stopped selling drugs because I didn't want to lose our house. My alcohol and drug intake increased, and I had to pay for drugs because I wasn't selling anymore. Buying alcohol and drugs got expensive, which led to a divorce. After the separation from my wife, I drank a lot. I was at the liquor store at least every other day, buying a half-gallon of Jim Beam.

I went to The Wolfeboro Inn every day after work, and if I worked Saturdays, I'd stop in for mimosas. I was living in a campground in a tiny one-room cabin. Everyone else in the campground was drinking, so I blended in. My drinking progressed to the point where I lost my job at that factory.

I moved to Rochester and found out that I was unemployable. I was young, had 18 years in the same position, and thought everyone was going to want me. I thought it would be effortless to get a job, but it wasn't. In the real world, you can't show up still drunk for work. It ended up with me starting at a heating company in a machine shop. On the very first day, the foreman, who was my boss, invited me to go to an AA meeting with him. My introduction to AA is what started my first bout of sobriety. I ended up having almost three years of sobriety.

Six months after my getting custody of my son, his mother called and wanted to take him for the weekend. Being alone is how my relapse started. I had it all figured out in my head; I was going to get a fifth, be hammered on Friday, hungover on Saturday, and Sunday I would pretend it didn't happen. On Friday, I went to the liquor store and bought a half-gallon. I didn't have another sober breath for six years. I drank every day. At first, it was a half-gallon every other day.

My drug use got excessive, too; I was doing drugs as often as possible. I had a relationship with three different women who were all over 75 years old. They were all overprescribed pills. They would buy me a half-gallon of vodka and give me around $200 worth of pills for prostitution favors.

When my son was 16, he poisoned my vodka. He was so sick of me drinking when he was living with me. He saved up those packets that come in pepperoni that say, "Do not eat." He put them in my vodka. He was trying to get me sick, so I would go to the hospital and get help. I knew it tasted funny, got angry, and called the police. I wanted someone to come fingerprint the bottle because someone had messed with it, and I didn't know who. I was not sober. I realized I had just called the police, and they were going to come and take my vodka. Even though I knew it was poisoned, I proceeded to chug the vodka as fast as I could. I didn't want them to take it.

These types of scenarios lasted six years. I ended up with my third DWI and could no longer tell myself I was a functioning alcoholic. I was drinking a half-gallon of vodka a day and continuing to use drugs. I would vomit blood and have seizures often. One day, during one of my seizures, as I was vomiting blood on the floor in my living room, my son came home. He saw me, stepped over me, and said, "Fuck you, Dad."

He had had it. His reaction was one of the most powerful things that has ever happened in my life. It hit me hard, and it got me back to AA meetings. I was still unemployable and a wreck. I was able to get a job at a car wash, which I had to hitchhike to both ways. I would go to an AA meeting at lunch break and got super active in AA. I'd go to at least one meeting a day.

I dove so much into AA that people started telling me that I had to back off. I overcommitted myself. They said you got sober to live life, and you're still hiding in meetings. I backed off quite a bit but always go to meetings today. I can't imagine how my life would have ended up if I didn't have the support of people in AA.

Looking back, when do you think it was the most out of control?

The end was, without a doubt, the worst. The time between my first sobriety until this sobriety. There were no morals, and it was horrible.

How are you able to not drink or use daily?

My job is helping other people. I get to spend all day trying to help other people get and stay sober. When things are going well in my life, the best thing is to do something for someone else. It takes me out of myself. I believe it's what keeps me in sobriety. My sobriety is as healthy as it is because I get to help other people all day long. I do it on my own time as well as at work.

What is your thought about medication-assisted treatment?

It has its place. I can't say I've seen it work very well. I don't want to say that it doesn't have its place, but it seems to be about people making money. How is someone supposed to get sober if doctors are prescribing five to eight different medications?

I started with cigarettes and alcohol simply because it was in my house and my friends' houses. We've flooded the streets with Suboxone. Kids have easier access to Suboxone than they do cigarettes or alcohol. It's a no-brainer that they're going to use that first. It's scary. I've been working with youth for over three years now, and the kids talk to me. I hear what's going on.

Is there anything you want those struggling with addiction to know?

There is hope. There is a way out. It will suck at first, but you're not alone. As long as you reach out, there will be people to help you. You do not need a drug to fix an alcohol or drug problem; you need people and connections. Having relationships with others is the opposite of addiction. Addiction is isolation. AA gave me people who understood how I was feeling, and that allowed me to open up.

<u>Eric S.</u>

Date of interview: 4/19/19
Sobriety date: 12/7/06, 12 years
Hometown: Salem

When did you start drinking or using drugs, and how did it progress?

I started using pot in fifth grade with some older kids in the neighborhood. I didn't feel high, and it wasn't a great experience; I just thought it was dumb. Not long after that, I drank vodka for the first time. We had a homeless guy buy it for us at a liquor store. I was an alcoholic from the get-go. I drank until I blacked out and threw up. That Sunday morning, I woke up and started to drink by myself. This led to drinking during school, which led to drugs, which led to smoking pot.

I did a lot of Ecstasy and was intoxicated as frequently as I could be. It brought me relief from a life where I felt uncomfortable. This discomfort in life had been around since I was born. I always felt displaced, or that other kids were ahead of me, that somehow they had life figured out better than I did. They appeared more comfortable in their skin. I remember being anxious all the time.

When I was 14 years old, a friend of mine came over with a 40 mg OxyContin. I had already taken Ecstasy and Vicodin, so taking pills for effect wasn't anything new. I didn't know when I sniffed half of this OxyContin that I was taking pharmaceutical-grade heroin. I had no idea it would change the course of my life forever. It became what I wanted to do.

In the beginning, it was fun. A year later, when I was 15, OxyContin (Oxys) was harder to get consistently. I needed to get high because I had a physical addiction to drugs, and there were no Oxys around. Even though I said I was never going to, I tried heroin. A girl I was friends with stuck a needle in my arm, and I shot a bag of dope. From that moment on, I was a full-blown IV drug user. I shot heroin as frequently as I could. I almost immediately dropped out of school at 15. Heroin became my master. It ruled me. My entire life revolved around finding the money, getting the money, getting the drugs, and doing them. I was stuck on repeat every day. I did this consistently until I got sober in 2006.

Just before my 22nd birthday, I had almost seven years of continuous IV drug use. I overdosed five times during that period. I died five times, and they brought me back to life. I would wake up in the hospital on breathing machines, after multiple shots of Narcan. Addiction devastated my parents. My father had a stress-related stroke when I was 19, due to all my use.

I tried to find recovery for the first time at 17 years old and did a year and a half at a methadone clinic. Every day I would wake up, drive to the methadone clinic, and they would give me concentrated methadone syrup. I'd sit there and drink it, make sure I got every drop, and then go home and drink alcohol, eat benzos, smoke weed, and be in a stupor all day long. I'd go to the methadone clinics and do all those other drugs during the day. Then I'd smoke crack and shoot cocaine all night long. I'd come down off those drugs and head back to the methadone clinic and do it all again. I would intermittently go to detox, go to treatment, go to meetings, therapy, and jail. That was always the struggle.

I've tried almost everything. Now I have a recognition that I am more than just a mind and a body, but that I have a spirit as well. As much as I need to take care of my body, I need to take care of my soul. I take care of my spirit by living with principles. I understand it is a life-long process. There's no graduating from this thing, and there's no hitting a place where you've done all the work you need to do. I'll be working on this until the day I die.

Looking back, when do you think it was mostly out of control?

From 17 until I got sober at age 22, it was all a nightmare.

How are you able to not drink or use daily?

I work a 12-step program. I pray, use meditation, take a daily moral inventory, admit when I'm wrong, and continue self-discovery.

What is your thought about medication-assisted treatment?

I see a whole lot of medication deployed, and I don't see an equal amount of treatment going along with it. Medication is taking over, unfortunately. I never thought being an abstinence-based recovery guy would make me the enemy of many people. I toe the line and take the heat just talking about what I believe in and my experience. I wish more people would come out and stop backing down.

All the people who are pro-abstinence and passionate about it are passionate about it because of their lived experience. There is very rarely anybody passionate about their medication-assisted treatment experience. You have so-called recovery advocates, and a lot of them aren't even in recovery, nor have they ever taken Suboxone. A lot of people passionate about abstinence, like me, are products of MAT, and it didn't work for them.

Is there anything you want those struggling with addiction to know?

There is no easy fix for addiction. There are so many people looking for an easy fix. People from the micro-level and people with personal experience are looking to get sober quickly. People from the macro-level who are legislators, policymakers, and the general society are looking to put a Band-Aid on this addiction crisis. To recover, it takes hard work, but it's open to everybody. Anyone can get better; it doesn't matter who you are. Absolutely everyone can recover if they are willing.

Erin M.

Date of interview: 4/2/19
Sobriety date: 12/26/09, 9 years
Hometown: Grafton

When did you start drinking or using drugs, and how did it progress?

I was nine and at my friend's house, and her mom made some wine spritzers. She made each of us one, and I loved it. I wanted more immediately. Next time was when I was about 13 or 14; my parents had a bar, and they'd have friends over occasionally. At night when they were in bed, and I couldn't sleep, I'd read the little bartending guide and make myself a drink. It helped me sleep. I did this about once or twice a week randomly.

Then, when I was 16, I started smoking pot. I smoked daily and all day long until I was 18. I was drinking on occasion, but it wasn't much. It was effortless to get. I graduated from high school, and when I was 20, I got pregnant, so I stopped everything. I did well for the first several years after my daughter was born and would drink or smoke on occasion but not around my daughter.

Drinking didn't become an issue again until I was around 27. I had just gone through a rough divorce and started drinking a lot, trying to cope with it. Eventually, I met someone else, and we started drinking just on the weekends. A few years after that, I ended up having endometriosis and became addicted to pain pills. I was 30 and using Percocet, Vicodin, and Valium. I can't remember what else, but they were all prescribed by my doctor. I just took them as a pill, usually a little more than I needed to, but continued to only drink on the weekends.

I had a hysterectomy and thoroughly cleaned myself of everything. I didn't drink, do pills, or smoke pot and did okay for a couple of years. I don't know what shifted, but I started drinking again and met people at bars who became my friends. They could drink as I did, and at some point, it shifted to where whenever I drank, I'd black out almost every single time. It got to a point, over the last few years of my drinking, where I specifically drank to black out. I was also smoking cigarettes this whole time, and if anyone had something else, I would do it.

I wasn't going out and seeking drugs. I drank daily though. My last night drinking was Christmas 2009; I went to my usual bar. I blacked out and was in handcuffs. I had no idea why. I remember being in the police car and asking the police officer if I had hurt anyone. I finally came to in jail and realized, "Oh my gosh, what have I done with my life?"

I went home that night and had this weird little area of stolen stuff in my bedroom, hats, pool table balls, etc., and it hit me. I tore everything down and threw it in a pile. Something told me the alcohol was making me do this, and I had a problem with alcohol. The next morning, I woke up and called a friend who I used to drink with. She took me to my first AA meeting, and I've been going ever since.

Looking back, when do you think it was mostly out of control?

The last year is when I realized that it was becoming an issue.

How are you able to not drink or use daily?

I have people in my recovery network that I reach out to, and I pray. Prayer and spirituality are a considerable part of my sobriety.

What is your thought about medication-assisted treatment?

I don't necessarily agree with medication. I did not need it, and I know many people who did not need it. Taking certain medications can cause one to have to detox, again. If someone wants to be sober and live a good life, there's a lot of help out there. There's AA, NA, and many other types of meetings. Many people have been through it and can help.

Is there anything you want those struggling with addiction to know?

Life can be a lot better without alcohol or other drugs. You don't need to feel the way you're feeling anymore. Some drink or use other drugs to mask emotions, but it also hides the good feelings. You can learn how to be truly happy; you have to allow yourself to feel.

Gary F.

Date of interview: 6/4/2019
Sobriety date: 8/15/85, 33 years
Hometown: Farmington

When did you start drinking or using drugs, and how did it progress?

It was Christmas Eve, and I was 13 years old. I stole a bottle of Canadian Club whiskey from my old man and met up with three guys at midnight mass. We snuck out and went to the all-night laundromat, where I had hidden the bottle. We drank, got drunk, and ended up in jail. I sort of ruined Christmas that year for my family. My father wanted to kill me. I remembered what the alcohol did for me; I could sing, I could dance, I felt great, and I couldn't wait to do it again.

From ages 13 to 18, I drank whenever I could get it, which was once a month or so. At 16, I got arrested again. Now pot and LSD were in the picture. I had a lot of arrests by the time I was 18. I was in my third high school at this point. On my graduation day, I got drunk, high, and then arrested. The guards didn't take my belt, and I hung myself in the cell. My brother and my dad came in and my brother saved me. I woke up in the hospital three days later.

Not long after this, I met a girl in a bar who later became my wife.

She got pregnant, and we were going to have a child. The night before we were to leave to move out west, some friends threw a party for me. On my way home, I got pulled over. The cop found marijuana, and I got arrested again. They allowed me to leave on a bond. She moved to Arizona, pregnant, and I went to Texas to get a job. Eventually, she joined me in Texas. I was still drinking.

My daughter was born, and I was drinking. I came home, and my wife said, "Something has to change, or we're all done." Eventually, she got a restraining order and I couldn't go to the house. The sheriff told me I had to leave. I reasoned my way back in when we had two children, but I had to go to AA.

I went to my first meeting in 1981 and went to the bar right after. I drank a reasonable amount, put gum in my mouth, and went home. When my wife asked how it was, I told her it was good, but they needed $10 a meeting. I told her this to get her to give me money. There is no cost, only donations. It wasn't even a month after that, I woke up on the curb with my nose busted and covered in blood. I had gotten into a fight. I remember my little daughter seeing me this way. It must have been frightening for her.

We moved back to Pennsylvania to be with my wife's mother. One night I came home in a blackout, and I remember her mother's foot close to the side of my head. She was telling me that she would raise my children and take care of my wife. She then proceeded to ask me to get out. I slept under a bridge that night.

I couch-surfed until my sister-in-law told me I could move to Derry, New Hampshire. I got a job and told her I wasn't going to drink again. I cut out the St. Jude prayer and started to say it every day. I was such an angry person sober. My job wound up letting me go, so I stopped and got a beer on the way home and drank it. Then I got a 12-pack. My sister-in-law walked in and asked what I was doing. I told her my job had let me go. She said, "I'd drink too if I were you," and so I did. That was right around Christmas time.

I drove back to Pennsylvania to spend Christmas with my wife and kids. I ended up drinking and falling down my mother-in-law's front steps. My family sat me down and told me I needed to grow up and stop all of this. Right then, the phone rang, and it was for me. It was a call from a job I'd applied to in New Hampshire. I went in for the interview and got the job, so my wife and kids moved to NH.

In 1984, there was a shutdown at the company where I worked. They gave us our regular checks, bonuses, vacation pay, and a keg party. The next thing I remember is waking up on the floor of a jail. I was 31 at this time. I called my wife, and she told me to get myself out and the divorce was back on again.

Shortly after that, I got a DUI, I lost my license and was charged with leaving the scene of an accident and possession. I told my wife I wasn't going to drink again, and I didn't for three to four weeks. However, I ended up drinking with someone who was giving me a ride home from work on August 14, 1985. I pulled up to the house, and I remember the disappointed look in my wife's eyes as she held our two children. I knew I had to do something. I called AA, went to a meeting, and haven't picked up a drink since.

Looking back, when do you think it was mostly out of control?

From 1977 up until 1984, it was the most out of control.

How are you able to not drink or use daily?

I wake up; I don't come to. I go to bed; I don't pass out. As soon as I open my eyes, I ask a power greater than myself to keep me away from a drink or a drug, just for today. I spend time with a group of sober guys. I go to meetings regularly, read the *Twenty-Four Hours a Day* book, and the *Daily Reflections*. I'm told that if I have a cold, I'm an alcoholic with a cold. If I lose a job, I'm an alcoholic losing a job. If I go through a divorce, I'm an alcoholic getting a divorce. It has allowed me to live a life I never thought I would.

What is your thought about medication-assisted treatment?

Medication prescribed by a doctor in specific situations is right. You're going to go through anxiety, depression, and everything else, but you don't need a drug to cover up those feelings.

Is there anything that you want those struggling with addiction to know?

There is a solution. You don't need a drug that's a crutch. You don't need a crutch. You need to get with people who are experiencing the same thing, sober people. Stuff your pride and become teachable. Realize you can have the best. Margarine tastes good on bread, but it isn't butter.

Glenn M.

Date of interview: 4/4/19
Sobriety date: 5/16/92, 26 years
Hometown: Undisclosed

When did you start drinking or using drugs, and how did it progress?

My first experience drinking was at age 13. I drank wine with a group of kids in junior high school. It was disgusting. However, magic happened; I finally fit in. I was a part of something, and it felt amazing. I was funny; girls talked to me. I chased that feeling from then on.

I played football as a freshman. After the first game, I went to a party. It was the first time I got drunk. I was 15. From then on, I got drunk every time I drank. I could talk to girls; I was somebody.

I looked forward to every Saturday night so that I could drink. I grew up wanting to be a professional athlete and said I'd never drink. Now, I'm drinking, and by the time I was a sophomore, I was drinking two nights a week. In my junior year, it progressed to three times per week. I was introduced to marijuana. Now I'm drinking alcohol at least twice a week and smoking pot. Senior year, I was buying pot, smoking it four times a week, and drinking during school.

One day, I hit a teacher with my car. He yelled, "You just hit me," and I was like, "You were in the middle of the road." I blamed him. I grabbed my gym bag and went off to the office. I placed the gym bag behind a door as I went into the office. Another teacher saw this, grabbed the bag, brought it into the office, and said, "Hey, he came in with this, and there are eight fifths of alcohol in it." My drinking progressed and was consuming my life. If I wasn't playing sports, I was looking to drink, smoke pot, or both.

I received a full scholarship to play football in college. It was very structured for the first semester. The second semester, they cut us loose, and that is where my drinking took off. I went from a 3.0 student to a 2.0 student, all in one semester. There were only two places I ever felt comfortable: in an athletic uniform or drinking. Other than that, I was scared and insecure, with minimal self-esteem. I didn't know how to be social.

By then, I was drinking five times a week. I got a head injury the last game of my sophomore year, which ended my football career. The team made me the manager. I was angry and resentful. I had started on every team, and now I was carrying dummy bags and water bottles and filming practices. It made me sick. I could not accept this and used booze to dull the pain.

I became a daily drinker from that point on. During my junior year in college, I broke my hand in a fight. The doctor gave me

Demerol. BOOM! This felt good. I wanted that shot, whether I needed it or not. For the next six months, I was prescribed opiates. I started taking two every four hours, then three every four hours, and then four every two hours. It was becoming a very dark and scary time. Eventually, I resorted back to alcohol.

I transferred to another college. I was accepted and had a great first game. My name was in the paper, and I was back. At least, it felt that way. The school I left called and reported me to the new school. They said I shouldn't be playing football due to my head injury. They took me off the field. I fought it, won, and got back into football, but I wasn't going to class. I was there to play football and to party. I didn't graduate. When the football season ended, a beer distributor was hiring immediately. I left school that day and was soon in charge of a 28,000-pound truck full of 1,000 cases of beer, Monday through Friday.

At that point, I was daily drinking and starting to make the police log regularly. I went to court for a drunk and disorderly charge, and there was a kid at court who said, "Hey, if you go to these AA meetings, get a paper signed and show the judge, he usually gives you a slap on the wrist." I started going to AA. I was the last one there and the first to leave. I got the paper signed and went to court; boom, it worked. Three months of AA, and I didn't drink. I felt better, I related it to these people, and it felt positive. However, once I stopped going to meetings, alcohol progression was in full bloom. Things got worse!

Driving under the influence was routine. I finally earned a DWI. I lawyered up but lost the case at the district court level. I appealed but suffered another defeat in superior court. Over $8,500 spent to lose. Ouch! I went back to AA meetings to restore my license. I had to attend and complete the First Offenders Program. I remained dry for approximately four months. I graduated from the First Offenders Program and celebrated at the Gas Lighter Bar.

A friend showed up at the bar and bought me a beer. The next thing I know, I'm at The Yard drinking in Manchester. Upon leaving, there was a fight regarding who would drive. I lost and began driving on 93 with five or six other kids in the car. I must have been in a grey out because it was as if I woke up and pulled over. I argued with my friends that I shouldn't be driving with no license. They convinced me I was okay, and I continued.

I got off at exit 10, and the blue lights came on. It turned into a 57-minute car chase with the police. I finally pulled over and attempted to run, but I had my seatbelt on and couldn't exit the car. An officer with a gun drawn yelled, "Did you have enough?" I fell back into my seat and, looking up, I saw myself in the mirror. Game over.

I thought to myself, "What the fuck am I doing?" I could no longer blame my life on losing football, never making Dad proud, never measuring up, or the world being against me. I realized the problem was looking at me in the mirror. An overwhelming state of calm and a sense of relief came over me. It was my first spiritual experience.

That night changed my life. The parents of the girl I was dating bailed me out, and her mother gave me a Big Book, a hug, and told me everything was going to be okay. Instead of my losing my job, my employer kept me on, paid the fines, and helped me get back on my feet. That is when I felt I had some purpose, and I dove into recovery full steam.

I accepted my alcoholism; my life was unmanageable. Once I understood this, I was finally free. I struggled with the spiritual piece at first. A guy took me off to the side and said, "There's a difference between spirituality and religion. Religion is for people afraid of going to hell, and spirituality is for the people who have already been there." I was afraid of going to jail, and one guy said,

"Pray about it. What have you got to lose?"

A door opened up for me right there and then. It started me on Steps 2 and 3. In Step 4, I learned who I was, and that good intentions aren't good enough. I learned about my hidden agendas, and this allowed me to change my thoughts. I also started to change my behaviors.

After six months of my being dry, my wife said that she wished I were drinking again. My sponsor suggested I do some more controlled drinking, come back, and tell him how it works out. I was devastated and confused; however, this helped me understand that just putting down the alcohol and drugs was not enough. I learned how staying sober works. I had to change myself.

Alcohol is only mentioned in the first half of the first step. The next 11 and a half steps are about making changes in me. I needed to do this to function in society and have sustained sobriety. Steps 1, 2, and 3 will get you dry. Steps 4, 5, 6, 7, 8, and 9 will get you sober, and Steps 10, 11, and 12 will help you maintain sobriety.

I made the journey through the steps. Each step is built on humility. I needed to get humble to get to recovery. This is how I stay sober. I genuinely believe that if a person does not get humility, they cannot stay sober. Whatever pops into my head, I am not responsible for; I am only accountable for what I do with it. There are days where if you knew what I was thinking, you would lock me up; however, the difference is, I am not acting on it today.

Looking back, when do you think it was mostly out of control?

The last two years of college were terrible. Once I started with the beer company, I was just so unpredictable. I would leave work on Friday and go to work on Monday in the same uniform. That's probably not manageable.

How are you able to not drink or use daily?

I get a daily reprieve based upon my spiritual condition. I pray and meditate to my higher power every day, sometimes multiple times a day. The steps, meetings, and helping others is vital.

What is your thought about medication-assisted treatment?

There's a place for medication, but right now, it is abused. Medicine has a purpose if administered correctly. You start on a specific dose and wean off. Now they're increasing the dose, not decreasing the doses. They're using it as a crutch versus using it for recovery. Something that wasn't supposed to be abused is being abused. I'm a big believer in the abstinence theory. It's a way of life for me.

Is there anything you want those struggling with addiction to know?

The disease is always there telling you you're no good, you're worthless, you don't count. That is a lie. If you don't practice humility, you won't get recovery. You cannot stay sober if you're not willing to put yourself under a microscope and come to terms with your dark side. You have to challenge the way you think to change the way you behave. You need to change your habits in areas such as nutrition, exercise, and sleep. Medication can be unnecessary. We have broken brains that are trying to kill us. There's a solution. If we are willing to do the work, the answer is free, absolutely free. It's amazing.

Grant O.

Date of interview: 6/7/19
Sobriety date: 12/5/14, 4 years
Hometown: Manchester

When did you start drinking or using drugs, and how did it

progress?

I used to finish my mother and father's beers when I was around six years old. I was trying to imitate what Mom and Dad were doing; they were both alcoholics. The first time I remember getting drunk was age nine. I was sick, and my father gave me NyQuil, two or three doses. I started feeling funny and liked it.

I was exposed to marijuana and alcohol at 15 in high school. Freshman year, I was partying on the weekends, and by sophomore year I was immersed in it. I could quickly get it from the people I hung around with. They were older and doing it more frequently than just on the weekends. Every weekend turned into before and after school. I was doing LSD occasionally, marijuana every day, and drinking a couple of times a week. On weekends it was sometimes all day, a 12-pack or more.

By the time I was 16, my mother was sober, and my father was on his way to sobriety. I felt the need to show them what an alcoholic looked like. Alcohol was easily accessible, and it was easy for me to get into bars. It was fun at first, but in my junior year, I started experimenting with cocaine. I went from getting honor grades to, at best, a C average.

It went from just cocaine to crack. I started hanging out with a different crowd. During my senior year, OxyContin had hit the streets. My friends started going into rehab for OxyContin and crack addiction. Alcohol was my drug of choice though, marijuana would accentuate it, and cocaine would allow me to drink more.

After high school, going to college was off the table, so I went into the restaurant field. There's usually alcohol on site and people who enjoy partying. It got to the point where I had to drink to function in the morning because I would be shaking.

I tried leaving Manchester and the people I was hanging out with and ended up selling magazines door to door in Florida. Florida is a hot spot for partying. I stayed down there for a year, came back to New Hampshire, and went back into the restaurant field and that lifestyle. I was 21 and a full-blown alcoholic.

Alcohol kept me in bondage. I had no brakes, no shutoff switch. I was now having seizures if I didn't drink and would get the shakes in the morning. I was terrified, but drinking was so ingrained in me; it's what I knew. Drinking alcohol was the only way I knew how to deal with things in my life.

In 2001, I got out of my first 30-day program, and I didn't drink. I wanted to get it together. I was smoking an ounce of pot a week, though, still self-medicating, but I wasn't drinking. I was working two jobs.

I got married in 2003 and had a daughter in 2004. The marriage didn't work out, and we divorced in 2006. In 2009, my father got very ill. I never dealt with death well. When he passed away, I coped by drinking. I did another 30-day program and a psych ward stay. My daughter's mother told me I had to get my life together. She said I couldn't be drinking like I was with my daughter around, and she requested the court only allow supervised visits.

The shame and guilt got worse. I had only supervised visits with my daughter, and I was still trying to deal with my father's death. I was completely off the rails. I thought I wasn't doing that badly because I was still holding down a couple of jobs.

I needed a six-pack in the morning before I could even brush my teeth. After a year of struggling off and on, my best friend and boss passed away from a heart attack. That night I was right back to the psych ward. Some of my friends did an intervention on me and helped me get into another 30-day program, but as soon as I left, I continued drinking where I had left off.

In 2012, I finally lost my job, was living in my car, and was using a lot of cocaine, marijuana, and alcohol. I went into the Concord Hospital psych ward, and they detoxed me. I was a frequent flyer there. I was still shaking, got out, and drank. I ended up living in a homeless shelter with good structure. I was able to start seeing my daughter again and started going to AA meetings. The folks at the meetings told me to put the bat down and surrender to the disease. I don't think I understood what that meant.

I was working two jobs while living at the shelter and my sobriety took a back seat to going to work. I ended up being able to get an apartment from working those two jobs and decided I deserved to celebrate. I planned only to have a couple of drinks, but when I got back to the shelter, I blew a .43 blood alcohol level They couldn't even kick me out until the next morning because I was so intoxicated.

After that, I was living on the streets, literally in the woods. The shame and guilt were so overwhelming. I was diagnosed with diabetes because alcohol had ruined my pancreas. The doctors told me that if I kept drinking, eventually it would kill me. I hadn't seen my daughter in a year, and it made me want to drink even more. I didn't want to feel this shame and guilt, so I drank. I was in and out of psych wards and homeless shelters. I knew if I kept drinking, I would lose my daughter or die from the effects of alcohol on my diabetes, and I still drank.

One time, I planned to jump off the top of a parking garage, and the next thing I knew, I was in the emergency room. I spent two weeks in a psych ward. I always felt okay in psych wards and enjoyed helping people there no matter why they were there. When I was left alone to deal with my problems and emotions, I drank and lost control.

In 2013, I had my last psych ward stay. I was strapped down, five-point restraints, trying to bite the doctors and security guards. I had psychosis from alcohol and thought they were trying to shoot medicine into my neck. My blood sugar was at 700; I should have had a stroke or heart attack. I was just terrified. When I came out of it, I thought I had had some weird dream and worried about what was going on with my life.

The things I thought I would never do I was now doing. I used to say to myself, "Well, at least I have never been to jail." I was going to jail every weekend now. I would say, "At least I've never been homeless." I'd been homeless for years. "I will never, never do this with my daughter." I hadn't seen my daughter in years now. I'm now just begging to die, and I can't even do that.

I had a friend who was sober and knew that I wanted to be a better person, so they called him, and I went to Teen Challenge. I had no idea it existed but decided to try it out. It was not like any other program I had experienced. Something was different; there was a strange peace about this place. I started seeking God and doing what they asked me to do.

After two months, I was getting some of my functions back, bodily and mentally. I had never dealt with anything head-on, but after a couple of months here, I started dealing with things, which got intense. I wasn't into praying, but the shame and guilt I had for not being there for my daughter were so overwhelming. I decided to make a deal with God if He lifted the shame and guilt from me. He lifted it right off me. I cried, and it felt so good.

This wave of emotions was a lot for me, and after three months in the program, I decided to get a job and take care of my daughter. I did what I knew how to do, and that's run. I made it two blocks away, panhandled a couple of bucks, and got a couple of beers. Within a week, I was back under the bridge where I lived. I knew I had something special going on at Teen Challenge but decided to take my old world back again.

I was on the streets for two months, went back to Teen Challenge, and got welcomed back with open arms. I had no more fight in me. I surrendered to this disease completely.

Looking back, when do you think it was mostly out of control?

From 2010-2014.

How are you able to not drink or use daily?

I needed to be done and had to be willing to get help. I have to do everything I'd be willing to do to get the next drink or drug, to stay sober. I enjoy the outdoors and hiking, being in God's creation. I do meditation. I read literature: Benny Hinn: *The Anointing*, books by CS Lewis, Charles Stanley: *The Gift of Forgiveness*, etc.

What is your thought about medication-assisted treatment?

Suboxone and methadone are harder to get off of than heroin. It's government-approved heroin. I don't think doctors understand. Doctors believe they are helping. Methadone takes a month to detox from, and Suboxone can take up to a week or two. You experience very tough withdrawals from both. I don't believe that it's the answer. Other chemicals aren't the answer, either.

Is there anything you want those struggling with addiction to know?

That as hopeless as it seems, there is a better life beyond anything that you can imagine. God's plan is better than your wildest dreams.

<u>**Jack Q.**</u>

Date of interview: 11/1/19
Sobriety date: 12/20/69, 49 years

Hometown: Thornton

When did you start drinking or using drugs, and how did it progress?

The first time I drank, I was 13 years old and in grammar school. My father was an alcoholic; he only finished a year of a grammar school in Jersey City. My mother graduated from high school in Boston. She would give in to my father all the time. Near the end of World War II, we lived in a 20-unit apartment building, which was emptying of residents so that the restoration could begin.

At one point, there was only one other family in the building beside us. Their father was also an alcoholic. Because there was heat in our apartment, vagrants would sleep in the space between our apartment and another. At that time, my father would work at night; there was no one to protect my mother and me. When relatives would say something about the danger, my mother would say, "Brother will protect me." My name was Brother, and I was nine years old.

When we moved three blocks away, my father would come home drunk, get me out of bed, and cross-examine me about every crime he heard in the bars. He would start by saying, "Where were you at four o'clock at such and such a date?" and then begin to hit me. I would run out of the apartment and spend hours in the streets until I thought he might be asleep. When sneaking into the apartment, I would hear every creak in the floors and be fearful of waking him. His bed was the first after the kitchen. I had to attend school the next morning.

We had no money, no food, no anything. I was one of the most impoverished kids in my Catholic school. The clothes I'd have on were hand-me-downs from strangers. I shoe-shined to make money. I would make $3.75, and my dad would take $3.25 and give me 50 cents, so I learned to lie about what I made.

My father never provided funds to have our clothes cleaned, so they began to smell. Our school nun told us a girl's mother complained that her daughter could not stand the odor from some boy in class. It happened to be a heavy boy who perspired, but I always was sensitive to the fact it could be me.

One time, I put on a burner to heat water for a bath, my father came home drunk and was annoyed it was on because it cost money for the kerosene. He then proceeded to stick my head in the sink as punishment. He kept up the abuse until I was 13 and started hitting him back. I began to drink alcohol to escape my unfortunate situation. I just wanted to feel like everyone else. I used alcohol to escape from age 13 to 17. I'd get into fights in high school and was encouraged to quit.

At age 17, I joined the Marine Corps and went to boot camp on November 20, 1952. I could not wait to eat three meals a day. I planned to finish high school and go to college on the Korean G.I. Bill. I did not drink or gamble while I was in the Marines.

When I got into the Marine Corps, a friend of mine—who was released because he was underage—sent me a package of booze in a cake. I sold it to make money. I was then stationed in Miami, and someone said, "I noticed you don't drink much," and I said, "I don't want to be like my father." When I finally got into booze, I thought it was wonderful.

Determined to do better than the way I was raised, I took an aptitude test. The results showed I should be a chemical engineer, so I entered Newark College of Engineering in New Jersey, which is now the New Jersey Institute of Technology.

In October 1960, while I was going to college, I got married. My wife came from a beautiful Italian family. We had our first child just about nine months later and two other babies shortly after that. In 1968 and 1970, we had two more children. It took me seven and a half years to get my degree because of my drinking. My drinking got me fired from my first and third engineering positions. I would return to my wife at night with no money; we were so poor. I gambled, lost money, and bought people drinks all the time. Eventually, they repossessed my car. I didn't pay attention to my responsibilities at home. My family rarely saw me, and the grass was overgrown in my yard.

In August, during a drinking episode, I slipped near the swimming pool and got hurt. My wife was so upset with me, she wouldn't help. I called my sister, who lived 35 miles away, to help me. I lay on the floor, recovering, and told the paramedics that I was a former Marine and knew what to do when wounded: keep the head down, feet up, and keep warm with a blanket. The medics thought I was a jerk.

I finally got sober and went to AA in October 1966. I was penniless and didn't have enough money to put in the basket at the AA meeting. I was in and out of AA until December 20, 1969 when I asked God to help me stop drinking. Life progressively got better. Everything was going great for the first five years, and people said I should do the steps. I didn't think I needed to. I was now going out of my mind. People in AA told me, "Either you get the spiritual thing, or you go bananas." I wanted to blow my brains out. I couldn't live in my own skin, so I went to see the Chaplain and told him all my dark stuff. I also started talking with my sponsor and helping others.

I got hired by the government as an engineer and had a great career. I never got fired again. In December of 1976, I went to the prison and started an in-depth step study with my sponsor, and I went every Sunday for a year. Then I began to work on the 12 Steps outside of the prison. Once I started doing the steps and incorporated them into my life, God came into my life. I kept getting promotions at work and became the head of Quality Assurance for the Communication System Agency. After 29 years, I retired. Then a former General wanted me to be an executive director of a company. I worked for a year to set up that office. I am now able to pay cash for things. I am no longer a devout Catholic but live a spiritual life and continue to attend church weekly.

When I was a kid, I was always skinny. Eventually, I realized I needed to take care of my physical health; I learned this while in the Marine Corps. After age 50, I started getting medals for my athletic abilities. I participated in the NYC Marathon four times. At age 68, I learned how to swim laps and participated in two sprint triathlons. Now, at age 84, I have a life beyond my wildest dreams.

I feel as if I'm 25. I am devoted to AA. If I don't go to meetings for seven days, I become a jerk. My wife and I have been married 59 years and travel often. I try not to be self-centered and appreciate all she has been through with me. I am so lucky she is in my life.

I do Step 10 a lot; I don't have to do it as much as I used to because I try to remember to treat people well. I don't gamble or drink, and I work on my spiritual condition regularly. The most important thing is my spiritual life. My kids are all grown, and all have graduated from college. They are pursuing great careers and live amazing lives. Everything I have is because of AA and God. I have been sober now for almost 50 years, and it gets better, with God's help, each year.

Looking back, when do you think it was mostly out of control?

Right before I got sober. My drinking was worse on my family.

How are you able to not drink or use daily?

I go to three to four AA meetings and church weekly. I share everything about myself with others, if I think it will help them. I read the St Francis Prayer, *Overeaters Anonymous*, and *Adult Children of Alcoholics* books. I also read Dr. Kent's *Paradoxical Commandments* and Mother Teresa's "Anyway." I have a lot of books on my Kindle and bring it with me everywhere. I like to read when I travel.

What is your thought about medication-assisted treatment?

I think total abstinence is necessary because getting sober is a spiritual process.

Is there anything you want those struggling with addiction to know?

Rely on God's help, put the effort in, refrain from retaliation, and you'll be rewarded.

Jane K.

Date of interview: 6/17/19
Sobriety date: 1/1/83, 36 years
Hometown: Pittsburg

When did you start drinking or using drugs, and how did it progress?

I drank a six-pack with friends when I was 15 years old. My parents were both alcoholics, so drinking was something I knew. I drank to lessen my anxiety and avoid the feelings of my youth. I had to save myself from the insanity I found myself and my younger brother living in every day. My first husband was my savior from this. I fell in love deeply with him, and we married that fall when I was 16. He was eight years older than I was. I met him in downtown Hampton Center. A man who lived there allowed us kids to go to his apartment and drink.

After we were married, I asked him not to drink. I didn't enjoy drinking then. He tried to quit, but this didn't work out very well. I gave birth to our two sons. We drank on weekends mostly, and we would have weekend parties with all our friends. During this time is when I began to have blackouts.

By age 25, I was drinking beer every day. I loved Scotch but didn't drink it often because whenever I drank it, I blacked out. Our marriage was a mess. I eventually left him and moved into my father's house because I couldn't stand to hurt him any longer. I was an emotional train wreck.

One night at my father's house, I had a horrible thought of my husband being killed. He had been drug dealing, and word came to me that his truck had been broken into while stopping at a popular bar on his way home one night. I worried he could lose his life. I cried out to God for help and experienced an incredible feeling of love encompass my whole being. I felt a sense of enlightenment. I have never been the same since.

I went back to my husband because I thought God wanted me to make it work. My Christian friends believed I should. Through my new spiritual self, I figured we could work things out. The reality was we couldn't make it work. It was way too broken, and we were in two very different places. I kept praying for direction. Eventually, it dawned on me that our other little house was empty, so my boys and I went to live there.

In 1979, I met my second husband at a bar. I was drinking a six-pack and half a day and using cocaine at times. Alcohol took away my reality. I was out of control. I was hoping to get sober and done with this alcohol stuff, and on New Year's Day at three a.m., it came. As I was trying to choke down one more beer, I could not swallow another drop. My aunt had always covered us kids in prayer, and I felt her prayers all around me at that moment. I finally surrendered. The desire to drink lifted from me; I was done with alcohol. I was delivered. I cried all that night, knowing I was finished. I've never felt the urge to drink since.

My second husband and I married after I got sober and stayed married for six years. He was drinking and using drugs, and I was not. This marriage was rocky. I tried with all that I was to make this marriage work. It was never meant to be because he couldn't, or wouldn't, stop using. I knew I needed to think of myself and my sobriety. While we were separated, a friend of mine asked me to go to Spain with him. I went, came home, and reunited with my second husband, desperately hoping he would get clean and sober.

During an AA New Year's Eve party, my husband left halfway through the night because he felt ill. I stayed and enjoyed the evening with friends. When I arrived home, expecting to see my sick husband there, he was not. I waited up for him and at four a.m., he came back. He had been out doing drugs with my sons and their friends. This behavior was the final straw.

By March of 1989, I moved in with my current husband, the guy who had been my dear friend from high school. He was also the guy who had taken me to Spain. He had been sober for two years at the time. We went to therapy together before we got married, which helped ground us and put us on the right path. We have had a great relationship together for over 30 years.

I got sober by the Grace of God. Going to AA and having supportive people helped. I lived through all kinds of amazing challenges; some I brought on myself, some came to me from outside. My Higher Power, whom I chose to call God, helped me find the authentic me. I'm sane and oh-so-grateful today.

I never thought of ever picking up another drink. I chose to go forward, day by day, and not backward. All the work I ever did, on my behalf, is mine for the keeping. I chose to lean into my Higher Power for the strength to get through each day. Taking one day at a time has brought me into this incredible place. I'm a lay minister now and lean into my Higher Power with every breath I take and for all that I need daily. I get to share this fantastic relationship that healed me and keeps me going.

Looking back, when do you think it was mostly out of control?

When I was 26, before my enlightenment, I was so out of control and made horrible choices for myself. My life and marriage were a total mess. The chaos of my drinking slowed down during my enlightenment. The progression picked up again, though, since this disease is progressive, not stagnant. I was changed because the lifestyle didn't fit with my newfound faith in God.

How are you able to not drink or use daily?

My connection with God is vital. It's a living, breathing relationship with a living, breathing God. I love my life and feel as if I live in constant prayer, 24/7, with this God who saved me from myself. The literature that helped me is *Breathing Underwater-Spirituality, The Twelve Steps* by Richard Rohr, and Carl Jung's Psychology books.

What is your thought about medication-assisted treatment?

I understand there may be a need for medical assistance when a soul is getting off of alcohol and other drugs, but if there is no end plan, how does that make sense? I don't see the purpose of a never-ending drug plan. People need to do it through a 12-step recovery program, therapy or both. God created us to live in a relationship with God, not doing drugs.

Is there anything you want those struggling with addiction to know?

There is hope. There is a way. There is a path our creator will lead us on to a place where we will rejoice every day about being alive. Hook up with your Higher Power. Life in sobriety is "second to none." Join us!

Jane S.

Date of interview: 3/27/19
Sobriety date: 2/5/09, 10 years
Hometown: Bristol

When did you start drinking or using drugs, and how did it progress?

Age 11. I used to steal my parents' booze and drink at my house or put it in jelly jars and take it to school. My friends and I drank and smoked pot at Kelly Park in Bristol around the grandstand. I'd get drunk before I got on the bus for a class trip. We did this once in a while and would party on the weekends.

I was on the honor roll, in the school band, and skied. In the summer, when I was 15, I started living at the Whip O' Will Motel in Hebron. I drank daily and smoked pot often. In the fall, I lived at home and drank mostly on the weekends. I didn't smoke a ton of marijuana because I got paranoid. When I drank, I didn't care and would just smoke it. I smoked pot right until the end of my drinking.

By age 19, I got my first DUI. I continued to drink and smoke pot the same way in college. When I was 24, I got married. I had my kids when I was 26 and 34. My first husband and I drank heavily for the six years of our marriage, but I didn't drink when I was pregnant. I married again within two years of getting divorced from my first husband. He smoked pot every day, so my pot smoking got worse. That marriage lasted six years. After this marriage, my drinking progressed. I drank everything and anything.

My alcoholism often caused me trouble in my jobs because I wasn't a very nice person. I was a kitchen manager in Florida and the president of the Chefs Association. I became a national account manager for Sysco and went on to work for Kellogg's. Kellogg's moved me back to New Hampshire. In the last 10 years of my drinking, I progressed to daily drinking. At this point, I had to drink. I was depressed, so I went to psychologists, and everyone was throwing meds at me. I added booze to the meds. It wasn't a pretty picture. I got to the point where I physically, emotionally, and mentally couldn't function.

In 2004, I thought if I got out of the corporate world, things would be better, so I bought an inn in Durham. I put my son on the school bus in the morning, drank vodka, and put wine in my coffee cup. I didn't know it then, but I had to have alcohol every day to function. I went to my doctor, and she referred me to a licensed drug and alcohol counselor.

One day a woman came into my inn. It was in September, and she wanted to know if I needed a financial advisor. I was about to lose everything, so I sat and listened. She said, "I think we met for a reason." I wasn't exactly sure what she meant. I met her again at a networking meeting, and she let me know she had been sober for six years, and I told her about my drinking problem. She called her sponsor right then. She and her sponsor tagged teamed me and brought me to my first AA meeting. I heard someone at the meeting tell my story and I wanted what everyone in the room had. I knew they had a solution. I felt it. I knew I didn't have to drink anymore and haven't found it necessary to pick up a drink or a drug since.

Looking back, when do you think it was mostly out of control?

The last 15 years of my drinking were crazy. I would get so drunk at events, and my son would have to drive me home. I couldn't stand up. I was mixing drugs and booze.

How are you able to not drink or use daily?

I pray a lot and meditate. I work a program of recovery. I practice what I was taught in the beginning by everyone who embraced me. I help others and have a very spiritual program.

What is your thought about medication-assisted treatment?

There are times and places for it. People may benefit from it. However, I don't believe it should be a requirement to get treatment. There are many paths to recovery, and not all include pharmaceuticals. There are plenty of us that got sober and stay sober by working a productive program of recovery, without any medication. I found the solution in meetings. I wanted what they had—they were not using meds— and they have a spiritual recovery program.

Is there anything you want those struggling with addiction to know?

There is a solution, you are not alone, and there is help. There are many pathways to recovery. The fellowship of Alcoholics Anonymous and the 12 Steps give a new design for life. It is a way to walk through each day, with its challenges and joys, and find inner peace and serenity.

<u>**Janessa F.**</u>

Date of interview: 6/10/2019
Sobriety date: 1/31/17, 2 years
Hometown: Hillsborough

When did you start drinking or using drugs, and how did it

progress?

I started drinking in late middle school. I was with a friend and we decided to try her parents' alcohol. After that, I didn't drink until my senior year of high school. It was still sporadic, but when I did drink, I drank excessively. Then I drank progressively more and more until my early 20s. I didn't drink all the time, but when I did, it was until I blacked out.

When I was 20, I had extensive surgery on my stomach and back. As soon as I tried pain medication, that was it. I loved it. I was prescribed five mg of OxyContin every couple of hours daily for my back and took it for two years. I never took it as prescribed though. I took more than prescribed. I liked the way it made me feel. It didn't even really help my back pain. As soon as I felt what I felt from the opiates, I thought I had found the solution to all my problems.

The drinking still progressed until I was 25. I stopped drinking then because I didn't like being sick and hungover. My opiate addiction, however, turned into a heroin addiction rather quickly since heroin was easy to access. Once I made connections with people who had it, I started using it all the time and got into many dysfunctional relationships. This was my life from ages 25 to 32. I would use as much as I could afford as often as I could. I did whatever it took to support my habit.

I tried methadone and Suboxone; neither of them worked. Methadone just helped me get through so I wouldn't be sick. I would still use drugs while on it. I got Suboxone and sold it for drugs. This was from 2011 to 2016, on and off. I tried to stop many times throughout these years. The relationships I was in were toxic. I burned every bridge I had. I also prostituted myself for four years to pay for my drug habit. It was a vicious cycle.

One day, I had this epiphany that I needed to get help. I knew I couldn't do it alone anymore and went to a sober house and started working the 12-step program. I was only clean for only a few weeks and relapsed. I didn't want to die, but I didn't care if I did. There were times when I hoped I wouldn't overdose, but then other times I felt like, "who cares?" I was so miserable.

I was in a program for seven months and stayed clean, but it didn't work. I just wasn't ready to follow what they were asking me to do. I used drugs up until the day I came here to His Mansion. I hit my rock bottom multiple times and it was the bottom of the bottom. It brought me to this program for a second time. After getting clean, I worked through my childhood traumas. The traumas I experienced made me so depressed. It would have led me to something else even if I had never been prescribed opiates after surgery.

Since coming to His Mansion, I can't even fathom living the life I led before. It's hard to even think about the person I was. I'm completely different. I don't have to wake up every morning in despair and wonder how I'm going to get high. It's the best thing I've ever done.

Looking back, when do you think it was mostly out of control?

When I got out of the treatment center after the seven-month stay. For two years after that, it was just hell.

How are you able to not drink or use daily?

Throughout the day, I stay in communication with the Lord. I've found my relationship with Him has grown tremendously since coming to His Mansion and working through my childhood trauma. I read the *Bible, Jesus Calling*, and *The Wounded Heart*. Sexual relationships, prostitution, and giving myself to any man for any purpose did a lot of damage to me. The book *Sex and the*

Soul of a Woman helped me work through some of this.

What is your thought about medication-assisted treatment?

It didn't work for me, and it didn't work for the people I surrounded myself with. The people I was around all tried it and ended up doing the same drugs I did. We manipulated the system and continued to use other drugs. I initially heard Suboxone and methadone were supposed to be used short-term. I'm not seeing that at all. I feel as if you're just trading one addiction for another when you take these drugs. One is just more socially acceptable and readily available. It's just another bondage. You're not looking at your stuff. Do you want to wake up every day and still be tied to a substance? I know I don't.

Is there anything that you want those struggling with addiction to know?

You need to face your pain and heal. I believe this healing comes from the Lord. It's tough work, but you get through to the other side. There is no Band-Aid you can put over the trauma. To be truly free, you have to face what caused you to use in the first place.

<u>**Janice H.**</u>

Date of interview: 6/13/2019
Sobriety date: 1/25/2007, 12 years
Hometown: Errol

When did you start drinking or using drugs, and how did it progress?

I was 11 years old. My mother had just been hospitalized for mental illness and I was left in charge, as the mother of the house. This was when I decided I could drink, so I went to the liquor cabinet, tried it, and loved it. From then on, I drank whenever I could. As a teenager, I'd go to sleepovers and bring liquor from my parents' cabinet. I knew it did something to me that it didn't do to my friends. I didn't care because I loved what it did for me. I was bulletproof, funny, and I could dance and sing. I could do anything if I had a drink. Drugs were also a part of my life. At age 17, I got pregnant and stopped the drug use, but I continued to drink.

My first husband drank like I did; we were heavy weekend drinkers. If we could get my parents to take the kids or we had a babysitter who would stay over, we would drink to oblivion. If something was important, I wouldn't drink. I knew if I drank, I'd lose control. I would be obsessed with wanting to drink, but I wouldn't drink.

When I was 27, I bought a house and a business. My drinking started to scare me. I was blacking out and afraid of losing everything. I'd drink if everything went well and if it didn't go well. I was also fearful of losing my kids, so I went to AA. I got sober and stayed in AA for a few years, but I couldn't get the powerlessness part. So, I convinced myself that I was unduly alarmed.

I had years of abstinence and convinced myself I wasn't an alcoholic. When I married my third husband, we decided we would get married and both not drink. After getting married, it was so hard not to drink; we were so miserable. We didn't last three years together. The first thing I did when we split up was drink. I'd drink, and then I'd stop. I'd drink and then stop. Eventually, I couldn't stay stopped.

I lost the ability to stop. I drank in phases: hard liquor and stop, drink wine and then stop. I was only drinking wine at the end, but I couldn't go a day without it. One day, I outed myself to a friend. Then she outed herself to me that she was going to AA. I didn't know she was not drinking and going to AA. I was shocked and said, "You should be taking me to AA." She said, "Really, Janice? Do you think you have a problem with alcohol?" I said, "Oh no, I'm not ready. I don't want to be an AA alcoholic." I didn't want to go to an AA meeting because I knew that meant I wouldn't be able to drink again, and I couldn't imagine my life without a drink. I thought I just needed to get my control back. From that point on, I drank around her every chance I got. I was trying to get her to tell me I had a problem, so I could prove to her that I didn't. She never mentioned AA or her sobriety again.

A few years went by, and the blackouts got worse. I was drinking every day. One day, I came to and was done with drinking. My husband was away on a trip, and I was sick and tired of being sick and tired. There was no trauma and no arrests. I was just done.

I called my friend and said I needed help. She asked if I had a drink yet, and I told her no. She said, "If you can stay sober until 11 a.m., I will have someone you know meet you at the 11 a.m. AA meeting in Plymouth." She wouldn't tell me who. I went to a meeting. I sat in the parking lot and thought, "I do not belong here. Going to AA is not what I want. What was I thinking? I shouldn't have called her." Then someone tapped on my window. It was a woman I had sat next to in church for years. The woman said to me, "I've been saving a seat for you." I had no idea she was a woman in recovery.

The woman who set up the meeting got a group of women to come to my house every week for a year. They took me through *The Women's Way Through the 12 Steps*. When I went to the AA meetings, I heard of a local place that was taking people through the AA Big Book 12 Steps. I thought it was a graduate course and I wanted it. I wanted to graduate so that I could control my drinking. I did not want to be one of the losers who was still going to AA after 15 or 20 years, so I chased that graduate program.

I also got involved in an AWOL (A Way of Life, an intense 12-step program) and was doing this at the same time as the Women's 12-step program. I wanted to do it right. I was committed, and I was going to do it right. My arrogance was out of control. I thought my sponsor was lucky to work with me. People just loved me through my recovery.

Eight years into my recovery, I had a surgical procedure. Before this, I had a real problem when I would hear how others came into AA and say they were addicts. When I had this procedure, I had a physical reaction, and I didn't know what it was. I was jonesing for something and didn't know why.

My sponsor told me it was the opiates. She told me I was an addict, and I can't do pain meds of any kind. When I talked to my aunt, she reminded me when I was three years old, my mother put paregoric on my gums for tooth pain, and I was scaling the cabinets trying to get more. I have a disease of more.

By chasing the steps, it brought me to a God of my understanding. Instead of helping me graduate, the steps brought me to the God of my understanding. I believed in God but didn't think he believed in me. AA gave me a God that loved me in spite of myself. If I want to stay sober, more than anything else, this higher power will help me stay sober. The critical factor in my sobriety is this AA God, and the directions for my life are in the Big Book.

Looking back, when do you think it was mostly out of control?

Just after my second marriage.

How are you able to not drink or use daily?

I go to meetings, pray, meditate, read, and go to church.

Books I read: *God Calling, Twenty-Four Hours a Day*, Melody Beatie's books on codependency and recovery, and Annie

Lamont's books. I read anything I can get my hands on. Right now, I'm learning about the Three Principles. I hear people are getting a lot from it.

What is your thought about medication-assisted treatment?

I can't work with anyone who's using another chemical to stay sober. That's not my experience, and I can only offer my personal experience.

Is there anything you want those struggling with addiction to know?

That no matter how far down you've gone, there's a way out. You are not hopeless. At my second meeting, a man spoke who I had known when he was using. He was so bad that you only whispered his name. When he told his story, he sounded even worse than I remembered. He talked about how he got clean and sober in prison. By the end of his story, I knew that I was in the right place. If he could find a God of his understanding and this God would help him, as low as he was, maybe there was hope for me.

<u>Jasmine L.</u>

Date of interview: 3/25/19
Sobriety date: 11/3/16, 2 years
Hometown: Nashua

When did you start drinking or using drugs, and how did it progress?

Age nine. My first drink was a Budweiser. A family member gave it to me and asked me if I wanted to drink like the rest of the family. I sat at the table and shared the moment with them. It was the first time I felt a connection to them. I remember how it tasted and how it felt. By the age of 12, I was drinking on the weekends. Age 14, I started experimenting with drugs: marijuana, benzos, prescription drugs, and cocaine.

My disease progressed rather quickly. By the age of 15, I was a daily drug user: cocaine, marijuana, and Ecstasy. I would do acid and mushrooms a lot. I would go to school completely inebriated. My guidance counselor would stop me and say, "What the heck is going on?" She'd tell me I had potential. I had no idea because I grew up in an environment where drinking was okay. What I was doing wasn't odd to me. It was odd that people were questioning what I was doing.

I started suffering consequences in my teens. I was getting arrested for anything to do with my SUD: drunk and disorderly, fighting, stealing, and robbing businesses. In my early 20s, I picked up a narcotic sale charge. If you add up all my jail time, it's a lot. I knew I was uncomfortable but didn't know what was wrong with me.

I was suffering and tried all kinds of ways to stay sober. I always thought alcohol and drugs were my problems. I tried everything outside of myself to stay sober. I tried Suboxone; it didn't work for me. I just lied to my therapist to get more. I found creative ways to pass my drug tests. I hated where I was and couldn't understand why I wanted to kill myself.

I was homeless, living on the streets, not showering, not eating, and my hair was matted. I was squatting in an abandoned house and would use a small pool to wash up. I didn't think I could change. I thought it was the deck of cards I had been dealt. I intentionally overdosed at age 32. I was so sick of life. People were trying to help me into treatment. I didn't think I was worth it and pushed them away.

One day, a woman called. She asked me if I wanted help and I said yes. I don't know why I said yes because I wanted to die. I got a scholarship to go to Granite Recovery Center for detox, the 28-day program for 60 days, housing, partial hospitalization program, and intensive outpatient program. I was in a meth-induced psychosis; I had to go to the hospital to get the abscesses off my back. This treatment center was an abstinence-based treatment center. They broke down the disease model for me. When they did this, I had this feeling in my heart. I knew this is where I needed to be, and this is what I needed to do.

I work in business development now at a recovery center. I am really active in 12-step recovery. I will do anything to help people to get recovery.

Looking back, when do you think it was mostly out of control?

I think it was always out of control. I was never okay. I was a child that was never okay. I was a little girl that went through so much trauma, I didn't know how to be present. I couldn't connect with myself.

How are you able to not drink or use daily?

Spiritual practices. I try to be a decent human being and live by spiritual principals.

What is your thought about medication-assisted treatment?

I had a previous experience where it did not work for me. My tendency was to abuse it.

Is there anything you want those struggling with addiction to know?

You are worth it. Reach out to anyone, someone who is sober. I love you.

Jason S.

Date of interview: 3/25/19
Sobriety date: 10/6/16, 2 years
Hometown: Manchester

When did you start drinking or using drugs, and how did it progress?

Age 12. I drank Irish Crème from my friend's parents. I would drink once in a great while. By age 15 or 16, I started drinking most days and weekends and would drink to get drunk. I was in and out of adolescent afterschool programs for being a troubled kid. I got my first DUI when I was 16, the second when I was 17, and the third when I was 18. At age 18, I got caught reckless driving. I was driving on people's lawns and had bags of methamphetamines on me.

I went into the military because I got into some legal trouble. After three years, I was discharged. I was kicked out for drinking and fighting. I came home and started selling drugs out of the back of my car to support my habit. I picked up using Hydrocodone, and as soon as I put it into my body, I got addicted within a week. I got caught and went to jail.

From the ages of 22 to 26, I was in and out of county corrections for selling drugs. I continued to violate probation because I couldn't stay sober. I was failing my urine tests, and I didn't get treatment. While in Rockingham County Jail, it was effortless to get Suboxone in mass quantities because it is for sale on the streets. People were selling their Suboxone to get heroin.

In 2011, I went to a 28-day rehab in the Rockingham jail. People from AA came in and spoke. As soon as I got out, I did the 12 Steps with a sponsor. He showed me the solution: the 12 Steps and how to grow along spiritual lines. I stayed sober for five years, stopped working the steps, stopped praying and helping other people. Then I started drinking again, which led to using hard drugs. I was in Lawrence, Massachusetts, and got arrested for drug possession. In 2012, I went to the VA Hospital in Bedford, Massachusetts, and have been sober ever since.

How are you able to not drink or use daily?

I go to AA meetings daily. I work the 12 Steps, take a daily inventory, pray, and continue to address the internal condition in order not to have the old behaviors.

What is your thought about medication-assisted treatment?

When I took Suboxone to wean off opiates, it made me sick, and I sold it. I don't want to put a mind-altering substance in my body. I didn't like that process.

Is there anything you want those struggling with addiction to know?

If you can find contentment and fullness in your life, you will never want to drink or use drugs again. Find a spiritual connection.

Jeff B.

Date of interview: 6/8/19
Sobriety date: 11/25/93, 25 years
Hometown: Nashua

When did you start drinking or using drugs, and how did it progress?

My first experience with alcohol was around the age of 15 or 16 years old. I was with my older brother, cousin, and one of my brother's friends. They had a bottle of vodka, and we all went out bowling. I drank way too much, got sick, and threw up. The next morning, I told my parents I would never drink again—that didn't happen.

During my senior year of high school, I partied, like most of my friends, on weekends. There were a lot of temptations throughout my teenage years, and no matter what the occasion, I most often drank and did drugs. This pattern continued into college—I would go out on weekends to drink heavily—the trend continued into adulthood.

When I started my career, I was goal-oriented like most and did not see or did not care to know the warning signs of my drinking— my goals and alcohol use were conflicting with one another. I worked hard and saved drinking for the weekends. The signs increased, such as being arrested, missing opportunities, and alcohol was always complicating my life. I continued to ignore the signs and kept on abusing alcohol.

When I hit bottom later in life, I found myself in a desperate state of mind! My insides were in a knot, my mind confused, and I was hurting from what alcohol was doing to me. My choice to stop drinking was an easy one and has been well worth it ever since. Not every day in sobriety has gone my way, and some days are harder than others – I'm good with this because I'm sober, and I know I have done my very best.

I have a good life and a great family! I have relationships with people I wouldn't have had if I were drinking. I've been all over the country on business and vacation. Because of my sobriety, I'm honest, trustworthy, and have integrity all the time. I don't miss the hangovers, the lies, or the guilty feelings. I work on my thoughts, and most days they're manageable. I do my best. I work hard at letting go.

I'm so thankful for my sobriety and for the person who was there for me when I needed someone the most. All I had to do was reach out, ask for help, and be willing not to drink. I'm so grateful for that someone and for the people in my life today who share the same path as I do. I would not change my sober life for anything.

Looking back, when do you think it was mostly out of control?

Right before I got sober, it was the most out of control.

How are you able to not drink or use daily?

Today, I have no urge to drink. I do one thing correctly every day, and that is "I don't drink!" I remind myself that I can have all the pain and suffering back whenever I want it—all I have to do is pick up. I also think of that special someone who was there for me when I got sober and who was there throughout most of my sobriety. I think of him often, our conversations, his shared wisdom, and his writings. I read them regularly. I have a circle of sober friends today, and I attend AA meetings when I can—I do my best to stay connected.

What is your thought about medication-assisted treatment?

I don't know anyone who's using medication to stay off drugs or alcohol.

Is there anything you want those struggling with addiction to know?

If you need and want help, reach out to someone—it's never too late for a new beginning.

Jennifer B.

Date of interview: 6/6/19
Sobriety date: 2/7/13, 6 years
Hometown: Lisbon

When did you start drinking or using drugs, and how did it progress?

I was allowed a cup of spiked punch at a family get-together for Christmas one year when I was 14. I got a second cup with help from a cousin. I was only supposed to have one cup and got busted with the second one. My stepmother made me drink a bottle of Reunite the next morning as punishment. I didn't drink again for a long time after that. My family was a little messed up. My parents divorced when I was eight, and I went to live with my dad and stepmother. My sister stayed with my mom.

I started drinking again when I went to Long Island for college, but not heavily. My downfall was my addiction to marijuana. I started smoking right after college and entered a career that became the love of my life. I was around people who worked in the woods. I guess you'd call them the hippie type.

In the middle to late 1990s, I experimented with pot and liked it. I drank a lot right before I quit. When I drank, I drank a lot. I didn't have the tolerance a lot of heavier drinkers had; I would get hammered. I would generally throw up, and towards the end, I was blacking out. I would do embarrassing things. I'd call people I hadn't talked to in years or kiss random people at the bar; it was ugly.

Life was getting unmanageable for me. It is a higher bottom than most people, but I was tremendously terrified by the time I sought help. I took a three-month leave of absence from work and went to treatment. I realized my life was spiraling out of control from smoking pot. I started smoking at work, which was pretty bad in my mind. It was a complete breach of my ethics.

My husband had already gotten clean, and I was seeing him as a buzzkill more than anything. I was having trouble with anxiety, and my mental health wasn't great. I never felt as if I fit in anywhere. I was always trying to be the coolest person I could be. I thought it was cool to be bad. I went to AA and NA. I didn't know what to expect, but I finally felt like I belonged somewhere.

Looking back, when do you think it was mostly out of control?

It was the most out of control in the two years before I got sober.

How are you able to not drink or use daily?

Recently, I find myself reaching out to God naturally. I have no religious background, and I don't feel as if I belong to any one faith. To ask for help was foreign before recovery. Developing this relationship is my number one go-to. I call my sponsor a couple of times a week; we did it every day for a while. I read the *One Day at A Time* book and sections of the Big Book, as well as the Narcotics Anonymous book, *Just for Today*.

What is your thought about medication-assisted treatment?

If someone can be on something that is less devastating than what they're addicted to, then whatever works for them. Experts seem to think it's worth a shot when other things have failed — being on it for the rest of your life would be a shame.

Is there anything you want those struggling with addiction to know?

There is a community of people just like you. You are not alone at all. There are tons of us, and we're everywhere. There is help.

<u>**Jesse H.**</u>

Date of interview: 4/19/19
Sobriety date: 12/18/05, 13 years
Hometown: Concord

When did you start drinking or using drugs, and how did it progress?

I was 11 years old and smoked some weed. I drank alcohol when I was in Lowell High School, but that was not the problem. I had other addictive tendencies that started well before drugs and alcohol. I was addicted to online games and internet pornography starting at around age 12. My coping mechanisms were isolation and avoidance. I would avoid eating in the cafeteria because my social anxiety was so high.

When I attended Plymouth State University my freshman year, I took 17 credits. College is where I discovered good weed and began regular alcohol use. I also started to notice there was something different about me. With my drinking and drug use, I had no shut-off button.

In my first semester, a state trooper arrested me, and I got in trouble in a dorm for drinking and had to take alcohol awareness classes. I failed my courses, got caught for plagiarism, and had to go in front of a review board. Causing this kind of trouble was not a great start to my college experience. My mom wrote a letter to the school to get me back in for my second semester. I did what I could to change, but it didn't help. I failed out of school and moved to Hampton Beach with my mom.

A year after we moved, my father passed away. He had fought in Vietnam and was part of the 20 percent that got addicted to heroin. When I was four years old, he left and never returned. From age five to 20, I talked to him a total of three times. It was as if I didn't even have a father. The night he passed away, I called my friend and did cocaine for the first time. I instantly felt a connection, and I wanted to feel this way from here on out. It set me on a destructive course to chase that feeling. It brought me into the darkest places, where I was shooting heroin, doing speed balls, drinking, and doing OxyContin.

I was doing things I said I would never do. Eventually, I found a way to order prescription medication. I could have unlimited quantities shipped to me anytime. When OxyContin got delivered, it was like gold. I knew I was going to die from OxyContin. I had an overdose experience from it and didn't tell anyone.

My plan to "escape" my drug-addicted hell was to move to Florida with someone from work. Florida was one of the worst places you could go in 2005, because of the pill mills. Two weeks before leaving, I went to get my package of pills and got a call from someone saying my box went to the post office. I thought to myself, "That doesn't make any sense, why would it go there?" I needed that sense of relief, so I went to the post office anyway, where I was arrested. It was a sting operation with federal agents and the local police. The exciting part is that they let me go.

I moved down to Florida shortly after being arrested and tried to manage my addiction. I said to myself, "As long as I stay away from cocaine, I'm going to be okay. I can take pills and drink." It took four months, and eventually, people offered me cocaine enough times that I just did it. The next six months were a bloody mess. I sold everything I owned and would go into work not having slept on several occasions. I had a near-death experience that prompted the concern of my roommate. He and my employer called my brother in New Hampshire and told him I would die if I didn't get out of there.

I was arrested again within two weeks of being back in New Hampshire. This time it was serious. In December of 2005, I was at an arraignment in the Concord Federal Court with a court-appointed lawyer facing seven years of federal prison. Someone told me we'd be facing the toughest prosecutor you could get, and he was going to crack down on me.

This serious action by the court was the start of my transition to recovery. I was 22 years old and finally woke up. I found myself in front of a federal judge, chained at my wrists and ankles. I looked at my mom, my brother, and his wife, and they were all bawling their eyes out. Right then, I thought, "What have I done with the last four years of my life?" I felt the need to change everything. I didn't know what that meant, but the court recognized my determination. The court officials said, "You're not going to drink or do drugs. You're going to go to a therapist, you're talking to your lawyer, and you're going to work full-time." There was no rehab for me, no drug court, none of that.

The court had a tough time believing that I took all the pills myself. I should have been dead a thousand times. They finally decided to give me two years of probation. I knew a miracle had just happened, a second chance. My faith got strong after this. I endured stress and pressure most people never experience in their first six months of recovery. I had severe panic attacks but didn't take any medication.

I started to do a set of routines, which turned into habits, and those habits created a new life. The first two routines were to focus on my recovery and do the next right thing every day. These new habits eventually led me to buy my first home at six years in recovery. They led me to get my degree in psychology and, ultimately, my master's in counseling.

I won the highest award possible at my job, which paid for a trip to Switzerland with the President and Vice President of the company. I eventually left this six-figure, secure employment and started my own business, which is what I do today. I published my first book in November of 2018 called *"Smash Your Comfort Zone with Cold Showers."* My Entrepreneurs in Recovery training and workshops continue to elevate the lives of people in addiction recovery. I'm all about helping the next person in recovery reach their full potential.

Looking back, when do you think it was mostly out of control?

When I was going to Lowell to score drugs, this was a dark place. You can get heroin in a few minutes. I would damage my nasal cavities by snorting drugs and still do it anyway. Eventually, even the dealers resisted selling me drugs at times.

How are you able to not drink or use daily?

I focus on my recovery each day. I have a morning and night routine. I practice meditation daily and visualize my life and my day. I attempt to show up as my highest self, my true self daily. I write down three things I'm grateful for and set my intentions for the day. I also take a cold shower every day and have for the last four years. I look at my goals for the day, week, month, and year every day. I look at my to-do list and ask myself if my daily tasks line up with my most important priorities for the year. I show up for others, sponsor men, and mentor/coach both men and women.

What is your thought about medication-assisted treatment?

Absolutely necessary. We are facing the most significant health crisis of our time. It's out of control and getting worse. When people are coming off fentanyl and other drugs, they're going to need a detox. If you believe you have to be on medication for the rest of your life to live your best life, I would question that. As far as Suboxone or methadone long-term, it would have to be on a case by case basis. I don't believe you need to be on these medications for the long-term.

Is there anything you want those struggling with addiction to know?

Focus on your recovery every day. Treat it as your number one priority through daily self-care. You are more resilient than you know. Tap into your inner resources and tell yourself you are capable of greatness. You are supposed to be here. You have unique strengths and gifts to bring to the world. If you are in recovery, you are the most resilient person on the planet. To go through what you have gone through and be on the other side is something to recognize. Tap into that resilience. When stuff gets tough in recovery, look back and be like, "Oh my God, I managed to get through all of that?" You can get through anything and use that strength to build the life you want.

Jaimie D.

Date of interview: 5/23/19
Sobriety date: 8/3/17, 1 year
Hometown: Plymouth

When did you start drinking or using drugs, and how did it progress?

I was 15. I used marijuana with a friend. Back in those times, it was just marijuana and alcohol. I lived in Plymouth, which is a party town, and I fell right in love with that. I didn't start getting into anything more until I was in my junior year of high school and began experimenting with Ecstasy and other party drugs. I was able to put drugs down at the time.

When I was 19, I was in a significant car accident. I broke my back in three places and got introduced to opiate pain killers. Percocet to start, but I quickly found out I was able to manipulate the system by exaggerating the pain. Within a short period, I was on Morphine and OxyContin. This use ended up lasting a very long time. The accident took place in Berlin, and the doctors who gave me most of my medications were in Conway, so I moved to Conway and lived there for eight years.

The last doctor's office I saw was a pain clinic in Somersworth. I eventually got kicked out of that practice, because I was on an array of medications, one of which was methadone. I was selling the methadone, so it wasn't in my toxin screen. Within 48 hours of discharge from the clinic, I made a connection and was driving to Providence to get heroin.

My narcotic use started in Conway in a regular doctor's office. They referred me to the pain clinic because they didn't feel comfortable prescribing me the array of narcotics I was on. I was taking 100 mg of Morphine three times a day and 15 mg of Roxicet four times a day. I was also taking 10 mg of Valium three times a day. This regiment went on for two or three years.

At this time, there was absolutely nothing wrong with my back. I had a significant injury which turned into significant drug addiction. By the time I got to the pain center, the only pain I felt was probably withdrawal pain when I ran out of medication. I would exaggerate pain that wasn't there. None of the doctors talked to me about addiction or withdrawal symptoms. They are part of what got me here. If I had known what was happening to me, I might have made different decisions.

I started shooting heroin right away. I snorted it in the very beginning but then watched other people shoot it. I had an uncle who had died of AIDS; he caught it through dirty needles in the 1980s. I told myself I would never do that, and here I was. I developed a significant heroin addiction. I also started shooting cocaine in my mid-20s.

I decided to go to a Suboxone doctor in North Conway and took Suboxone for three years. I weaned down and was doing well. I was working and all this other stuff. One day, I was not able to make an appointment due to a snowstorm. At this time, I was living in Plymouth, and my doctor was still in North Conway. They wanted to see me face to face before they would call in my prescription, and I couldn't make it. I didn't drive up there, and they didn't call in my script. Immediately, I started to withdraw from the Suboxone, which was worse than dope, and I relapsed back on heroin. I was off and running. I also got introduced to methamphetamines, and my whole life fell apart for six years.

On August 3, 2017, I got arrested in southern New Hampshire. I was on the news for three days for trafficking methamphetamines. I had warrants out on me in Grafton County because I was on the run from probation. I went to Rockingham County Jail in Brentwood. It was awesome, actually, but I had no intention of changing my life.

In October of that year, I called home, and my mother was crying. She said, "The jail didn't get through to you?" I said "No, Ma, the jail doesn't give messages to inmates." My father had passed away. I can't explain it. Something inside of me changed, and I knew that from this point forward, I was going to try to figure this addiction thing out. I worked out a plea with the court.

I started to learn about withdrawal. I didn't go to treatment and did it on my own. Yes, I learned through experience what withdrawals are. Nobody identified what I needed. Once my dad passed away, something changed. The court tried to hit me with distribution, but they couldn't prove distribution. They wanted to scare me with 10 to 30 years in prison but could only prove possession. They gave me time served as long as I went to a program. I tried to go to the Salvation Army program in Massachusetts. Grafton County said, "Absolutely not. He's a flight risk." I entered a program called The Firm. It's almost like being in rehab, but it's in jail.

I came to Littleton, moved into the sober house, and the rest is history. I eventually moved into leadership at that sober house. I'm now the regional house manager for six of their homes: four in Littleton, one in Plymouth, and one in Northfield. I'm also the center manager for the North Country Serenity Center. Being part of other people's recovery helps my recovery.

I have a fiancé and a three-month-old little girl. My 15-year-old daughter is back in my life. However, I lost custody of my two younger kids because of my last meth run. It was awful, and there is irreparable damage that I couldn't fix. I hope I can rectify this in the future.

I tried to get clean two times before this. I would sit in front of somebody that was book-read and had no lived experience. I didn't want to hear anything they had to say because I didn't respect them. How is someone going to tell me about recovery when they have no idea what it feels like to be an addict? People in recovery share their experience, strength, and hope with each other and it helps us stay clean. There is nobody I won't talk to about their addiction. I don't care how heinous their story. I'm able to relate to them and gain their trust. It worked for me, and I'm going to continue to save lives.

Looking back, when do you think it was mostly out of control?

The last two years of my use were when it was the most out of control. The meth took my soul. A week or two without sleep doesn't produce rational thought. When I was on the opiates, I wasn't healthy either.

How are you able to not drink or use daily?

I go to meetings and practice the 12 Steps. I come to work at the sober house and recovery center and help others. I am active in Narcotics Anonymous. I have a sponsor and four home groups. I also have a service position in each of my home groups. Because of being right in mind, body, and spirit, this keeps me clean, I go to the gym, and I'm involved in other outside activities. I enjoy life on life's terms.

What is your thought about medication-assisted treatment?

It has a place if it's utilized proactively to help someone sustain active recovery. People are coming out of jail and being forced to start medication, even if they are clean already. It is causing more harm than good. Many of us abused it, traded it, and used other drugs while on it. Until you completely surrender to this disease and are abstinent from all mind-altering substances, you can't truly move forward in your recovery. Being on a substance makes it too easy to go back to your drug of choice. I'm glad I can wake up every morning and not have to worry about a substance.

Is there anything you want those struggling with addiction to know?

You are not alone. Some people have lived your life and know what you're going through. You've just got to seek us out, and we will help.

Jill K.

Date of interview: 4/15/19
Sobriety date: 1/1/14, 5 years
Hometown: Auburn

When did you start drinking or using drugs, and how did it progress?

I was 13 years old and with a bunch of friends. I drank a beer and thought it tasted terrible, but I loved the way it felt. I was part of a group of people who raced sailboats, so there was a lot of beer available in the summer. I took great advantage of that. At age 15, I started drinking a lot on weekends. I had a boyfriend who was 19, so he could buy beer legally. My parents trusted me. I didn't drink at all during my junior and senior years of high school because we moved to Utah. The drinking age was 21 there. It wasn't readily available to me.

Then I went off to college at the University of Utah. That's when it all took off. I started drinking as much as I could whenever I could. One of my roommates was quite wealthy and introduced me to cocaine. I never bought it, but I loved using it. I was someone who would get sick and sleep through classes. I didn't know what I wanted to do with my life, so I drank to numb that feeling. I never felt as if I fit in. Drinking was the one thing that made me the same as everybody else.

My junior year of college, I moved back to the East and went to the University of Maryland. I got a couple of jobs as a waitress and a bartender, so drinking was easy. I eventually got engaged at the same time I was ready to graduate. We married and both drank a lot. We knew drinking was a problem, so we agreed not to drink hard liquor and only on weekends.

I decided to go back to school to become a teacher, and shortly after that, I chose to have kids. I didn't drink during pregnancy. I stayed home with the children and couldn't afford to buy it. I had one son, and then two and a half years later, I had twin boys. All the boys were under the age of three. I would limit myself to a glass of wine after they went to bed.

My drinking wasn't out of control. I had rules for alcohol. I always figured out a way to hold it to just this side of catastrophe. Then when my sons were five and seven, I divorced and was drinking pretty much every day, but I limited it. My twins had a rough time between the ages of 11 and 17. Without going into the details of that, I can say that suddenly, my life was in chaos, and my drinking picked up.

I would hide my booze in my room because I didn't want the boys to get it. I would sit up in my room and drink, and then go storming out if something happened. When the twins were 17, they moved to Virginia with their father. Being without them is when the switch flipped. I could drink the way I wanted to. I was lonely and felt as if I'd been through a lot. I thought, "If you had my life, you'd drink too." I started going to bars and became a regular at a couple of them.

Eventually, I met my second husband in a bar. We drank a lot together. I never entertained the notion that I was an alcoholic because I had a job, a car, and a house. I deserved to drink. The interesting thing is, I knew for sure that my husband was an alcoholic. We were married 14 months, and his health declined. He started walking with a cane because he had neuropathy from his drinking.

One night, after 14 months of marriage, he didn't feel stable enough to go up the stairs, and he decided to sleep on the couch. The next morning, I came down, and he couldn't walk. The ambulance took him to the hospital, and he died a month later of liver failure from drinking. We were only together for four years.

Before I knew he wasn't coming home from the hospital, I pulled all the liquor down from the cabinet and told my sons, who were 21 at the time, "Hey, if you want any of this, take it." I was so in love with alcohol, I didn't even think of pouring it down the drain. I knew I couldn't drink anymore if I was going to be a good wife. Then I thought, "Well, maybe I can go out drinking with friends," and wondered if he would be upset.

I was already bargaining with myself about how I could keep drinking, even though I knew my husband might die from it. I put the alcohol back in the cabinet, and there was a sense of relief. The day he died, my friend picked me up, and we drank three bottles of his favorite wine.

I had a 25-year career in education at this point. I quit drinking. I didn't intend to stop. Even once I quit, I didn't think I had a problem. I thought it just wasn't so good for me. One day, I decided to go to yoga because I had enjoyed it when I was young. I was extremely fortunate because I wandered into the River Flow Yoga Studio in Hooksett. At the time, I didn't know spirituality was anything I was missing. I also didn't realize that being a part of my community was anything I needed. I found both of these things in that studio.

The more connected I got to the people at the studio, the more connected I got to myself through spirituality. It didn't make sense to have this wonderful yoga class, feel all spiritual, and then stop off at the bar and get drunk on the way home. I started feeling a little ashamed and I remember the day I decided not to pick up a drink. It was January 1, not because I'm a person who makes New Year's resolutions, but because I am a person who had just sat at home for two weeks drinking and felt awful. I felt miserable and lonely.

I Googled alcoholism on the internet and started entertaining the notion that maybe I had a problem. I didn't drink that day and then didn't drink the next day. I started writing a blog because I read other people's blogs and commented on them. I started connecting to people in sobriety online. After about a week of that, I was part of a 12-step fellowship. I knew enough about 12-step fellowships to ask someone where to find a meeting. A woman told me she was going to a meeting, but I couldn't go because it was a closed meeting. I asked why, and she told me you could only go to a closed meeting if you don't want to drink. I told her I quit a week before, so we went together.

I sat in that room and heard people talk about the way I felt. I felt a little bad because I was lying to these kind people; I didn't think I was an alcoholic. I kept going because I wanted to know more about this fellowship. There was something there. A week later, I knew I had a problem and kept going. I was very stubborn. People would suggest things, like, "You should go to 90 meetings in 90 days." I'd think, "Well, that's fine for you people," but I counted yoga classes as meetings. I could do it my way, and maybe sometimes, I still do.

I found something by connecting to people in sobriety. People allowed themselves to be vulnerable and talk about the way they felt. I had never seen that before in my life, outside of my relationship with my mother, who passed away the same year I divorced. I never allowed myself to be vulnerable with anyone. I allowed myself to be vulnerable then and admit how I felt without shame. I realized people accepted me exactly how I was and didn't try to change me. I learned how to accept other people exactly as they are too.

Looking back, when do you think it was mostly out of control?

After the twins left, I had ebbs and flows because I still kept making rules about how I was going to drink. In the end, the absolute desperation was there, and there was nothing fun about it. I had a blackout, and it scared me. I was 52 when I finally put the drink down. I drank for 39 years.

How are you able to not drink or use daily?

The fastest way to get out of my head is to reach out and help somebody else. I connect with my soul. I talk to a lot of people about doing things that feed your soul. I paint, hike, and kayak. I go to concerts with a group of people. I enjoy music and have season tickets to Broadway in Boston. I keep connected to my spirituality, practice yoga, and meditate. I connect to my best self, my spirit, and think about us all as being connected.

I've studied Reiki, Buddhism, and *A Course in Miracles.* I take opportunities to do as much spiritual learning as I can. I read every day. I participate in a sober fellowship and go to meetings at least two or three times a week and then socialize with those same people another two or three times a week. I've learned to be grateful for the things I have and greet moments of discomfort as teachable opportunities.

What is your thought about medication-assisted treatment?

I have seen medication help a lot of people past the initial cravings, long enough to get into treatment and get their life in a stable place. I've met many people that are starting their journey with nothing and homeless. If that's where you're beginning, it will take you longer than 28 days of treatment to get your life in place. I've seen people do this quite successfully but as a short-term thing. Thinking a pill or a strip can fix the hole in a person's soul worries me. They need to find a way to do this by connecting to people and their souls.

Is there anything you want those struggling with addiction to know?

It gets better if you allow other people to help you. Let go of all the negative emotions long enough to reach out and let somebody walk beside you on the journey.

Jim G.

Date of interview: 4/22/19
Sobriety date: 4/27/93, 25 years
Hometown: Londonderry

When did you start drinking or using drugs, and how did it progress?

I was 12 years old. I've always had an infatuation with alcohol,

169

since being raised in a French-Canadian home. Alcohol was something we did as a family when everyone got together. I've always had a feeling of not quite fitting in and insecurity.

One night, I had friends over. We had a party with the disco light going and played disco music. I remembered my parents had a half bottle of slow gin in the refrigerator. I picked up the slow gin, started pouring it in my Coca-Cola, drank it, and my brain lit up like the Fourth of July. I drank more and more. I asked a girl I had a crush on to dance with me and kissed her. It was awesome.

I continued to drink more. The room started spinning; I threw up all over the place and passed out. The next morning, I promised my parents I'd never do it again. The following weekend, friends arrived at a party and said, "Hey Jim, your neighbors are gone for a couple of weeks, and they've got a case of booze in their basement." We broke in and got the alcohol. I started drinking, had the euphoria, loved it, and drank more. I threw up all over the place and passed out. This behavior was the beginning of my journey into using substances.

I remember saying to myself, "I'll drink alcohol, but I'll never do drugs." But at 15, I tried marijuana and loved it. I was now smoking cigarettes and marijuana. I drank and smoked pot for several years, and then at the age of 17, I tried cocaine for the first time. By the time I was 18, somebody had turned me on to freebasing cocaine, and I ran with that for the next eight years. I was also using heroin.

I would go on benders for four or five days, using crack cocaine and then two to three days using heroin. I would typically drink alcohol and get intoxicated, and then go out and acquire cocaine, start freebasing, and be up for days. It's similar to shooting because your body absorbs the cocaine more quickly. It's in a pure form and is distributed in your body a lot faster than if you were snorting it.

The turning point of my addiction was when I lost both of my parents three months apart. I lost my father in December of 1988. He died of a massive heart attack, and then I lost my mother in March of 1989 due to lung cancer. My addiction ramped up after this. I felt as if I were out in the deepest, darkest parts of Africa, and I did not have a clue about responsibility. After I lost them, everything went downhill. I had a large inheritance and depleted everything as a result of doing drugs and alcohol.

I ended up in Valley Street Jail with multiple felonies. My brother hired a lawyer, and the lawyer got me out of that jackpot. I was on probation for a year and didn't have anything other than an apartment in Manchester. I'd squandered everything. I violated probation because the probation officer dared to tell me that alcohol was a drug and I couldn't drink. I said, "My charge had to do with guns, drugs, and possession of stolen property. There's nothing there about alcohol." He said, "Alcohol is a drug. You can't drink." I told them they might as well violate me right then because I wanted to continue to drink. I was willing to do three and a half to seven years in state prison to defend my right to drink. I ended up drinking and using drugs, so they violated me, and I went back to jail.

I did 12 months and was court ordered to go into treatment. I got out of Valley Street Jail and tried to avoid treatment. I started using crack cocaine, heroin, alcohol, and marijuana. I was not going to go into treatment, but a supervisor encouraged me to. He said, "You need help. You're a good worker. I don't want to lose you, so get into treatment."

I went into the Sobriety Maintenance Center, which is now Serenity Place. I was there for seven days and then went to the Farnum Center for their 30-day residential program. Something happened while I was there. I found out that I wasn't a bad person, just a sick person trying to get well. I always felt I was a bad person because of the guilt, shame, and remorse from the things I put people through. It shifted my perception of myself and my struggle with drugs. They suggested I go to Alcoholics Anonymous meetings. I started to learn about responsibility.

At the first AA meeting, I asked a guy to sponsor me. He asked me, "Are you willing to go to any lengths to stay sober?" I said I would do anything; I didn't want to go back to using drugs. He suggested that I go to 90 meetings in 90 days, don't drink, ask for help, join a group, and get active. I did all of this and never said "no" because I started to feel like a person again, not my addiction. In combination with going to meetings, I went to outpatient counseling for two years. I had a lot of trauma that I needed to work out. My lifestyle was very traumatic.

After about two years of working in construction, a woman from the Farnum Center reached out to me and said she had a job opportunity for me. I let her know of my criminal background and told her the only job I deserve is construction. She told me to come in and talk. She believed in me and told me I had potential.

She offered me the job if I worked toward my GED. I started working there, got my GED, and loved working in the profession. I loved the idea of helping others. I started going to school at Hesser College and took some free courses. Then I went to Springfield College for my undergraduate degree. I also went on to get my master's at Boston University and recently acquired my LICSW. I've been working in the addiction profession since 1995.

Looking back, when do you think it was mostly out of control?

When my mother was diagnosed with cancer, I was angry. It was a three-year process. The jackpots started when I was 19. I had trouble with the law, I was using, and all my money went to using drugs and alcohol.

How are you able to not drink or use daily?

I pray every day and try to grow along spiritual lines. I accept the Lord as my savior. I go to church and belong to a church community. I also read the *Bible* and teach kids about it. I have a sponsor and sponsor other people. I've built my life with recovery supports and go to AA meetings. Everything I do today has nothing to do with substance use at all and has everything to do with recovery. I'm also very involved in the community at large because I believe in giving back. I can't keep what I have unless I give back.

What is your thought about medication-assisted treatment?

People can benefit from medication-assisted treatment. Our agency utilizes MAT as the last option. Typically, it's Suboxone. We may utilize Suboxone if someone has a long-term opiate addiction and has failed treatment in the past. We use a collaborative approach to the client's treatment: the clinical team, participant, family, and the doctor.

We also utilize other MAT options, such as Naltrexone and Acamprosate. Participants report that these are very effective in helping them decrease cravings. If there is a bump in the road and they end up using again, they don't experience the pleasure of substance use as before, so they will tend to choose to go back to abstinence.

All of the research I've looked up concludes that providers don't believe Suboxone should be used throughout a lifetime, a year or two tops.

Is there anything you want those struggling with addiction to

know?

There's hope. If I can do it, anybody can. I was homeless, struggling, and had nothing. Today, I live a life that's second to none. I'm blessed immensely, and that's really what I want to convey. No matter where you are, if you get into treatment and start doing the things you need to do to maintain your sobriety, anything is possible.

Joe K.

Date of interview: 4/20/19
Sobriety date: 3/13/95, 24 years
Hometown: Lisbon

When did you start drinking or using drugs, and how did it progress?

I was too young to remember. We lived on a ranch in southwest Texas on 195,000 acres. We were 120 miles from the nearest town. It wasn't uncommon for Mom to put a little whiskey in our bottle to help us sleep. When I was four years old, I would fetch beers daily from the fridge for the grownups. I took sips. I thought it was disgusting, but it made me feel important.

When I was 13 years old, I had free reign to run around. Being raised in the country, we did a lot of camping, hiking, and hunting. One time, my friends and I went camping. I raided my parents' liquor cabinet, took a bunch of different kinds of alcohol, and put it in a curd jar. My dad showed up and threw it in the trash and said, "That stays there." I didn't dare disobey him.

Not long after that, we were visiting some friends in Texas, and I went out with a group of older teenagers. They stopped and bought beer, so we drove around drinking, and I experienced getting drunk for the first time. I was blackout drunk. I can't tell you how much I drank. I remember waking up in the middle of the night, vomiting all over the room, and cleaning everything up. I thought it was a great experience and couldn't wait to do it again.

It would be a while before I got in trouble again because I got involved with a church. It kept me out of trouble for several years. A Christian boy brought me there, and we became friends. He was a good athlete, and I was trying to be. Every Saturday night, the church would have this big barbecue, and the adults would get drunk. The kids would swim and stay the night at the lodge. The next morning, we would get up and do a devotional with the grownups. Someone said, "This should be a church." Eventually, I helped build one there.

I went to school and studied to be a minister but came back to help the church. A young girl showed up, and it wasn't long before we were married with three kids. She had trouble with infidelity, though, so it wasn't long before I couldn't deal with it and walked out. Coping with the infidelity was what led me to turn to the bottle. I jumped in with both feet. A month before our separation, someone said, "Why don't you have a beer?" I opened the beer on the ride home, took two swallows, and instantly all the knots in my stomach relaxed. I knew I'd found the solution to my problems.

I felt guilty for leaving my family at age 27. I was a whiskey drinker and progressing with my alcoholism. Weekend drinking wasn't enough for me. It went from nightly drinking to all day, except for at work. It wasn't long after that I married a party girl. We were together for two years. She got run over by an 18-wheeler that put her in a wheelchair for the rest of her life. After that, I wasn't just drinking to quell the feelings inside me anymore; I was drinking because I didn't know how not to drink. I was drinking a case of Jack Daniels a week.

My drinking progressed into a lot of blackout drinking. Several years went by, and my father passed away from cirrhosis. My family and I were sitting around after his death, and my mother said, "You know, we are all alcoholics." I thought, "Well duh, aren't we supposed to be?" It wasn't long after this I was put into a nuthouse because I got suicidal. They were trying to convince me I was an alcoholic, and I was trying to convince them I was a nut. I spent three months there, got out, celebrated by drinking, went into a blackout, and didn't go home until three days later. I lost my job, and my wife ran off on me because of my drinking. When I wasn't drinking, I was intolerable to be around.

I recall sitting at home on a Thursday, and a friend was visiting from Florida. He came over, and we went to the liquor store and got drunk by the time we got home. He took all his clothes off and chased my wife around the house. I had to stop drinking and hide the booze and keys. I was trying to keep him under control. He finally left on a Saturday night. That whole experience was like holding a mirror up to me. I felt terrible about it.

Someone called looking for this man and said, "He can be a handful, can't he?" I told him that after that experience, I might quit drinking. He seemed to get excited for some reason. He said, "Well, I go to these meetings and would be happy to take you to one." That started me on a quest to quit drinking. I knew this was a bigger monster than I could handle by myself. Over time, I tried to control my drinking or not drink at all.

I called a pastor of a church nearby, and he said he would be happy to counsel me, but suggested I go to Alcoholics Anonymous. I wasn't sure what it was, but I didn't go back to him. I called a psychiatrist. The psychiatrist suggested I go to AA, so I didn't go back to him either. Then I found a substance abuse counselor in a center in Dallas. They had a good program. The counselor I spoke with said, "You can pay $35 and go to a group or meet one on one with a counselor." She said they also work closely with AA, so I didn't go back to her. My plan was, if I had someone to talk with, it would be someone who could help me get over that knot in my stomach, and then I would drink less. I didn't realize I wasn't just drinking because of the knot.

Since I hadn't worked in a while, I decided to go to school. I figured most of my problems were at home, so I went one hundred miles from my house. I stayed at the school during the week and went home on weekends. I noticed they had a drug and alcohol counselor at the school, and it was free. He had to listen to me.

After I registered, I went to see him. He said, "I would be thrilled to listen to you all you want, but it won't help." He said, "I have been going to AA for 35 years, and it is the only way I have seen an alcoholic like you get sober." I finally conceded. I found the noon meeting that day and went. I had quit for 10 days by that point and was going crazy. Going to AA this time was my last stop.

I remember walking up to the door of AA. It took everything I had to turn that handle and open the door. I was so full of shame. Everyone was friendly; they got me a cup of coffee and made me feel comfortable. They went around the room and shared a little about themselves. Each one of them seemed as if they were telling my story. When it came to me, someone asked if I wanted to share, and I did. I said, "I don't know what you all are talking about, but if it is alcoholism, I might be one of you."

As I was going out the door, a man walked up to me and said, "Joe, are you willing to go to any lengths to stay sober?" This guy later became my sponsor. What was going through my head was that he didn't know what it took me to walk through the door here. I said, "There is nothing you can ask me that is harder than what it took to get in here." I had to stay away from a drink. I was desperate at this point. On my way home, tears were coming down my face. An incredible feeling came over me. I knew everything was going to be okay. I remember going to a meeting the next time and letting someone know what I had felt that night, and someone said, "It's hope." I didn't know that.

When I had been four years sober, my second wife and I divorced. I got sober and found out we were very different people. A few years later, I met my current wife. We've been married for 15 years. She is entirely different than anyone I had ever considered being with before. We disagree, but we don't fight. We each have three kids and have 32 grandchildren.

When I got sober, I was employable. I was a police officer for 21 years and have now retired. The knot in my stomach has not come back. I found freedom. The chains fell off. I couldn't look people in the eye before, and now I get excited to see people. My relationship with God is deeper and more meaningful than ever before. I am involved in the church. My kids want to be around me now. I have real friends; many of which I found in the fellowship of AA. It is indescribable.

Looking back, when do you think it was mostly out of control?

After my second wife got hit by a truck, I was home alone while she was in the hospital. I spent most of my time out drinking whiskey.

How are you able to not drink or use daily?

I work with other alcoholics, and I'm involved in Christian 12-step recovery and Life Recovery groups. I maintain myself as an active member of AA.

What is your thought about medication-assisted treatment?

I never saw a lot of sense in it. Drinking and drug use is a symptom of something being wrong. Medication only treats the symptoms; it doesn't address the core of the problem.

Is there anything you want those struggling with addiction to know?

There is hope. You don't have to die. You don't have to worry about what other people think. There is hope in AA. Being an alcoholic is not a bad thing; it's a sickness, and there is treatment.

John B.

Date of interview: 6/3/19
Sobriety date: 5/20/18, 1 year
Hometown: Nashua

When did you start drinking or using drugs, and how did it progress?

I was 13 years old and hanging out with a friend. His dad had a pretty extensive liquor cabinet. We didn't know how liquor worked. We were trying to be stealthy and took a little out of each bottle. There was whiskey, vodka, and a couple of others. We took just enough so he wouldn't notice. We mixed it all into a Thermos with a straw on it. I'll never forget it. As soon as the mixture touched my tongue I threw up, even though the substance never really went into my body. After I threw up, we drank more and got a buzz. It immediately relieved my problems.

After that, I obsessed about it; I couldn't wait for it to happen again. Throughout high school, I drank more and more. I'd skip school to drink. I had one day where I didn't go to any of my classes and just got drunk at 7:30 in the morning. I had basically checked out of school. I was uncomfortable all the time, and drinking was the only time I felt okay. Naturally, I obsessed over it. It was the one thing I could do to make myself feel good.

As a kid, I was diagnosed with depression and general anxiety disorder. Doctors prescribed me benzodiazepines my whole life. I didn't go to college, drifted around a lot, and worked at different jobs. My 20s are a blur. It was a series of having jobs, starting a relationship, then making a mess of the relationship, running away and starting all over again. When I was 20 years old, I broke up with my girlfriend, quit my job, and moved across the country to Utah. I just had no life skills. I didn't drink for a while when I first moved out there and felt out of my mind. After a few months, I started drinking again and found new drugs. That's when it escalated for me.

I was using cocaine one day and went to get a bag. The bag was the wrong color from what it normally was, and my friend told me it was heroin. I decided to try it anyway. From that moment on, it was at a whole new level. The next 10 years of my life were a series of finding heroin, going on a tear with it, and trying to get away from it.

I never had the resources to go to rehab. The options were either you went to the methadone clinic or you went on Suboxone. I didn't even know abstinence was an option. I figured I would just do methadone for the rest of my life and that's how it was presented as a solution to me. I went to the methadone clinic for three years consistently and was on it before and after that. There wasn't a feeling of being high; I just felt like a zombie.

After three years of being on methadone, I decided to take Suboxone instead. I was in my mid-20s at this point. While on Suboxone I went to college. I went to a new place where I didn't know anyone. It went well the first term. The second term, I started to slip and started getting high again, then dropped out. I ended up back at my parents' house. I tried to be on Suboxone again and got back into school. I just couldn't handle it anymore and decided to just do heroin. It was the lowest point of my entire life. I was so depressed. I couldn't eat and could barely bring myself to go upstairs to go to the bathroom. I didn't want my family to even look at me. It was terrible.

My brother is my best friend, and he said he worked with a guy who might be able to get me into a treatment center. He brought me to a police station in Scarborough, Maine, where there was a safe station, and they found me a place in Florida. There weren't many options in Maine at the time. I didn't have benzos for the first time in my life. It took me months to recover because I was taking a lot of benzos on top of what I had been prescribed.

Detox took a long time; my brain was so messed up. I tried a couple of different rehabs down there and then they sent me up here to New Hampshire. The rehab I went to was filled with people making their lives better and guys who helped me. They showed me how to lead a happy and successful life. They guided me on how to live without drugs. Things started to click for me, and I got relief for the first time.

Looking back, when do you think it was mostly out of control?

Toward the end, right before I went into treatment, when I was living at my parents' house.

How are you able to not drink or use daily?

I'm involved in AA meetings, sponsor other guys, and have a sponsor. I'm connected to a higher power. I pray every morning and read Hazelden's *Twenty-Four Hours a Day* book. Prayer has become a part of my daily regimen.

What is your thought about medication-assisted treatment?

I did it for a long time, and my life didn't change. I was hoping it would. I have seen other people use it and get their life better. I don't want to disparage it. I just never got to connect with the beauties and mysteries of life until I stopped all drugs. When I was taking medication, I felt as if I had been missing out on all these things. I let the discomfort I had been experiencing all my life happen and didn't pour something on top of it to make it go back down inside me. I was never really able to connect with life until I was completely abstinent. So, for me, the only answer was abstinence.

Is there anything you want those struggling with addiction to know?

I didn't believe that life without drugs and alcohol was a possibility for me. I was 100 percent sure of that. I know how it is when it's dark; it sucks, and it seems insurmountable, but there are so many people out there that want to help you.

John C.

Date of interview: 3/25/19
Sobriety date: 8/13/12, 6 years
Hometown: Merrimack

When did you start drinking or using drugs, and how did it progress?

At age 15, a friend of mine, at a football game, gave me a couple of beers. When I drank them, I got the feeling like this is who I am. I was an introvert and guarded. Even though I played sports, I had a low self-image. When I drank, those things went away. By age 16, my drinking started to pick up. I could drive and go places. At that time, I drank every weekend and would get drunk. At age 21, I discovered Percocet and would use it one to two times a month. That was even better than drinking. It boosted my energy level, and I could be more productive. It wasn't as readily available as it is now.

From age 25 to 28, I was a police officer, which curtailed my use. I was very busy. By age 28, I found a regular hook-up, and my use snowballed into every day. It took off after my kids were born and gave me the energy to take care of them. I thought it made me more efficient. The more responsibility I had, the more I used. I was married and had two kids, but when I was 32, my wife and I separated. At one point, my wife said, "Either you go to treatment, or we're getting divorced," so I moved in with my parents. My dad suffered from chronic pain. I started to steal his morphine. I changed my profession and was now a maintenance man at a private school.

I went to the IOP in Concord, Fresh Start, but never stopped using. I thought I could control it. I wasn't going to get sick and could do it on the weekends only. After the IOP, I came clean to my wife and went through the IOP again. At that time, they introduced me to a Suboxone doctor. I was two weeks clean when I met him. He gave me half a tab, and I felt as if I got high. I thought, "Yeah, I'll take this." My intentions were to use it as prescribed. After four to five months, I did that. I had my mother give it to me. After a while, I would hold off on taking them, on the verge of getting sick, and then I started trading them for Percocet.

The last straw was when my dad passed away. I used his death as an excuse to go out. I stole a Home Depot credit card from a friend, and they told me to go away to treatment, or they would talk to the police. So, I went to treatment in Connecticut. I knew I had to get out of the area. I knew if I went home, I would use again.

My sister's best friend worked at Hampstead Hospital, and she recommended Granite Recovery Center. I got introduced to Alcoholics Anonymous and the 12-step process there. I went there for six months, then went out and relapsed. I tried to manipulate the 12-step process but found out you can't. I drank and used Percocet for a month, went back to Granite Recovery, and went through the program again.

Looking back, when do you think it was mostly out of control?

Between age 28 to 32, it was a downward spiral.

How are you able to not drink or use daily?

I practice all aspects of the 12 Steps daily. I also utilize a clinical approach.

What is your thought about medication-assisted treatment?

My experience with medication-assisted treatment wasn't good. I didn't work on the underlying issues. It was a Band-Aid for me. I didn't want any medications. Instead, I wanted to come to it on my own.

Is there anything you want those struggling with addiction to know?

Enjoy life. There are a lot of good things out there. You can stay sober and not use drugs. There is happiness.

<u>**John M.**</u>

Date of interview: 6/15/2019
Sobriety date: 6/20/75, 43 years
Hometown: Portsmouth

When did you start drinking or using drugs, and how did it progress?

My father was a physician and an alcoholic with a brilliant career. After his drinking progressed, he was reduced to having a medical office in our home. To get my mother out of his way, he often drugged her. Every day when I came home from school, she was in bed upstairs. Sometimes she would come down for dinner. He would make the dinner and drink while he did the cooking. By the time dinner came around, he was drunk. Occasionally, he would erupt and explode against my mother. I told myself I would never drink like that guy, and I'm sure I meant it.

When I was a senior in high school, my father was drunk one night and fell down the stairs. At three a.m., my mother came and woke me up. She told me he had fallen and wanted me to help. Blood was everywhere. I told her to call an ambulance. She said, "We're not calling anybody." We pushed him up the stairs and put him in bed. The doctors came the next day and caught the broken hand and the abrasions, but they never realized he had a fractured skull.

He was never taken into a hospital and examined. That day he was cleared, but three days later he started to get foggy. By the time they relieved the pressure on his skull, he was too far gone. He went into a coma from which he never came out. The death certificate says, "Killed in a fall, fractured skull." It didn't say, "Years and years of alcoholic drinking." I remember when my aunt came to tell me my dad had died. When she left, and I looked in the mirror, I thought to myself, "Why do I not feel like crying? Why do I have no feelings for him?"

May of my last year of high school, three of my friends asked me to go to New York to drink at a bar. I had a fake ID, so I went. Somebody said, "Why don't you have a vodka and orange juice?" I had my first drink and felt a sense of heat, and I thought, "Wow." It was a new feeling. I went off to college and within a month, I was hanging around with people who smoked cigarettes and drank. I was asked to leave my sophomore year because of a drinking incident. I went to another university and got kicked out of there for stealing from a liquor store and getting caught. They let me back in, but they wouldn't let me live on campus. I didn't drink every day at this point. When I went to law school, I waited on tables, made good money, and drank after the restaurant closed.

That's how I got through law school.

I came to Portsmouth in 1969. By 1970, I was making money and drinking in bars. I had arrived. I had charge accounts at various bars and felt terrific. By 1973, I was drinking every day. I met a guy who started telling me how his wife had kicked him out; he lost his business and was sleeping in his car. His friend asked him if it was related to alcohol and told him to go to an AA meeting. He just talked about himself; it was perfect. He must have known I was an alcoholic. He went out of his way to tell me how AA had saved his life. I said, "Well, I'm happy things worked out for you, but I've got to go." I left but never forgot him.

I started drinking every day. Intellectually, I knew I should do something about my drinking; I didn't want to. There was one event where I made a fool of myself. I called up that friend who told me his story, and he told me he would send me a bunch of books in a brown bag. No one would know. He sent it to my law office so that I could read them in my own time. I got them and never read them. I tried not to drink, and it failed. I'd go to the bar and have one, but then I'd have another and another. Night after night, I came home when the kids were in bed, and I didn't think much of it.

One night, I was at a restaurant, and there was a couple in the corner. They said, "Hey, come on over." I started to walk over. When I got halfway there, her eyes changed; it was the recognition that I was drunk. I went outside and started to cry. I called the friend who gave me the AA books. He said, "I know just the guy in Portsmouth for you to talk to." He asked if it was okay for him to call me. It ended up being a guy I knew well. He was Mr. AA in Portsmouth and lived across the street from me. He took me to my first meeting. I knew this was where I should be. This guy who brought me asked me to go the next day and the day after that. He took it one day at a time. He just wanted me not to drink that day.

After five months, I was having trouble with the concept of accepting I am an alcoholic. I voluntarily signed into Beech Hill Rehab for 10 days. I walked away feeling, in my gut, that I'd accepted the fact that I'm an alcoholic and cannot drink. I never questioned it again.

In 1990, I flew over to Ireland, went to a pub, and was sitting down by myself. I was hungry, angry, lonesome, and tired. A woman said to me, "Have you ever had any Guinness?" and asked me to try hers. My first thought was, "Who would know if I drank it?" My second thought was, "I would know." I didn't pick up that drink. I left.

The next day I found myself on a golf course, and in the middle of a game, a guy was talking about drinking, and I said I didn't drink. The caddy said he didn't drink either. I asked him if he was in AA, and he said, "No, I'm a Pioneer." Pioneers are prominent in Ireland. They all swear in front of the church's guidance that they won't drink. He introduced me to a man who gave me a book about AA in Ireland. For the rest of the 25 days, I went to AA meetings, introduced myself, told everyone I was looking for someone to play a round of golf, and someone would always be waiting at the end of the meeting to schedule a game. I spent 30 days in Ireland golfing all over with people in AA.

I am always close to a drink. I don't have a desire to drink now, but circumstances could change, events could occur, and I am not far away from a drink. I can feel as if it's impossible, or that I'm not interested, but in an instant, that could change. I preplan an escape route if I have this threat.

Looking back, when do you think it was mostly out of control?

I was a daily drinker. It was probably the worst right before I got sober.

How are you able to not drink or use daily?

Being in AA is the best decision I've ever made, more important than my marriage, more important than anything. I wouldn't be married to the woman I am today, and I wouldn't have the life I have today if I hadn't gotten sober and stayed sober through AA.

I start my day with a meeting. I go to meetings every day. I go and listen to how people live. It's not just about alcohol. It's how to be a better person through following the 12 Steps: when I'm wrong to promptly admit it, treat people as best as I can, and do an inventory of my life regularly. I have gone to AA Monday through Friday for the last 20 years. I got emotionally confused about different things when I wasn't. AA is the platform upon which all other good things grow or exist. I am embedded in AA, golf with people in AA, and go to movies with people in AA. I have friends that are not in AA and friends in AA.

My wife and I have a pretty quiet life. I must say that AA is quite Christian based. I'm not a Christian; I'm a Unitarian. My Unitarianism is based on doing social justice activities. I'm driven daily to be involved in a humanistic approach to life, non-profits, and helping people individually, financially, or any other way. I spend no time at all thinking about the afterlife, if there is one. I certainly hope there is, but I'm betting that if I am kind, treat people well, live by the Ten Commandments, and there is a God, he or she will treat me well. I pray as if it's all up to God but work as if it's all up to me. I don't go out of my way to deny the existence of God. I turn my will and my life over to God.

What is your thought about medication-assisted treatment?

I believe medication can help. A psychiatrist diagnosed me as being clinically depressed and thought I should be on an antidepressant. Since 1990, I have been taking an antidepressant daily. However, I believe using Suboxone or methadone is putting off a solution. It is essentially buying into another solution, and I think the incentive for totally getting off everything may decrease. I would not be in favor of it. I think it's better than heroin, but you're not putting yourself in a position to have an examined or informed life. You're not clear-headed. There's something that's keeping you together. Being in AA allows you to explore who you are, how you live, and what you should do. When you take a substance that dulls that, the result isn't as rich.

Is there anything you want those struggling with addiction to know?

You are not alone. With the help of others, you can recover from addiction. You can live a meaningful life and help others. You will increase your worth and be a credit to yourself, your family, and society. Develop an escape route from an event where there is drinking. Even if you don't think you need it, develop it.

John P.

Date of interview: 4/7/19
Sobriety date: 10/6/88, 30 years
Hometown: Campton

When did you start drinking or using drugs, and how did it progress?

The first time was June of 1973, at the end of sixth grade. At the time, the drinking age was 18. I had friends who were 16, and they had friends who were 18. They asked me if I wanted something from the package store. Someone asked if I wanted a bottle of wine, so I paid for it, and they got it for me. I felt as if I'd arrived. Even before I picked up the bottle, I was hanging out with older kids. I was small for 13 and now I felt as if I belonged to something. When I drank that bottle down, everything changed.

The next morning, I woke up with a hangover and threw up off the side of my bed. I said to myself, "I'll never do that again."

From that day forward and into the 1980s, I was a weekend warrior. I looked forward to Friday and Saturday nights, getting together with friends, and getting drunk. I started to recognize that some people saw me as having a Dr. Jekyll and Mr. Hyde personality. I was a big-time blackout drinker. I would do things when I drank that I usually don't do when not drinking. I didn't understand that alcoholism was a disease or that alcohol made it that way for me. Alcohol was making all the choices and decisions in my life. What I did in my life was based on drinking. I was a drink and get drunk kind of guy, or I didn't drink.

I went into the military after high school for a geographical cure. I wanted to get the heck out of my hometown. I did very well as a young fellow in the military for a reasonable amount of time, until I got stationed and made friends. When duty ended for the day, we would head to the local pub and drink.

I got into a relationship, not based on what I now understand is true love. We married, and we had a child together. In August of 1986, my wife left me and took our infant daughter with her. I was devastated and did what I do best. I drank four to five nights a week. The progression of my disease got worse and worse. My friends were getting worse, and the bars I went to were worse. I tried cocaine and acid a couple of times but never got into it regularly. I paid my rent, paid my child support, had a job, so I didn't believe I was an alcoholic.

In November of 1986, my mother and father died. It was like a rug was pulled out from underneath me. I didn't deal with it well. I had no coping skills. My coping skill at that time was to drink. I don't know if there was a night when I didn't drink. There were times I'd tell myself, "I'm not going to drink tonight," only to wake up the next morning after having drunk all night. I couldn't understand how I could get drunk again.

Eventually, I met an honest girl. She told me she had a couple of cousins in AA, they had straightened out their lives, and one of them wanted to talk to me. She also told me she thought I was a great guy, but when I drank, I frightened her. I started to wonder what she and others meant by that.

From 1987 to October of 1988, I started drinking and wishing I would die in my sleep. I was in my head and wasn't talking to anyone about what I was feeling and thinking. My thoughts were taking over. I thought, "If I could drink myself to death, my troubles with everybody else would be over." October 5th, 1988 was my last drink. I tried to take my own life. In a blackout, I went to the basement of my home with a 12-gauge shotgun, wedged the gun between the wall and my chest, and pulled the trigger. I don't remember what happened. I do remember walking up the basement stairs and holding myself. My brother was home when it happened, and he called the police. I remember the police officer said, "If I knew it was this bad, I would have gotten you some help."

I was in intensive care and a coma for two weeks. When I came out of the coma and on full life support, the first thing I thought of was, "I want a drink." Then I thought, "Look where I am. Maybe I shouldn't be drinking." Somehow my brain opened up to the truth, and the truth set me free. A few weeks later, a couple of friends came to see me. They were sober and shared their experience with alcohol, the strength it took them to get sober, and their hope for me being able to do it too. It set my sobriety in motion. They left me an AA Big Book, and I started reading it. I identified a lot with the stories in the book. There was a person in the book with a story just like mine. He got sober, and his life changed for the better.

I had a spiritual awakening when I woke up from the coma. The

God of my understanding had allowed me the opportunity to become the man I was supposed to become. I'm a sober member of Alcoholics Anonymous. I'm spiritually grounded in my life and trust the 12 Steps of Recovery.

Looking back, when do you think it was the most out of control?

In the end, with the suicide attempt.

How are you able to not drink or use it daily?

The first thing I do is put my life in God's hands daily. I go to weekly meetings of Alcoholics Anonymous. I communicate with other recovering alcoholics and help them to the best of my ability.

What is your thought on medication-assisted treatment?

I think it's a substitute. All you're doing is changing seats on the sinking Titanic. I'm not a doctor, but when a chemical alters your mind, it will be tough to receive a spiritual message.

Is there anything that you want those struggling with addiction to know?

You are not alone. You never have to be alone again. There are other people just like you, people who understand, and there's no reason to be ashamed. Whatever your addiction may be, it's a disease of the mind, and you can get better. Recovery is a gift, and we do it one day at a time.

<u>Joseph K.</u>

Date of interview: 6/4/19
Sobriety date: 12/10/14, 4 years
Hometown: Nashua

When did you start drinking or using drugs, and how did it progress?

Growing up, I felt as if I didn't belong, didn't fit in, and didn't feel a part of anything. My first real drink was when I was 12. My friends and I found a bottle of Hot Damn liquor in the woods. I'd seen a bunch of my older friends drinking. I never got into it, but I said, "This bottle here, this is made for me." I took a sip and felt it go down my windpipe. It was disgusting. I hated cinnamon. I wanted to spit it out, but that warm, fuzzy feeling I felt down in my chest as it went in my stomach, wow, that's what I wanted. It instantly made me feel as if I could get what I wanted. I blacked out and ended up doing a bunch of stupid stuff. To me, it was exciting.

My parents drank. I watched them enjoy it but didn't see the adverse effects. At age 13, I started to plan my drinking, smoking weed, and hanging out with the older crowd. Eventually, at age 15, I found Vicodin and Percocet. One time, I had tooth surgery and took a whole bottle at once. I felt a different way with pills. I had arrived. I liked the combination of opiates and drinking. It was a match made in heaven. It made me feel like Superman, invincible. I'd work a 14-hour day, and it didn't matter.

I lost my license at age 16, at 20 for DWI, and again at 32, all because of drinking. Opiates weren't the problem, right? It's drinking. I tried lengths of time where I was only doing opiates, but it always led me back to drinking. I didn't get in trouble every time I was drinking, but every time I got in trouble, I was drinking.

I started to catch charges and wound up in jail a bunch of times. I would show up to work whether I smelled like a brewery or not, and OxyContin got me through the day. I had to work to have money to buy drugs. Eventually, working wasn't enough. I started robbing from my family, breaking into houses, and selling drugs. Cocaine, Molly, Ecstasy, I was doing all that stuff. It didn't matter what drug it was. It got progressively worse and led me to choose heroin. I thought I wouldn't shoot it; I'll sniff it. The thing about OxyContin is, you looked for the drip after you sniffed it. I'd do heroin and didn't like that drip. It was disgusting to me. I knew I was doing this dirty drug.

My justification for taking pills was, "Hey, they're pharmaceuticals. It's not a drug, right?" One day, I was inebriated, and my buddy loaded up a rig for himself, and said, "Come on, you've got to do this." I said, "No, I don't want to," and went upstairs. When I came down again, he had loaded the rig for me, and I said, "Fuck it, let's do it." This started my obsession with needles. I was putting cocaine or whatever I had in a syringe. My disease took off. I was 25 years old. OxyContins were gone, and now I was shooting heroin.

I spent my entire day consumed by getting and shooting up drugs. I overdosed several times in the next few years and was brought back from the dead more times than I want to count. I had always gone to court-ordered AA meetings and tried to take the suggestions, but never felt as if I fit in. I wasn't ready and didn't have enough pain to change. I'd see people transform their lives in AA, but never thought I could.

I went to jail for the fifth time, got out, and said, "That's it, I'm going to stay clean." I went to meetings and started to like going to them. I met a girl and wanted to impress her, so of course, I drank. I told myself I wouldn't shoot heroin again but started. I never got the full effect of alcohol alone. This girl and I ended up having a baby a couple of years later and decided that would be the reason to stop.

I thought this girl was my soulmate. We loved the same things, especially the escape dope provided from reality and our trauma. We fought this disease together and separately. Our daughter is eight years old now, and we've always fought for her, even when we didn't fight for ourselves. Our daughter was a reason to stop for good. "This is it," we said when she was born. Finally, I didn't need to be selfish anymore. I tried to stay sober to be a good dad and couldn't. I couldn't stop.

I was taking Suboxone when we had her, but a week after having our daughter, my girl and I were both shooting heroin again. This disease is so selfish. I put my family through a bunch of pain. One time, I lost track of my daughter. She was three years old, and I couldn't find her. She was safe and in the care of her mother, but I was blacking out towards the end. I was doing fentanyl and all sorts of crazy illicit drugs. I lost my daughter. Losing her was demoralizing and just enough pain for me to start to consider a new way of life. I knew I needed help.

In 2014, I was ready. I was beaten down and broken by this disease. I didn't want to live and didn't know how to die. I had lost my job, my kid, my girl, and my house. I went to rehab for 30 days and realized 30 days wasn't enough. I saw people going into sober homes and figured I would try. I talked to the founder of GateHouse in Nashua. He told me they would show me how to live again, and if I wanted to recover, there was a way out if I could follow directions. I thought, "What's the worst that could happen?"

I lived at GateHouse for a couple of months, got better, and became part of something I never knew was out there. I became a productive member of the community and started to show other guys how to do it too. I've been here for four and a half years now and have made this my permanent home.

I was sober for 12 months when the worst thing in the world that could happen happened: my sister died of a fentanyl overdose.

After a year of sobriety and because of the tools of the 12-step program, my AA family got me through it and supported me the whole time. I got to be there for my sister. I'm an advocate for people who think there's no hope. There is hope. My little sister was 32 and had two babies. She had a C-section, and the doctor gave her Dilaudid. I saw her develop a mental obsession with the drugs and called her every day. I tried to be there for her. It was a little too late. She did fentanyl one time and died. One time and it was over.

This experience strengthened my recovery. It gave me a reason to fight, being there for her kids and my daughter. I'm there for my family and all the guys I sponsor. I have so many reasons to fight. I have a purpose, and there is meaning in my life today. I care about other people and want to be part of the solution, not part of the problem. I want to do the right thing and have found a way to do this with the help of others.

Looking back, when do you think it was mostly out of control?

Right before I got sober, my life was so out of control. I didn't care if I lived or died. I lost respect for myself and my family. I was at a turning point; I was either going to die or fight for life.

How are you able to not drink or use daily?

I practice the 12 Steps, have a sponsor, and go to AA. I lived with a bunch of guys when I first got sober, who were all doing the same thing. Most importantly, I talk to people about decisions and feelings in my life. I find prayer and meditation to be fantastic tools to ground me and calm my fears and doubts.

What is your thought about medication-assisted treatment?

It wasn't the route I took. I took Suboxone off and on my whole life. I also used other drugs while taking it. A drug is a drug is a drug. I didn't want to be a slave to any drug. I have seen the research that shows people severely addicted being stepped down from their drug use while taking Suboxone. If prescribed by their doctor or administered by a treatment center and then you go entirely abstinent, I agree with it for some cases. It works if you get them into a recovery lifestyle so that they don't have cravings. They need to develop a recovery network, be provided resources, and have monitored care.

Is there anything you want those struggling with addiction to know?

There is hope. There's help out there. You are not alone. It's tough to go to a meeting and open up. Most people at a meeting are coming together because they know we recover together. For people who have a severe addiction like mine, I needed sober living. We need the support of others in recovery. I formed healthy habits and reshaped my perspective on life. This change takes a while, so give yourself a chance.

Left to my own devices, I don't go to meetings. If I don't have a sponsor, I'm not held accountable. With almost five years sober, I have people that keep me accountable and make me show up. I don't do it on my own. Reach out; there are so many people that can help you. Tell somebody. You are as sick as your secrets.

Joshua T.

Date of interview: 6/10/19
Sobriety date: 1/10/13, 6 years
Hometown: Deering

When did you start drinking or using drugs, and how did it progress?

At age 12 I started smoking marijuana. I was home with

pneumonia and told a buddy I wanted to smoke pot. He was five years older. His mom and dad were never home, so he was always at our house. He was like an older brother to me. He took me to the woods and made a makeshift bong out of a jug, and I took a couple of hits. When I got home, I laid down and felt like I was in a tunnel. I started freaking out and having panic attacks. I went into the room where my dad was and just paced back and forth. Then I lay down and tried to calm myself. I had panic attacks consistently after that; it wasn't enjoyable for me. The reason I wanted to try it was to belong.

I grew up going to church with my parents. When my father started smoking pot and my mother started taking pills, everything became chaotic. We stopped going to church and started to have a lot of social get-togethers with alcohol. My family was falling apart. I tried alcohol a few times at one of the gatherings and tried marijuana again. I had more panic attacks.

I went home, freaked out, fell on my knees, and asked God for help. Right then, I realized the last time I smoked pot I told God I would never smoke again. I broke my promise to God. At this time, I didn't understand the gospel. I didn't understand grace. I didn't know we are saved by grace alone. I didn't know that I'm not going to hell, and God forgives me.

I was having panic attacks and not doing well in school. My parents were getting divorced, and I felt guilty all the time. One time, when I was getting in trouble, my mom said, "Why do you think your dad left?" She wanted me to believe that he left because I was a bad kid, and I believed her. I felt as if I had a shameful cloak over me. I felt repulsed by my father and mother. My mother was hooked on Xanax. I saw what the pills were doing to her and vowed I would never do them.

I smoked weed and had anxiety attacks every day, so eventually, I stopped smoking pot. Anxiety, fear, and shame ruled me. I liked playing sports, but I started having too much anxiety on the baseball field, so I stopped. I started playing guitar and got involved in a band when I was 16 and started smoking pot again. I thought I could master the drug. I said to myself, I'm just going to smoke weed and fight through the panic attacks until they go away, and I did. I mastered the fear of death and was able to not have panic attacks. I started to love pot.

My thoughts consumed me with, "I'm not going anywhere, I'm stuck, stagnant, and a loser." All my friends were doing painkillers and benzos, and even though I said I never would, I tried half a painkiller one day. Right then, my drug of choice became opiates. I thought I had arrived, and I was going to do this forever. My friends and I were getting opiates from pill mills. I would take 5 mg of Hydrocodone in the morning and 5 mg at night. It gave my attitude and personality a boost. I felt great, but I started to get jaded and bitter towards life and God.

I moved out of my house, used painkillers daily, and got up to 250 mg of opiates a day. I overdosed a few times and had a lot of blackouts. I thought it was a spiritual thing. It alleviated the burden of my soul. Drugs were a father, a mother, and a god to me. I worshiped them. They touched my heart and made the pain go away.

When I was 19, I took a bunch of pills one night, went to a bar with friends, and had some beers. I got messed up and was blacking out. I left the bar, blacked out, and ran my car into someone's house. I woke up with the owner and the cops in my face. I got arrested for underage drinking, possession with intent to distribute, and a paraphernalia misdemeanor. It was my first arrest. I woke up in jail and was thinking, "Oh my God, this is real."

I was terrified and had no idea what was going to happen to me.

All charges, except the misdemeanor, were dropped. They gave me probation for a year and did random drug tests. I failed the first two drug tests. I went to court again and told them I didn't have enough time in treatment to get off the drugs because I had been taking them for a long time. I told them the next drug test would be good. The next one wasn't good. I couldn't stop. I wanted to, but I couldn't. I thought I had to keep doing them, and the cops were going to have to catch me.

I moved in with friends who also did pills. I started going from job to job, always looking over my shoulder for the police to show up. I started abusing Adderall and cocaine. I just went to the doctor and told him, "I'm in college and I'm having trouble studying." I wasn't even in college. He wrote me a script for Adderall on the spot. One night after I'd been up for two or three days, I used my sister's car, was speeding, and got pulled over. The police said, "You have four warrants out for your arrest, and you can get 10 years for using a controlled substance." Of course, I told them the pills were not mine. I went to jail. There was a big black man in my cell, and he re-introduced me to the *Bible* and the Lord.

The court allowed me to do the STOP program with daily reporting. I was clean for five months. On the Fourth of July, I relapsed. I showed up and told my caseworker that I used. The court made me go to 90 support group meetings in 90 days. I said, "Yeah, I'll do that," and didn't follow through. My caseworker called me, told me I could start the program over or go to jail. I decided to go to jail and did five months. In late August, I got out, and my goal was to stay clean. I moved in with my sister. My mom was homeless and sleeping on the couch there. She had Adderall and other pills, so I started taking her Adderall and ended up homeless.

My grandmother took me in; she was a southern Christian woman who loved the Lord. She was sick with cancer but said she would

200

take me in if I got help. She told me about His Mansion in New Hampshire. We were in Louisiana. I fell asleep that night, woke up in the middle of the night, and read the *Bible*. I slept with it under my pillow. Another night, I fell asleep watching TV, and woke up to the 700 Club. They were selling Elvis Presley music, and I listened to How Great Thou Art. The next morning, I woke up, and the only thing on my mind was, "I'm going to His Mansion."

The intake was in January. I showed up and had to detox. It was painful. I felt as if the Holy Spirit were taking me over. I was a resident of His Mansion for two and a half years. After this, I started teaching the first phase of the program. I love to learn and have a passion for teaching God's Word. I taught for another two years. Then they asked me to be the program administrator, and I've been doing that for a year and a half.

Looking back, when do you think it was mostly out of control?

Towards the end, it was the most out of control. I stole my grandmother's gold and sold it for drugs. The last thing she did before she died was to get me into His Mansion.

How are you able to not drink or use daily?

I get into the Word first thing in the morning. I ask the Lord to illuminate my heart and reveal himself to me. I pray for the Lord to help me love others. I read a daily devotional by Charles Spurgeon and have critical friends I can be honest with, who tell me the truth. They pray for me and pronounce forgiveness over me, and they confront me if I need it. I try to stay open and vulnerable. I talk with my friends about what I'm feeling, either good or bad, so a bitter root doesn't grow and lead me back to addiction. The gratitude I have fills me. I know Christ transcends suffering. I love the Lord with all my heart. I have joy, and I'm grounded.

What is your thought about medication-assisted treatment?

Suboxone and methadone are bogus. It's the golden calf. It's trading one drug for the other. You're playing with fire and giving yourself an out. If you are in detox and the medical professionals say you'll die if you don't use the medication, then that would be the exception. It's too strong of a pull, and we are too weak. It's a false god, slavery, and bondage. Christ comes to liberate the captives, and it's not in a Suboxone strip.

Is there anything you want those struggling with addiction to know?

You can stop using drugs. Come to Christ, and you will have a lot more than freedom from addiction. Christ is the answer. He has always been the answer. Come to God and experience freedom. Get into treatment or a church where people can walk alongside you and care about you on your journey out of addiction.

Jules R.

Date of interview: 6/14/19
Sobriety date: 6/23/84, 34 years
Hometown: Pittsburgh

When did you start drinking or using drugs, and how did it progress?

I was nine years old. I grew up in an alcoholic home and was full of fear, doubt, and insecurity long before I took a drink. At nine years old, I stole two beers from my house and went into the cornfield next door and guzzled them down. That's how I saw people drink, so I thought that was how you drink. I loved the way it made me feel; it made me forget about everything. I didn't particularly like the taste, but the effect was magical. I thought it was what I was missing in my life.

By the time I could remember, I felt as if something were wrong with me, but I didn't know what. I was so full of fear, insecurities, doubt, and self-pity. From the minute I picked up alcohol, I thought it was a cure-all and chased it. It was effortless to get alcohol in my home; my three brothers and I had our bedrooms in the basement, and we had a cooler that was always full of beer.

At a very early age, 11 years old, I was sedating myself to sleep with two to three beers and that progressed. From that time on, nothing else mattered, absolutely nothing. I went to school, but it didn't matter. When I was 13 years old, I discovered whiskey, which was quicker than beer. I would keep that close at hand, and at night I would sip some whiskey and down a couple of beers. I grew up in a big family. There were alcoholics all over the place, so no one knew.

I wasn't interested in anything except music. I taught myself how to play guitar at age nine. At 14, I started playing in a band at clubs. My biggest aspiration in life was to become a rock star, which goes hand in hand with alcohol. I never got into drugs. I tried pot a little bit at 13, and all it did was make me sleepy. I made sure I went to school every day, only because my mother was an art teacher and would make sure I was there.

When I turned 16 and got my license, my friends and I would head up to Canada; they would serve us at the bars there. We would drink and drink and never remember driving home. I'd drive home in blackouts. After high school, all my buddies went off to college or did other things. I stayed, got drunk, and played rock and roll in bars, usually Thursday through Saturday nights.

From the time I was 18 until age 20, I drank a fifth of Jack Daniels every day and as much beer as I could. I had thoughts of killing myself. I hated myself. I hated everything, so thoughts of suicide kept coming. I wished I were dead every day. I was deeply depressed and didn't know it. I was either excited or sad. I was excited when I drank and depressed when I wasn't. It was a horrible, horrible life.

When I was 20 years old, I was supposed to be having a band rehearsal on a Sunday morning and showed up drunk, so they told me to leave. I left and hooked up with a buddy. We took off and started drinking, and he purchased some acid. I had never done anything like that before, but I took some of it. I woke up two days later at my girlfriend's parents' house, and everyone was at work. I woke up and was completely horrified. The desperation and loneliness were horrible. I had insane thinking and thought I was possessed.

I screamed out, "God, please help me," and the first thought that came into my head was about a gentleman I'd met in a bar two years before, who was now sober. I bugged that man that whole night about how he couldn't be having much fun while being sober. I remembered his name and called him. He and his wife were both home and invited me over.

I stopped at the store where my girlfriend was working to tell her that I was going for help and she was so happy. I went to their house, and they pulled out a bunch of literature, and we talked all evening. He asked me if I could stay sober and meet him at a meeting that night. I showed up at that meeting, 20 years old and a mess. When I walked in, I thought to myself, "What am I doing here?" I sat down and had a cup of coffee. They started telling me their stories. I had never heard such honesty in my life; it blew me away. Towards the end of the meeting, one of them stood up and pointed his finger at me and said, "Young man, let me tell you something. There's a God, and he loves you." I'd never experienced hope in my life until that night. At the end of the meeting, I was so relieved that I'd finally found out what was wrong with me: I'm an alcoholic.

Off and on for a couple of weeks, I'd try not to drink, but there were a couple of graduation parties I went to and got drunk, even though I intended not to drink. This inability to stop drinking convinced me that I was an alcoholic. I couldn't stop once I started. Going to those meetings paved the foundation, but I had a hard time leaving the party life and all my friends.

After the first month, I stayed sober for seven months. I moved to Florida where my brother was living, looking for a geographical cure. I waited for three months and drank a couple of times. When I came back, I met up with some of my buddies, and we got hammered for a couple of months. I don't remember much about what happened during that time.

After that, I decided I needed to leave again, so I moved to southern New Hampshire to my other brother's house and started going to meetings there. I went to meetings for three months and stayed sober. I got a real job, started working, and asked my girlfriend to marry me. I stayed dry for almost a year, and on June 22nd, 1984, friends and family took me out for my bachelor party, and I got drunk.

The next day I got married, and two weeks after our marriage, this impending doom hit me again out of nowhere. All the despair I felt as a kid came back. I knew it was God calling me. I took out a card with the serenity prayer on it, went into the bathroom, got on my knees, and said that prayer. I said it all night long. The next day I went to work and went to a meeting that night. I got a sponsor and went to meetings every single night for two months.

Looking back, when do you think it was mostly out of control?

After I turned 18, it was every single day. I didn't draw a sober breath for two years.

How are you able to not drink or use daily?

Every day I get up, start the coffee, walk into my office, and read Hazelden's *Twenty-Four Hours a Day* book. I pray and meditate after reading. I also work a lot and enjoy being very, very busy.

What is your thought about medication-assisted treatment?

I never believed in it. I don't think God made us to take a drug to keep us happy, joyous, and free. We have nobody staying in AA anymore. They're just so addicted to opioids that they destroy everything. They're so lost. They go to doctors for help, and they're giving them more drugs. It's so crazy.

Is there anything you want those struggling with addiction to know?

There is always hope. I hope you give it a chance. A lot of people can quit drinking and drugging but are not happy. Faith is what saved me. It allows you to live a fulfilled life and brings you happiness.

Karen P.

Date of interview: 5/29/2019
Sobriety date: 6/30/89, 29 Years
Hometown: Franklin

When did you start drinking or using drugs, and how did it progress?

I was four years old, just tall enough to reach the table. My mother was drinking blackberry brandy; she was an alcoholic. I couldn't get her attention, so I grabbed her glass and made a run for it and got a couple swallows down. It was painful going down; it exploded in my belly, and then I felt invincible. The next time I couldn't get her attention, I did the same thing. It wasn't long before I started doing it with other family members. I liked Grandpa's rum better than I liked Mom's brandy. I tell people now if your drink of choice at four years old is rum, it's not a good sign of what's to come.

I didn't get drunk until I was 12. I knew my mother liked to drink, but I didn't know she was also using drugs. I knew she didn't want to drink, but she kept doing it. I couldn't understand why she would keep doing something if she didn't want to. One day, my parents were out grocery shopping, and I was home alone. I had some chores to do while they were gone and rushed around to do them. I took out an eight-ounce tumbler, filled it with rum, and drank it down. I'd been a really angry kid and gotten in tons of trouble with my anger: fights, starting fires, all that kind of stuff. When the rum hit my system, I wasn't angry about anything. I had a feeling of relief and fell in love with drinking.

The next week my parents went out shopping. I volunteered to stay home to vacuum and drank again. It wasn't long before I figured out that hiding a bottle in the basement was a way to not wait for them to leave. I could drink anytime. When I was 14, my friends were already giving me a hard time about how much I was drinking. One friend had started going to Narcotics Anonymous meetings at 14, and she was trying to convince me that I was an alcoholic. She thought I needed help. I had none of that.

By 15, I was drinking every day. My mom had a big bottle of Valium that she was getting from a family member. It was in the medicine cabinet, and I would take three or four and drink on top of it. I was in terrible shape. By the time I was 16, there was a judge in town who was pretty insistent I go to AA meetings. I wasn't going, no matter what the consequences. At that time, in Vermont, there were no juvenile detention centers for girls, so I wasn't scared. What consequences were they going to give me? Tell me I shouldn't drink and to shape up?

I was drinking and popping pills all the time. I tried cocaine and speed but didn't like anything that brought me up. I couldn't deal with the crash afterward. Alcohol took away the angry feelings, and I liked that. I was 16 when I had my first suicide attempt. I turned my family in for physical and sexual abuse, and there was a massive court case. It involved the uncle who was giving my mother the Valium. I turned him in because of what was happening to my younger brother. My brother experienced the same kind of things as me. I couldn't let that happen to him.

When they started the investigation, they uncovered a sex trafficking and child pornography ring in New York, Massachusetts, and Vermont. They arrested several people. My father got arrested; not for that, but stuff that was going on in our family. I couldn't drink enough to drown it out. I had no hope, so I took handfuls of everything that was in the medicine cabinet and downed it with a lot of booze. I woke up the next morning in a big mess of vomit; everything had just let loose. I was in my room with the door locked. I lived, but it messed up my kidneys. I had bruising all through my face, and my kidneys were shutting down; they weren't functioning. I couldn't keep food down. My doctor told me, "If you don't stop drinking, you're going to die." I just kept drinking.

It didn't matter how much I drank; I would still feel the feelings. I couldn't drown them out anymore. I started taking Quaaludes and all sorts of stuff. I couldn't find relief, and everyone was on my case. I thought, "Maybe I need to stop for a while and get a handle on things." I'd make it two or three days and wouldn't use; I'd be a mess. It felt like the very fact that I breathed air was a problem. I was enraged, raw, and acted out in violence. I figured I might as well be drinking, so I drank again and took Valium.

I would get into trouble and say, "Okay, I'm going to stop," then I'd drink again, and the cycle would repeat itself. I did this for two years. I had lots of suicide attempts and lots of getting in trouble.

The court made me see a counselor, and the counselor tried to convince me that alcohol and Valium were a problem. I didn't see it that way. I saw it as the only thing that worked for me.

After the last suicide attempt, I woke up, and I screamed at God to leave me alone. I knew it was divine intervention that saved me, and I was pissed. I decided if I couldn't check out, then I was going to have to find a way to live differently. I decided to stop but didn't realize that meant completely stopping. I thought if you didn't have blackouts, then it didn't count as drinking. I controlled it for almost three months, and on the 89th day, I dropped a TV dinner on the floor; mashed potatoes and gravy spilled all over the carpet. I yelled, swore, and kicked a hole in the wall. I grabbed a bottle of gin, and life was blank for two weeks. I'd come out of a blackout just long enough to go back in.

One day, my father said something I didn't like, and I went after him with a knife. My mother managed to talk me down. The look on her face made me put down the knife. I ran out of the house, got a bottle, and called my counselor. I told her I thought I had a problem with alcohol. She said, "I'm on my way over to take you to an AA meeting." I said, "No, you're not." She then said, "What excuse do you have not to go?" I said, "I'm too young and don't belong in AA." Instead, I camped out in the rail yard. No matter how much I drank that night, I couldn't shut my head off.

My bottom was the horrified look on my mother's face and not being able to shut off my head, no matter what I put in my system. I called the counselor back and she took me to rehab. I stayed for two months. My detox was horrible; I shook and sweated for six weeks. We had school every day, and I studied Buddhism for schoolwork; this turned me on to meditation.

I moved from the rehab to college and was in a suite with five other people. No one in my suite drank. There were 14 students on campus in the 12-step programs, and we supported each other. I stayed for two years. After a couple of years, I ran out of money. I also had problems with my mental health that the 12 Steps weren't going to help. I was hallucinating. Things were talking to me that shouldn't be talking to me. They were yelling at me, so I started to flunk out of school and ended up leaving. I was on the streets for two years, sober. My AA sponsor convinced me to see a psychiatrist who put me on some non-addictive meds that helped. I needed professional help.

Looking back, when do you think it was mostly out of control?

When I first tried to stop drinking at 16. I was drinking around the clock. I couldn't sleep for more than two or three hours without getting up and putting something in my system.

How are you able to not drink or use daily?

I know at my core that I can't drink; it's not even an option. I start my morning with prayers of thanks. Every morning I say, "Thank you, God, for giving me everything I need for the day ahead." It reminds me that I can trust that everything I need to get through that day, I receive. I stay in touch with other people, so I don't isolate.

What is your thought about medication-assisted treatment?

I'm concerned about answering a drug problem with another drug. It just doesn't seem to make a whole lot of sense. It seems like another temptation. It doesn't get you out of the addiction mentality that fed the substance abuse issue. Treat the underlying causes and conditions. methadone and Suboxone are like putting a Band-Aid on a problem.

Is there anything you want those struggling with addiction to know?

You can live life in your own skin. It's possible to live life without chasing after a substance. There are other ways of getting relief, like prayer and meditation.

Karin B.

Date of interview: 4/22/19
Sobriety date: 3/27/85, 34 years
Hometown: Bedford

When did you start drinking or using drugs, and how did it progress?

I was 10 years old, and it was my parents' 20th wedding anniversary. They had a party, and I remember having three to four beers, going outside, and getting sick. It was a few years later before I drank again. On the first day of high school, I went over to a friend's house to drink beer and was very anxious, so I drank to calm my nerves. Then we went to school, and I ended up going to the bathroom in the men's bathroom. I remember this distinctly.

I drank every weekend throughout high school. I would drink until I passed out. I would get caught, something else would take precedence over my drinking, but then I would drink again and repeat, and drink and repeat. In my senior year, I met the man that would become my husband and the father of my son. We married a year out of high school.

I would drink, but not all the time. I held a job and drank on weekends. After three years of marriage, we divorced, and my drinking picked up. I was trying to control it and was able not to drink if I couldn't get wasted. I remember thinking, "If I can't drink as much as I want, I might as well not drink." I would start drinking on Thursday night after work, and my parents would watch my son. Then it turned into Thursday through Sunday.

I was dating a guy from high school, a student at UNH. I tried cocaine with him a couple of times and remember thinking I couldn't do it anymore because I loved it too much. I remember picking up my son from my parents, being wasted, and putting him in the back seat of the car. One time I hit his head on the door and drove home wasted. It was before the time that drunk driving was talked about a lot. I don't know how I got away with it, but I did.

It was not long before I was in another relationship, and my drinking went back to weekends. I was happy, so I didn't need to drink as much. He was verbally abusive, so I started drinking in order not to feel the emotional impact. My sister-in-law reintroduced me to cocaine, and it quickly became a daily habit. I was obsessed with it. I felt as if I had arrived, could go anywhere, and talk to anyone. It was a false sense of self-esteem. My cocaine use went on for years. I was living with my fiancé and spending most of my time in the bathroom doing cocaine. He thought I was having an affair. We eventually broke up, and he found someone else.

I dove deeper and deeper into my addiction, and on my 30th birthday, I fell down a flight of stairs and hurt myself pretty badly. I couldn't breathe and had to see a doctor. This situation was a wake-up call. I knew I couldn't do this anymore and needed to stop. I went to counseling for almost a year and tried to stop every week. She would ask if I used, and I would tell her yes. Then she gave me the number 1-800-COCAINE, which I dialed. I finally realized I needed to change my life.

Something needed to happen, or I was going to die. I used everything I could imagine and still couldn't get wasted. I felt sober. Nothing worked, so I decided I could either die or change something. The only reason I got sober at first was for my son. I didn't want my ex-husband and mother going to court over him. I couldn't do that to him. I called the 800 number, and the woman said that she thought I needed inpatient treatment. My parents were living six months in Florida and six months here. I thought I needed a vacation and to lay by the pool.

That's not what happened; I ended up in Hampstead Hospital. I told my son I was going on vacation to visit a friend. My mother flew home from Florida to take care of him while I was in rehab. He eventually found out where I was and came to visit me. When I went into rehab, they tried to give me Librium. I told them, "No, if I needed another drug to get off of a drug then I was walking out the door." They didn't make me take it.

I met my first therapist there and finally let it come out that when I was a kid, my best friend's father molested me. He was friends with my parents. He was also the police commissioner in our town. When my mother found out, she went to the police and told them, and he lost his job. I remember being angry that I couldn't be the one to say something, to let my voice come out. It took me years to forgive her for telling the police.

I didn't want to leave the program. I felt safe and comfortable there. Eventually, I had to leave and went back to my job. I started going to meetings, but I was also back with my old fiancé. He didn't think I was an alcoholic and didn't want me going to AA, so I stopped. He drank and I was a year sober. The relationship finally ended, and I went back to AA. My sister asked her friend at work to take me to AA. This woman ended up becoming my sponsor.

At first, I was obsessed with meetings. I didn't know how to live without going to a meeting and would call my sponsor before doing anything. I had this fear that would take over whenever I had to make a decision. When I would call her, she helped me tremendously. By doing the 12 Steps of recovery, I learned to let go of fear, embrace it, and walk through to the other side. The more I did this, the more I knew I could.

In 2009, I got a job in the addiction profession but was burnt out by 2015. It was hard emotionally, since so many people were dying of overdoses. I left the business and worked as a landscaper. I spent time taking care of myself and was enjoying weeding gardens. It was therapeutic for me. I am back in the addiction profession today and keep a healthy balance between work and self-care. I got sober for my son; I now stay sober for me.

Looking back, when do you think it was mostly out of control?

When I turned 30, it was the most out of control.

How are you able to not drink or use daily?

What helps me now is working in the addiction field. I see what the people are like coming in, and I don't ever want to go back there.

What is your thought about medication-assisted treatment?

I don't believe that you're sober. You don't feel the pain of giving it up. This pain helps you not use. I see instances where it is beneficial for a percentage of people. Pregnant women on methadone are safer for withdrawals, both mother and child.

Is there anything you want those struggling with addiction to know?

There is a Spirit within you to help you get and stay sober. Sometimes it's moments at a time, but those moments add up.

Katie N.

Date of interview: 5/21/19
Sobriety date: 7/11/16, 2 years
Hometown: Franklin

When did you start drinking or using drugs, and how did it

progress?

A couple of weeks before turning 15, my brother came home under the influence. He was drinking and smoking weed. I was like, "You're so stupid. Why would you do that?" The following weekend I was home, and he was out with his friends. I felt alone and as if I were missing out on something. The very next weekend, when he went out, I said to him I was going with him, or I would tell our mom.

We went to a campfire, and there were a whole lot of people from high school there. Days later, I was on the patio with him and his friends smoking pot. I don't remember being substance-free for more than a week-long period until I was 24 and entered my first rehab. The progression of my substance abuse went from drinking to smoking weed, to psychedelics, and to opiates. Ecstasy and alcohol would determine any choices I made in life from the ages of 18 to 23.

At 21, I got into my first legal trouble, aggravated DWI. It was the first time in all my using that I had had any consequences. I remember getting arrested on multiple occasions when I was younger but went to anger management or a diversion program. I tried hard to straighten my life out and told people I was only using alcohol, but in reality, my life was unmanageable. I traded one substance for another, and that's how my story looked until I got clean.

When I was done with the diversion program, I paid them all the money. I completed all my community service and classes. I got a phone call in the middle of the night that my brother had been in a car accident and wasn't going to make it. He passed away on October 13, 2014, and from that day on, I had hate in my heart. I wasn't a very hateful person typically, but now I had hatred.

Hard drugs came back in full swing. I was using intravenously, any substance mixed with any substance. Four months after my brother passed away, I was unemployed and unemployable. I was homeless and lost in the world. A year after he passed away, I entered my first rehab in New Jersey. I was going to change my ways, get a job, be a better person, a better daughter, and a better sister. It wasn't eight hours after I got out, I was back to using. I wasn't ready. I didn't have a spiritual solution.

It was through being incarcerated that a woman came in and spoke at the jail. She looked at me one day as I was sharing a story about my brother, and she said, "You know your brother is not coming back, right?" That was the moment I felt peace and serenity. It was real, and I accepted it. I let him go to rest. Once I let go, a higher power started working in my life, who I choose to call God. A chain of events and opportunities began in my life.

I was 25 when I got clean and sober and have not found the need to put any substance in my body since. I believe God placed people in my life to keep me alive until I got to a point where I was ready to surrender. Jail is where I surrendered. The woman who told me my brother wasn't coming back gave me a *Bible*. I sat on my bunk with that *Bible* and read it while everybody else got high, and I didn't. Everybody got drug tested, and I passed my test.

The using lifestyle was all I knew. I went to any lengths to get substances. I got into a sober house when I was released and started going to meetings. I started taking a lot of the suggestions from people and worked the 12 Steps. Working the steps is where I developed a relationship with a higher power. I have relationships with my family today and attend church on Sundays. I don't go to church because I like to consider myself a religious person. I go because I know it's God's grace that saved my life, and because before July 11, I was literally on a suicide mission. I had acquired as much heroin as I could to overdose and kept it at my parents' house. When released from jail, I went to my parents' house and threw it away. It was throwing away my death certificate.

I made a pact with God that I would live. I was ready to live. Holding onto the loss of my brother was holding me back and weighing me down. I was unwilling to do anything to help myself because I didn't feel worth it. I struggled with getting clean, sober, and into recovery because of this. I convinced myself for years that I was going to die in active addiction, and I was okay with that.

Since I've been in recovery, my sister has passed away too. She was in a sober house in Tennessee when it caught on fire. She and two other women didn't make it out. I was in the process of writing my fourth step and was able to let go of a lot of resentment towards the sober house. They had no working smoke detectors while she was there. There were 16 girls housed there, and they all paid a substantial amount to live there, but there were no working detectors. I was able to go out and meet the survivors of this tragedy. It was one of the most beautiful experiences I've ever felt in my life. A lot of the women had bumps and bruises, and a couple of them had broken legs from jumping out the windows. I made it through all this without picking up a substance.

I praise God for carrying me when I didn't even know what to do. I have a sponsor and a fellowship who love me when I'm unable to love myself. My sister's three-month chip is on my bureau at home. I hold it sometimes in the morning when I start my day. It reminds me that just because I'm clean and sober doesn't mean I have a promise of tomorrow; it's one day at a time.

When I wake up from a bad dream, or can't sleep, I can talk to people who are trying to live a life of not just abstinence but recovery. There's a considerable difference between abstinence and recovery. Recovery is engaging in a process, like a 12-step program. Drugs were my solution to everything until they became my problem and turned on me.

Today, I have the support of people who attend Al-Anon and other groups. I have people in my life who battle the demons of addiction every single day, and through God, a lot of that pain and suffering of the obsession to use is lifted. I have my triggers, but I also have solutions. From going to meetings and speaking with other people who are battling the same things, I hear a lot of what I've done, and it helps me. I travel all over the world today. Last year I went to England and last week I was in Arkansas. I went from a girl who wasn't allowed to leave the county and shackled to a wall with bars, to freedom.

Looking back, when do you think it was mostly out of control?

The second year after my brother passed away, because I don't remember a lot.

How are you able to not drink or use daily?

As soon as I open my eyes I get up and make my bed. I'm grateful I have one. I hit my knees and ask God to guide me through the day and place somebody in my way that I can serve. I have a few readings I do, one of them is the AA *Daily Reflections* and another is a women's recovery book. I reach out to a few alcoholics and drug addicts daily. We all get up around the same time, and we send out messages to each other. I have some faith-based and Christian music I listen to, like Lecrae, Bryann T, Tripp Lee, ASAP Preach, and Colicchie. I also listen to artists in recovery, Macklemore, Cooly, etc. It gets me in the right mindset for the day.

What is your thought about medication-assisted treatment?

I don't get it. Doctors are over-prescribing it. Maybe it can be used in a detox center. People need to be comfortable coming off it and not pressured to stay on it. It's substituting one thing for another sometimes. I've seen people mess up their lives more on these drugs than on illegal drugs. A lot of people shoot it; this is defeating the purpose. A guy at work, who was on methadone, got fired because he was always sleeping at his machine. He said they wouldn't lower his dose because the last time they did, he picked up heroin. Bringing people off it unmonitored is setting people up for failure. What plans are in place to get people off it?

Is there anything you want those struggling with addiction to know?

You don't have to use. There are other outlets, other ways. People care and will answer your call at two in the morning. It is possible to live a life without putting a substance into your body. There is a fellowship and promises of freedom. You cannot regret or shut the door on the past.

Keith A.

Date of interview: 4/16/19
Sobriety date: 5/15/03, 16 years
Hometown: Littleton

When did you start drinking or using drugs, and how did it progress?

I was 11 and camping with my father. He gave me a couple of beers, and I remember enjoying it. I also drank one time when I was babysitting. When I was around 12 years old, my father and stepmother thought that instead of me drinking outside with friends, they would let me drink at home. A lot of people in my family have the disease of addiction, whether it be to alcohol or drugs.

When I was 13, my father was diagnosed with cancer, and two months later he died. It was a tragic event, and my stepmother was actually his common-law wife, so she had no parental rights. She became active in her addiction and went off the deep end. I was supposed to start an excellent school that year and take auto mechanics, but when my father passed away, I couldn't cope and wanted to die. I had faith in Jesus, so I believed if I took my own life, I would never see my father again. I hoped that someone else would kill me.

I drank alcohol and smoked weed for a while, and I eventually got arrested. I refused to go to school, stole cars, carried guns, and got into a lot of trouble. As a result, I went into locked facilities, boot camps, rehabs for kids, etc. I was miserable right off the bat. I wanted to numb myself. That's all that mattered to me throughout my teenage years.

I was smoking angel dust daily and at age 17 I dropped out of school and got incarcerated. After jail I ended up going to a halfway house in East Boston. I stayed there for six months and then went into a sober house. I got a girlfriend; someone I'd known since I was 14. She was pretty strait-laced. At the time, I thought she was what I needed to stay clean. The relationship ended, and as soon as things started not working out, I "used at her." I drank and got high on purpose to spite her.

In 1997, heroin was everywhere in Boston. I started sniffing heroin and eventually started shooting it. I fell in love with it. I shot heroin and cocaine. By 1998, I was in jail again. I did six months and couldn't wait to get out and get high. When I was 21, I got out and used. I was getting high, stealing cars, and walking out of stores with whatever I could sell. I lived to use and used to live.

I went back to jail in 1998, got out again in January of 1999, and went back in March of 1999. I had no desire to get clean. When released to the community, a girl picked me up and brought me dope and a pack of Newport cigarettes. I got high in the parking lot and stayed high for a few months after that. I ended up getting charged for armed robbery on July 4, 2002 and went into the Cambridge jail for a year. After I fought it, they dismissed the case.

I went into the Salvation Army and started to pray. I thought it was a miracle that they had dismissed the case. I had one of the best summers I'd had since I was a little kid. I wanted to stay clean. I planned to get a job and find a girl. Then I went to court for a stolen car charge, and they offered me a year. I left that day so depressed, a case of self-pity kicked in, and so I went and did what I know how to do: I got high. The plan was to get some drugs, tuck them, and go to jail with the drugs. That didn't happen.

Two months later, I got arrested again for a stolen car and got three and a half years. Doing time was what I knew and where I thought I belonged. I got high as I usually had in the past, but something was different. I didn't feel this was where I was supposed to be. I took some Vicodin and drank a ton of water. I had an unexpected drug test two days later. I made a deal with God: if the drug test comes back negative, I will stay sober. It did.

My sobriety started when I began to pray privately in my cell and started reading recovery literature. That was it; I just surrendered. I knew I wasn't living right. I knew I had a lot going on inside of me, and my thoughts were distorted. I didn't understand what the disease of addiction was. I didn't realize that I had an obsession with using people, places, and things. I dove into the 12-step recovery process and followed every suggestion.

Looking back, when do you think it was mostly out of control?

I'd have to say immediately. Immediately I rebelled. My dad was gone, and I was so angry. I didn't want anyone to tell me what to do.

How are you able to not drink or use daily?

I'm a member of a 12-step fellowship. I pray daily and consistently, all day pretty much. I surround myself with people who are living life in a way I want to live, people that have what I want. I'm involved with my faith and spend time with members of the church. I take time for myself. I take time to enjoy this beautiful place God allows me to live in, even though I'm busy.

What is your thought about medication-assisted treatment?

I had no experience seeing anyone with success on methadone before I got sober. When I was two years clean, I had a young kid come to me on Suboxone. He wanted me to sponsor him, and I judged him and said, "This kid's not clean." I prayed on it, and I decided to sponsor him. The first six months, I watched him wean off the medication, and he's 14 years sober today. I've seen both outcomes, those who stay clean, and those who don't.

It is way over-prescribed and distributed all over the streets. It's easier to find Suboxone than it is to find dope. People are using it now to make money. It can work for some people, but therapy, a sound support system, accountability, and short-term dosing is needed.

Is there anything you want those struggling with addiction to know?

There is hope. No one thought I was going to stay clean, because I was a bad kid. If you find God and seek Him in all things, you can get and stay clean. Get involved in a 12-Step recovery. It's not just a spiritual program; it's a behavior change program. Do everything, go to therapy, go to the gym, meditate, and do things you enjoy, but have a foundation of recovery. Make the 12-step program your foundation.

Kelli K.

Date of interview: 6/4/19
Sobriety date: 4/17/17, 2 years
Hometown: Effingham

When did you start drinking or using drugs, and how did it progress?

I grew up in a white picket fence family. Both of my parents were active in AA recovery, and my younger brother was my best friend. I excelled in sports, got straight As and never went without anything.

By age 13, I started drinking and smoking pot. My parents went out and bought a new dress for me to wear to the winter formal. I never made it into the dance. My girlfriends and I sat behind a dumpster, drank, and smoked pot. It should have been a red flag. The second I started drinking and smoking, nothing mattered to me.

When I was 14, my parents got divorced. Before then, I had never been to a barbecue where I'd ever seen a beer. Then I was smoking pot with my dad and drinking wine coolers with my mom. We moved a lot. I went to four different high schools, and in my senior year, they told me I wasn't going to graduate, so I went to night school. I never walked with my class. Going to night school and not graduating with my class isn't the way I envisioned my life happening.

At age 19, I met my son's father. It was just a typical case of sweet, isolated girl meets bad boy. All we knew how to do was party. The first time I took an opiate was with him: Vicodin. I snorted it and hated it. After a year and a half, we had a bad break-up. I was devastated and started experimenting with anything I could get my hands on.

On my 21st birthday, I got kicked out of four different bars. I blacked out and had no recollection of what happened. The only reason I know this is from everyone telling me. From age 20 on, my drug use was daily. It started with Vicodin and Ritalin and then progressed to Percocet. My brother took Ritalin, so of course, I'd have him share it with me.

At 21, I worked for a school and met one-on-one with an autistic boy, I loved it. My drug addiction got terrible. I took drugs before work to get through the day and ended up quitting the job before I got fired. When I stopped going to work, I lied to my boyfriend about where I was. I would get up every morning and make it look as if I were going to work. I'd go to my sister's and use drugs all day. He eventually found out, and that was the end of us.

I got right back with my son's father. I was a full-blown drug addict, and he was an alcoholic. I couldn't keep a job, and at 27, I got pregnant with my son. As soon as I found out I was pregnant, I stopped drinking, smoking cigarettes, and doing drugs. I didn't want my son to wind up like his father, who had grown up in foster care. By the time I was three months pregnant, I was clean but with no support. I had an emergency C-section, and the second they put those drugs in me, it was like a light switch went on. I can't even explain it. I remember sitting there and holding this beautiful boy, who is completely healthy, and thinking, "I wonder what drugs they're going to send home with me." They'd give me a pill to take at the hospital, and I'd cheek it so I could go in the bathroom and snort it.

After my son was born, I had back surgery and put on fentanyl patches and took Dilaudid. I diagnosed myself as having ADHD and anxiety, so they gave me Adderall for the ADHD and Valium for the anxiety. I took these pills every day, all day.

When introduced to the needle, it was a complete game-changer. Not knowing what I was doing, I started shooting up. I wasn't hitting my veins and ended up with seven abscesses at once. One day, I got an infection, collapsed, and was rushed to the hospital in Lewiston, where they lanced my arms and filled them. My arms bubbled up; I have scars all over them. They put me on a gurney, strapped me down, took a scalpel, sliced it open, and pressed on it till the puss came out. They inserted a wick down into this hole to feed the infection out. I had seven of these on my arm at once. I was there for 11 days straight, under a false name, because I was afraid my son was going to get taken from me. My mom got wind of my hospital stay, took my son from me, and got temporary guardianship. I put down the needle right then and there. I did not put down the drugs though. Within two months, I had my son back. I was still a mess, but a prescribed mess.

My son's father was on Social Security because of his health problems, and we lived off the state. I was using prescription and street drugs all day, every day. Drugs were getting shipped right to us. DCYF was called on me 12 times, and after dealing with them, I would put the hard drugs off to the side and reel it back in when things blew over. I was barely taking care of myself or my child. I was an absolute mess. I needed to start using a needle again because I saw my fiancé got an entirely different effect.

I didn't want him to know how much I was doing, so I took off with my sister. I shot a gram of heroin, smoked a bunch of meth, and then went down to put gas in my car at the Irving in Ossipee. I was at the gas pump, and my sister was in the bathroom using. I'm under the vehicle trying to fix the exhaust, and the next thing I know, I see four sets of cop boots. I hear, "Miss, do you want to come out from underneath the car?" I ended up getting arrested for an OUI.

Our purses were both in the vehicle, filled with scales, baggies, and drugs. We weren't allowed near the car, and it got impounded. She walked away. I tucked two grams of heroin up my lady purse while cuffed in the back seat of the cruiser. They asked if they could search me, and I had a bag of heroin residue in my pocket, probably 25 cents worth. It turned into a strip search, cough, and squat. Then they threw me into a holding cell. My bail was only $40, but nobody came to get me. It just shows how many bridges I had burned.

The bondsman came in and said, "No one's coming to get you, are they?" I thought, "You don't even get it. I'm at the height of my addiction, and no one's going to come to get me." He says, "If you promise me, you'll come back with the $40, I'll let you go." I instantly thought, "What can I pawn, steal, or sell to come back here and pay bail?" I left, and the first thing I did was climb over the impound fence and get into my car. I didn't get caught. I had no idea where my son was—none. Everything was just such a blur.

My son's father died of an overdose, and it rocked my world. I had been with him for 10 years on and off. This is when my drug addiction plummeted out of control. I didn't care anymore and didn't want to be alive. I was now living at my mother's house. My mother and brother were using needles with me, and my poor son was living with us. The final straw was when I overdosed twice in 24 hours. The next day, a state worker and police officer came knocking at the door. I thought to myself, "What the fuck am I doing? This kid just lost his father." I said to my son, "Buddy, you're going to have to go away for a little while. Mommy's sick and needs to get better."

I detoxed at home and was able to get all the drugs to do this off the streets. My mother and father were sober, and I was going to

AA. I was told to go to 90 AA meetings in 90 days. I did 180 meetings in 90 days. The judge said I had to go to therapy and bring in the documentation. I went to the White Horse Addiction Center's IOP in Ossipee. My son lived with my mother, and I worked in the addiction center's thrift store. I developed a relationship with my son and got my license back. I got a promotion at my job, got an apartment of my own, and started to pay my bills. After two years of staying sober, I have my son back and have been free of drugs and alcohol ever since.

Looking back, when do you think it was mostly out of control?

Right after my fiancé died of an overdose.

How are you able to not drink or use daily?

I get up in the morning and pray. I pray about everything, and it works. If I'm anxious, I pray about it. If there is an obstacle, I pray about it. I'm grateful. I exercise at 4:30 a.m. every morning with amazing women, and I have people who support me. I go to three AA meetings a week, have a sponsor, and work the 12 Steps.

What is your thought about medication-assisted treatment?

I am entirely abstinent and grateful. While taking Suboxone, you're still wrapped up in addictive behavior. People taking an addictive medication for this disease don't have mental freedom. The freedom of not having thoughts rent space in their head. When was the last time I took my dose? When am I going to take the next dose? You don't have to get up in the morning and chase the need for the drug. I have thought, "If I got kidnapped right now, I would not get dope sick." I don't want to have to worry about dope sickness.

Is there anything you want those struggling with addiction to know?

227

There is hope. If I can do it, anyone can. You can have true freedom.

K.H.

Date of interview: 5/28/19
Sobriety date: 5/21/07, 12 years
Hometown: Manchester

When did you start drinking or using drugs, and how did it progress?

I was in third grade. I was reading a comic book, and someone had slipped acid to a character in the book. The next couple of pages were all cool looking. I remember thinking to myself, "I can't wait to try drugs. That seems so awesome." The first time I drank was in eighth grade. I was in a high school play and went to a high school party. I ended up face down in my vomit. I remember waking up the next morning with a hangover and feeling like I had arrived. I had gotten messed up with high school kids.

I may have gotten drunk a few times over that summer. I had just become someone who was going to use, and that followed me into high school. I stepped away from alcohol and moved towards the drugs. I was into a lot of psychedelics. I was smoking weed every day, doing acid or pills four to five times a month, and drinking two to three times a month, usually only drinking when nothing else was available. I used drugs this way all through high school.

When I was 17, I went into the Army and was addicted to heroin by the time I was 19. I got off heroin using a now-discredited program that used scream therapy. I was the only one in that group to stay clean off heroin, and the only way I did that was by switching from heroin to Johnny Walker Black. I just switched addictions. Then I stopped doing drugs for the most part and continued drinking. I always had negative experiences. By the time

I had reached the age of 48, I had gone from being a school principal, married with three children to living on the streets, stealing mouthwash from dollar stores for the alcohol, and contemplating suicide.

In May 2007, I had a bus ticket in my hand to carry out my suicide plan. I planned to go to the Dartmouth College campus, where the Appalachian Trail crosses, walk down the trail, and commit suicide. I had a moment of clarity and walked into the VA hospital instead. I told them, "I don't want to be alive anymore." I didn't recognize that alcohol was part of the problem. I thought alcohol was the only solution in my life; it was the only time that I would feel significantly better.

I was taken by ambulance to a hospital and physically detoxed off of alcohol. They kept me in the psychiatric unit on a suicide watch. There I was introduced to a recovery program, which remains the center of my sobriety. From that day, May 21, 2007, until today, I have not found it necessary to take a drink of alcohol or use any other mind-altering substances.

From the beginning, I was looking for a way to make life better through chemistry. Now, I treat my alcoholism with AA and address my other mental health issues with traditional forms of therapy.

Looking back, when do you think it was mostly out of control?

The end of my drinking.

How are you able to not drink or use daily?

Just as I created a life where alcohol made sense, now I have created a life where alcohol would not make sense and does not fit. I went to an AA meeting daily for the first year I was sober. After that, I cut it back to four to five a week, and now the number of meetings I go to ebbs and flows over time. Now, I go to a group with eight to 15 guys who have been in recovery. We get together every week, read the Big Book, and then talk about recovery.

When I first got sober, my sponsor told me that a grateful heart would never drink. I practice gratitude all the time and throughout my day. I always thank God for the life I have. The simple act of being able to express gratitude cleans out all the bad things that are in my soul. Every night before I go to sleep, I go over my day, and look for where I've been at fault and need to make amends. I think of ways I may have been less generous or kind and try to make amends wherever possible. I read a lot of spiritual literature; I'm fascinated by the early church, so I read a lot of church history.

What is your thought about medication-assisted treatment?

I see it as a possible step for people to take, but also as a potential trap. My goal for everybody is that they stop trying to find a better life through chemistry and instead develop the resources within themselves. So, any form of recovery that says, "Continue to take this outside chemical," is not going to be satisfactory to me as a form of healing.

People are finding their way instead of taking the chemical pathway. On the other hand, given a choice between someone using methadone or using dope, their lives will likely have some freedom and meaning using methadone. I wish that people didn't have to use it, but I like having people alive. The only way to find recovery is if you're living.

Is there anything that you want those struggling with addiction to know?

It's possible to get clean and sober. I believe, with every fiber of my being, there is some mystical connection that can almost instantly develop between one alcoholic or addict and another—

one who is in recovery and one who is struggling to find it. Talking with cool people in recovery is the best way to find out about recovery. It's not reading books, watching videos, or doing web searches. It is a human connection. You find a person you identify with in recovery, and a relationship will develop almost instantaneously.

Kim C.

Date of interview: 3/26/19
Sobriety date: 5/19/10, 8 years
Hometown: Campton

When did you start drinking or using drugs, and how did it progress?

I was the youngest of seven children. The next to the youngest was my sister, who is developmentally disabled, and my brother, the third to the youngest, was born deaf. I felt I always had to help take care of them. When I was 11, my father died, and I became my mother's right-hand person, supporting her even more. I grew up doing for everyone else.

When I turned 16 in July, my brother had a party, and he gave me two or three beers. I loved the fact that I was enjoying myself. It painted a new picture of who I was inside. I drank on the weekends and would get drunk occasionally. We had bonfires in the woods, and it was a big deal that we scored booze. My brothers would buy us alcohol; they weren't old enough, but they never got carded.

Sunday meals, my mother would have sombreros and red wine with my aunts and uncles. I would have a glass of wine, and I never felt as if I had to have more. In August of that year, my first boyfriend introduced me to pot and cocaine. Drugs didn't interest me as much as alcohol. I felt different when I drank. I felt safer. Pot made me paranoid, and cocaine made me high. They were not what I craved.

I continued drinking until I was 22 and met my husband. I felt needed by him. I found someone who would love and protect me. I was brought up to believe you meet the guy you marry, and you stay in that relationship for the rest of your life. I helped raise all three of his children. In my late 20s and early 30s, I drank heavily. The relationship turned into me being verbally and emotionally abused. I didn't want anyone to know, so I put up a false front, but was dying inside. I became a daily drinker around age 32 or 33. By the time I was 35, I was drinking a bottle or two of wine a night. I didn't eat much so that the food wouldn't ruin my buzz. I felt as if I deserved to drink. I worked hard, and I had a paycheck. While that was going on, I started hating myself.

I hid my drinking and drank alone. I felt as if alcohol were a shield that protected me. I didn't think it was terrible until I started to drink without my permission. I began to keep the buzz going all day. Once I took a sip, I wanted more and more. Then I was afraid I would get too drunk. It became a full-time job to buy it, hide it, and to forget where I put it. I thought I was going out of my mind.

At the end of my drinking, I realized I could drink half as much with vodka. I would put a pint in my pants, bring it upstairs, and hide it. If people were around, I would go upstairs, guzzle vodka, and only let them see I was drinking wine.

At age 44, I started blacking out nightly. One night I was in a blackout and cut a phone cord with a bread knife. I didn't remember doing it. My husband told me I did. I knew I wanted to quit drinking, but I didn't know how. I thought my life was over if I couldn't drink. I would have no happiness—everything I had to do related to alcohol, except for my job.

My husband was on my back to stop drinking, so I quit drinking for six months. I thought I was going insane. I drank again, and it was worse than ever. I wasn't going to any support meetings and didn't know anyone in recovery. I had heard about people going to a treatment center but didn't have the guts to go. My reputation would be tarnished. I thought people would think I was a loser. I got so sick of being sick and weighed only 90 pounds. I'd pray to God every night to help me.

On the morning of May 19, 2010, I got on my knees and asked God to help me stop drinking. I then made a call to a woman I'd met at an AA meeting. She had taken me to a couple of AA meetings prior. She told me she needed to make a few phone calls and would work on finding me a bed in rehab. I hung up and called my aunt, who I knew was in AA and had 30 years of sobriety.

I wound up going to Valley Vista in Vermont because New Hampshire did not have a bed available. I almost didn't go because I wanted to drink. I checked in at 5 p.m. that night and stayed for 12 days, then went to Nathan Brody in Laconia for their Intensive Outpatient Program.

Between Valley Vista and Nathan Brody, I learned more about this disease than anywhere. I also went to counseling for two years for underlying issues that contributed to my alcoholism. From the time I went to Valley Vista until now, I have not found it necessary to pick up a drink or a drug.

Looking back, when do you think it was mostly out of control?

When I hit age 40, because I think my tolerance level went up. I could drink a lot more. I wasn't getting the effect I needed without drinking more. Drinking was all I thought about, all day long. I couldn't wait to get home to drink. I was spending about $200 a week on high-end alcohol. I couldn't control it anymore.

How are you able to not drink or use daily?

233

First and foremost is God. I know AA is a God-given program, a divine intervention. It isn't about religion; it's about faith and a relationship with God. I bring Him into every aspect of my life. He loves me, no matter what.

What is your thought about medication-assisted treatment?

I was diagnosed with severe depression when I first got sober and didn't realize alcohol was adding to the misery. I thought it was helping. I take Celexa for depression but am currently weaning off.

Is there anything you want those struggling with addiction to know?

It's okay to reach out. Alcohol is just a symptom of our disease. There is a program of recovery. Abstinence is the only thing that will guarantee that this disease will remain dormant.

Larry G.

Date of interview: 4/22/19
Sobriety date: 10/6/83, 35 years
Hometown: Bedford

When did you start drinking or using drugs, and how did it progress?

The first time I drank, I was in high school and got drunk. Neither of my parents drank, but most of my uncles did. I drank with some buddies who were two years older than I was. They got it from home. It was after Thanksgiving, and we drank bourbon and coke. It was a terrible combination. I can still taste it. Terrible, terrible. I went home, threw up, and my mother got up out of bed. She was a trusting soul. She never worried about curfew and thought we were good boys. I was throwing up and kept blaming it on my friend's mother's cooking. She could smell it though. She had brothers, and she'd done it before, so she chastised me the next day. I was in the eleventh grade and didn't drink again until college.

At age 18, I started drinking in the fall at the University of Virginia. I was lucky to get to go there. I had a scholarship and worked my way through. There was a lot of partying. I'd never seen anything like it. I was getting rushed by fraternities because I was a baseball player; there was a lot of fraternity drinking. I loved it. It got me out of my shell. I was never shy again, as long as I was drinking. It was all fun the first year, and I didn't get into any trouble. We could walk down the street in Charlottesville, drinking and riding on the back of convertibles. Our mantra was, "When you're young and foolish, you might as well be a young fool." I thought everybody was like this. It wasn't until I quit drinking many years later that I realized not many people do it this way.

I was a binge drinker and had terrible hangovers. Even though I was in shape, I would wake up feeling as if I'd had a heart attack. I tried to quit drinking for two, three, or four days and then do it again. Every time I felt better, I would do it again. I could always drink a lot. We would have big parties with grain alcohol and grapefruit juice in a big garbage can. Of course, you can't even taste that. All of a sudden, you're blind, and you don't even know why. After a couple of mixed drinks, I would switch to beer. There was always a keg or a six-pack around. I was drinking alcoholically before I got out of college.

After I got out of college, it was terrible. I drank whenever I could. I married a woman who drank too. She wasn't an alcoholic but close. We would sometimes take the test to find out if we were alcoholics. I'd get a seven or eight, and she'd get a six. I'd always think she was lying. My boss was a heavy drinker too. We drank during the interview, and he hired me. We drank at the bar at night and did a lot of work while drinking. We were functional alcoholics. We came to work the next day, so we didn't think we had a problem.

I went to graduate school at the University of Virginia. Here I was a poor kid on a scholarship, and nobody in my family had ever been to college. At a bar in Virginia, we loved the long-neck beers they served. It was a badge of honor to have six to eight beer bottles on the table. It was a way of showing off. You never let the waitstaff take the bottles. We thought it was cool. I remember being in there one day, by myself, with six bottles on the table and asking her to take them away. I knew then that something was wrong. I also knew I'd have a bunch more.

Drinking and graduate school went hand in hand. I was 21, athletic, and worked out all the time. I also smoked and drank daily. I have the top pitching record for earned run average at the University of Virginia until today. I was there for a degree in special education and wanted to be a teacher my whole life if I went to college. Nobody had expected me to go to college. Nobody in my family had gone to college. I was scheduled to work in the shipyard and go to an apprentice school. My father would have been very proud of me if I'd gone to the apprentice school because I would have been a boss. Nobody in my family had ever been a boss. I didn't even apply to college, but the University of Virginia coach came to see me play baseball and wondered why I wasn't going. I had an excellent high school career, good enough that I could have played in the pros. I might have made the major leagues, but we'll never know.

During the day I taught in the projects in Gary, Indiana, and worked in a bar at night. The customers at the bar were old veterans who lived upstairs in a flophouse. They lived off each other's pensions. They had a pool on who would die in their sleep next because that's what they did. They drank, they ate a little bit, and they would never give me a tip. Instead, they would buy me a drink. So, I took no money home, got plowed every night, and went to work teaching kids in the projects the next day. It was an incredibly self-destructive life.

I took Valium for hangovers. I was getting it from a guy who got it from the VA. I never went anywhere without a 5 mg Valium in my pocket, in case I hyperventilated or got nervous. I had horrible hangovers and would feel as if I had had a heart attack. When I was young, I went to the ER twice for hyperventilation. I would sit in a meeting rubbing my chest. Eventually, all my shirts went thread-bare right above my heart from rubbing them so much.

Ironically, in 2012, I had a cardiac arrest and almost died, although I was in perfect health. No drinking, no smoking, exercising, it was just one of those things—eight percent of the people who have it survive. I had a lot of stress in my job; we were running programs all over New England. I was driving 30 to 40 thousand miles a year and was on call seven days a week.

My first recovery was in 1978, and I took to it. I loved the 12 Steps and was speaking at commitments. I had a sponsor and went to four or five meetings a week with AA people. I didn't have a good home life, so I was happy to get away. I was progressing, and after a year, I got involved in church and away from the program. I started thinking about drinking, and then one day, the third anniversary of my sobriety, I was on an airplane with my boss, and he bought a couple of beers. We sat in the back of the plane, and I said, "Bring me a scotch." I hadn't had anything in three years. It was just as if I had never quit. It was precisely the way people that relapsed said it would be.

Later, I got kicked out of a bar when my money ran out, but I had enough to buy a six-pack. I was walking back to the nice convention hotel where my work had put me up when I met some street guys. We sat and drank the beer together. I was sitting there in my suit with these guys who didn't have anything. I was out of money, and I was looking across the street and could see the top of my hotel. I knew I was back at my drinking bottom. The only thing that separated me from those bums was that I could walk across the street and have a room in the hotel, and I wore a suit. I drank for three or four more days and tried to sober up on the plane home.

When I got home, I went to meetings. Once I lived three years of sobriety, some of it white-knuckled, drinking was never the same. By the grace of God, I checked into Beech Hill rehab in 1983. I'm now 75, retiring from my job, and still sober.

Looking back, when do you think it was mostly out of control?

At the end of my drinking, it was the most out of control.

How are you able to not drink or use daily?

I have two or three different people in recovery that I call my best friends. A guy my age is my sponsor. I wouldn't tell people to do anything I wouldn't do myself, so I still consider him my sponsor. I may talk to him once a month, and he'll get mad when he doesn't see me at a meeting for a long time. I go to maybe four or five AA meetings a year. I might step into the treatment center or a group to converse with people working on recovery. I sit down in the cafeteria at the treatment center with a bunch of people. I love to say, "I'm not only the President, I'm also a client."

What is your thought about medication-assisted treatment?

I'm an abstinence person; I don't think you can drink or drug a little bit. I think you're sober or you're not. I see a lot of people on medication-assisted therapy. My staff tells me the client would probably be dead if they weren't on it. I'd rather see them taking Suboxone but with an exit plan.

Is there anything you want those struggling with addiction to

know?

You're not alone. You're not unique. There are 23 million others in recovery. These are people who have just said, "I've had enough and don't want to do this anymore." It takes control of their lives. It might take some time, but never give up. People won't give up on you. It's a great life, eventually. I don't miss drinking. I had some fun and did things I would never have dreamed of having the courage to do. I've also escaped drinking and doing ridiculously crazy things.

It's all about support groups and people. I would never have stayed sober if I hadn't had the first intense 10 years of conscious association with people in recovery. You meet people you might not ever think of having as friends. You learn more from them than you ever could learn in a book. I wouldn't trade it for anything. Find somebody to guide you.

Leslie G.

Date of interview: 5/7/2019
Sobriety date: 12/16/08, 10 years
Hometown: Meredith

When did you start drinking or using drugs, and how did it progress?

I was 11 years old. My friend and I were hanging around town. We rounded up a fellow who was going into the liquor store, and we asked him to get a pint of cherry vodka. We went behind the library, drank it, and I blacked out. The very first time I drank, I blacked out, went to my sister's husband's work, and he drove me home to my mother.

The next time I drank, I blacked out again. It was at my parents' house. My cousins were there, and I don't remember what we were drinking. I don't know if we smoked marijuana. I didn't remember anything. From the beginning, it increased my inability to control my propensity to dissociate, which was my trauma.

I was 13 when I met my husband. He was 22. He is a Mormon, and we married in the Mormon church. We dated for three years and rarely went out. When we did go out, I drank and blacked out. We never had fun and it was always a disaster.

After we got married, I didn't drink for 10 years. Nothing changed, except I lived in a constant state of dissociation. I didn't know it at the time though. I don't remember hardly any of my marriage and found out later it was a result of living in a chronic state of dissociation. I was never present and had no control.

Percocet came in when my oldest son was four, and I was 21. I didn't get high, but it dropped those barrier walls that were around me. I could see how cute my son was, and I felt love for him. It was the first time I had felt anything at all. Percocet helped me do this. I knew nothing about addiction back then.

I got involved with a neighbor and had an affair, which excommunicated me from the church and separated me from my husband. I was continually drinking, blacking out, and having bad stuff happen. I was always in the bars and had no idea how to take care of myself. We eventually divorced in 1987. Then I was partying all the time.

Somewhere between 1987 and 1993, I ended up seeing doctors for severe anxiety. They prescribed Xanax. Within a short period, I stole a prescription pad from my doctor and wrote my own prescriptions. I went right to the pharmacy in town to fill it and got arrested. My arrest led me to my first treatment center in 1993.

It took nine days to detox off the Xanax before going into treatment. The treatment center wanted to put me back on Xanax, afraid I would have seizures or something. It had already been nine days, so I told them I wasn't going back on it and checked myself out. I had five more years of drinking, dating, arrests, DUI's, and trouble with prescription medications. I was chasing medicine and trying to create physical problems to get it. This drug chasing lasted between 1993 and 1997. I was using every day.

I started dating an incredibly violent guy. I was going down and had a sense I would die. In 1998, I packed up my son and came to New Hampshire. Once I got stabilized in another relationship, I manipulated enablers around me. On December 15, 2008, I went to a Christmas party with my then-husband. I drank, made a fool of myself, and had no idea what happened. I called my oldest son on the way home from that party, who I was lying to about being sober. He knew I wasn't. I came out of the blackout with him on the phone saying, "Mom, Mom, are you okay?" The next morning, I woke up and was done. There were jails, institutions, near-death experiences, arrests, horrible times alone with my children, rapes, and all of it.

In 2008, something changed. The doctor gave me pain medication for ruptured disks in my back. My sponsor told me I had to get off it. To manage the pain in sobriety, I had to get involved with my physical body. I started doing yoga and slowly walking every day. I fell in love with my body and decided to get to know it.

Looking back, when do you think it was mostly out of control?

Right after I got off the Xanax, between 1993 and 1997, it was the most out of control.

How are you able to not drink or use daily?

Every morning I wake up, get out of bed, and make a big cup of tea. I get back in my bed, read meditation books, and talk to my higher power. I travel and try to explore new things. I am free.

My morning readings are *Each Day A New Beginning* and *The Language of Letting Go*. The first is for women in recovery, and the second is the language of codependency.

What is your thought about medication-assisted treatment?

If someone has had a chronic problem with opioids, they may need something in the beginning, in a hospital or clinical setting where it's very controlled and only for a very brief period. Nothing afterward because it takes the magic out of life.

Medication-assisted recovery takes the magic of being your true, authentic self. The psychic change comes from real, authentic living and all the wonderfulness that comes from being able to listen and pay attention. It comes from being aware in our skin and bones, and taking things in. This ability to feel and comprehend is not available with the use of medication. It cuts you off. It robs us of the truth about ourselves.

Is there anything you want those struggling with addiction to know?

Don't drink, and don't use drugs. Stay in recovery, and you will be amazed.

Lewis H.

Date of interview: 6/4/19
Sobriety date: 10/31/94, 24 years
Hometown: Nashua

When did you start drinking or using drugs, and how did it progress?

I was eight years old. I was an addict before touching a substance. When I was young, I needed to have more Crayola crayons or more Matchbox cars. I always needed more of everything and didn't care about the consequences. I tried model glue before I drank alcohol. I saw someone show someone else how to sniff glue and get silly, so I did it. This behavior set off a chain reaction of doing something that I knew wasn't right.

I came from a middle-class family and always pushed the limits. My defiance took root at an early age as I tagged along with my older brother. My best friend's brother hung out with my brother. We thought they were cool, but they didn't want us around. So, after they left, we would follow them and pretend we were them. Eventually we hung out with them. I was always doing things for them, so one day someone handed me a beer. Before this, I remember sitting with my dad, and he let me sip the foam off his beer. It never really did anything then, but this time it did. I got sick, and my parents said not to do it again.

I dropped out of school and thought getting a job would be smart so I could have money to drink. This led me into adulthood at an early age. The drinking age was 18, and I acted as if I were older to buy it at the local corner store. Soon, I was hanging out with people my brother's age, and they considered me one of their peers. I was socializing with them; there were marijuana, pills, speed, acid, mushrooms, etc.

In my 20s, I got introduced to cocaine, which eventually took control of me. I began freebasing, and the next thing you know, I graduated to doing it daily for a couple of years. While visiting friends in New York, I tried crack cocaine and came back from there with a severe crack cocaine habit. I used it every day for four years. I was also drinking and occasionally smoking pot.

By 1989, I knew my disease wanted more. I knocked at my parents' door, and they took me in. By the summer of 1990, I put crack down and just smoked pot and drank. I was also going to a 12-step program, where as long as you weren't doing drugs, it was okay.

Eventually, smoking pot and drinking was happening every day. I needed to drink to function. I tried to stop many times but couldn't. My average day was to come to, turn on the TV, go to the pantry, and grab a beer. There were many times when I told myself I wasn't going to do this anymore, but my body would go through withdrawals, and the next thing I knew, I had a beer in my hand.

My significant other recognized I had a problem and knew people in recovery. She'd have them over to the house. I didn't particularly like them, primarily because they were happy and poised in life. Misery was a step up for me at this time. I remember hearing people laughing and joking in the living room. I would walk through, and no one would say anything.

There came a day like any other day; I came to, in the same misery as usual, and told myself I needed help. I walked into our living room, and there was a 12-step meeting list on our table. I decided to go to my first meeting in October.

I was physically deteriorating. My skin was turning yellow, and I couldn't drink more than a half of a beer at a time. During this meeting, someone said, "You never have to feel this way again." That's what sold me. I was too scared to go back to drinking because I knew I was dying. I couldn't do it anymore. I continued to go to meetings and didn't drink, even though I wanted to. I stayed in meetings and stayed sober.

Looking back, when do you think it was mostly out of control?

It was the most out of control near the end of my drinking and using drugs.

How are you able to not drink or use daily?

When I wake up, I read spiritual poems and prayers. I read the AA

Daily Reflections book and pray; prayer is vital to me. I've had the same sponsor for 24 years. On my drive to work, I call him to keep connected.

What is your thought about medication-assisted treatment?

I don't think it's helping. I've worked with people who had a doctor or treatment facility suggest they be on it, and they just wanted to be sober. They wanted to be off drugs and alcohol. What I see for long-term success is sobriety. Using medication to comfort people through a transition to abstinence-based recovery, then that's different, but that's not what is happening.

Is there anything you want those struggling with addiction to know?

There is a way out, a solution. It comes with work and sacrifice. It comes with letting go of your ego and self-centeredness. You don't have to do it on your own. Talk and pray to something greater than yourself. Talk to other people in recovery.

Lou P.

Date of interview: 4/5/2019
Sobriety date: 10/04/76, 42 years
Hometown: Holderness

When did you start drinking or using drugs, and how did it progress?

I was in the military at 19 years old, the Air Force. I had my first drink after basic training. We had just transferred from basic training in New York to Mississippi. The oldest guy in our group was 25 and had been put in charge of us. Labor Day weekend, we got to Mississippi, and the base was unable to process us because of the holiday. They gave him a Class A pass, which allowed him to go off base. He asked us if we wanted to get some booze and have a party. He asked me what I wanted to drink, and I didn't want to be embarrassed, so I said gin. He asked me what I wanted him to get for a mix. I let him know I would get something out of the machine. In those days, the vending machines only had Coca-Cola. He said, "Boy, you guys from Boston are tough." I drank about half the bottle of gin and was physically sick for three days, throwing up and all.

After that, in 1952, I said I'd never touch it again. About six months later, I transferred to another base in Kansas. In Kansas, they had 3.2 beer. I didn't know the difference. Today, beer is six percent. A buddy and I would go into town and drink beer. I would not get stupefied drunk, just mellow.

A guy assigned to my barracks started bringing cases of beer back to the barracks and put them under his bunk. We had very few inspections, so we could get away with it. He would drink in the morning, and sometimes when I had a hangover, he'd encourage me to have a can of beer. It was warm because we didn't refrigerate it. I liked it in the morning. He used to call it, "the hair of the dog."

We would drink pitchers of beer when we went into town. By now, I was drinking daily. I drank one or two to get that buzz. I was drinking more than six beers, even on weekends. If I went into town with the guys, they got big pitchers of beer. It didn't affect me at the time; I had no reason to stop. I felt good. I kept getting promotions. I was a good worker and made staff sergeant within six months.

When I got out of the service in 1956, I met this young lady. We fell in love, and in 1958, we got married. We had our son and I went to college. I drank throughout all of this but never did any drugs.

I got a degree in business and then got a job at a major manufacturing company as a contract negotiator. It was a Fortune 500 manufacturing company and they gave me an expense account. I negotiated millions of dollars with government agencies. I took people to martini lunches all the time. The only people I offered to take to lunch were the ones who drank.

In 1970, I was drinking more and more every day. I would drink either a 12-pack or a fifth of gin a day. I used my ability to travel as a time to drink. It was out of control. I could tell I wasn't paying any attention to my kids. I wasn't a good family man or a good father. At this point, I had three kids. I took them places out of guilt and preferred to be away from the family because I needed to drink. I would also visit my mother on Saturdays when I was home and keep beer in her refrigerator, so I could drink when I was there.

About five years before I started the AA program, I realized I had a problem with drinking and used my mother's phone to call AA. I didn't want to say I was an alcoholic, so I'd hang up when someone answered.

On September 3, 1976, I was home alone in the morning and couldn't remember if I was getting up or going to bed. I had come back from a trip to Washington, DC. I got up, went into the kitchen, and put rum in my coffee. After having several cups of this, I sat there alone and wrote out a suicide note to my wife and kids, telling them how much I cared for them and how I couldn't care for myself anymore. I was going to run my car as fast as it would go into a bridge on route 495 to kill myself.

I cried out, "If there is a God, help me." I meant this with all my heart. I picked up the phone instead and called AA. The woman on the phone said she would have someone call me back. I waited between 10 to 20 minutes for someone to talk to, and because of

247

my remorse and sadness, I decided no one was going to call me back. I thought no one cared about me, so I headed out the kitchen door. Before I could make it out the door, the phone rang. It was a woman from the Spindle City Group in Lowell, Massachusetts. She talked to me for an hour and told me where the AA meetings were. She was doing 12-step work. Shortly after the call, I went to a meeting. It clicked for me, and I didn't drink.

On October 3, 1976, I left a meeting thinking all the speakers were wrong. I thought there's no reason I can't have a drink now and then. There was booze in my house, so when I got home, I grabbed a bottle of scotch, put it in my suitcase, and told my wife I needed to go to Washington for work. When I got to Washington, I got drunk in my room and did things like tear the wallpaper off the wall. I ended up calling my sponsor. My sponsor said to get back on the plane, go home, and don't drink. I got home and called the manager at the motel and told him I wanted to pay for the damages and didn't want my company to know. It cost $2,000. I stayed with my company, got better, and retired after 38 years.

From this point on, I went to meetings and talked to my sponsor. My sponsor knew Bill Wilson. I felt if he knew Bill Wilson, he was an exceptional man. I would meet with him at least three times a week; we didn't have cell phones in those days. This man saved my life.

Looking back, when do you think it was mostly out of control?

When I started drinking in the morning, the last five years. I had severe hangovers, and all my feelings were negative. I knew the drink would take away the negative thoughts.

How are you able to not drink or use daily?

I read the Hazelden *Twenty-Four Hours a Day* book daily and go to AA meetings. AA keeps me alive and keeps me in an emotionally good zone. I share my story to help others and make amends to people I hurt.

What is your thought about medication-assisted treatment?

When taking a medication, you have to have a doctor who fully understands addiction, and you fully trust your doctor. You want your doctor to find a medicine that works, and it doesn't have to be an opiate. Ask others in sobriety who the doctors are that they trust.

Is there anything you want those struggling with addiction to know?

There's hope. You can feel hope by getting a sponsor and going to AA. Get out of negative situations, calm down, and talk to someone regularly. There's help out there. Go to rehab if you need it. There is a life beyond drugs and booze.

Mark B.

Date of interview: 6/6/19
Sobriety date: 10/15/09, 9 years
Hometown: Lisbon
When did you start drinking or using drugs, and how did it progress?

When I was a little kid, I would sip my dad's beer. Both of my parents were alcoholics; they both quit when I was 11. After my parents got sober, they tried to warn me I might be one as well, so I only had a couple of tastes here and there because I thought I would immediately become an alcoholic.

While I was unpacking my bags at college, someone said, "Do you want to go to a party and get to know people?" I went with them, got drunk, and stayed drunk. Three months later, I was asked to leave the college. I had flunked all my classes because I hadn't bothered to attend. I went home and didn't tell my parents why I had been kicked out, and I drank for 20 years after that.

Eventually, I graduated from college. I didn't like my degree. I ended up working for an alcoholic painting houses. After that, I worked for a high-tech construction company and was on the road a lot, living out of hotels. We drank in bars every night. I was a daily drinker by my late 20s. I then took a job in northern Vermont for three years, drinking every day. I'd get up, drink coffee until I could stomach lunch, and go out drinking again. I'd drive home hammered every night.

I'd have periods when I would tell myself I needed to slow down. I would backpack or ski and wouldn't drink during those activities. After a few years, a girl who I had gone out with called me, and we got together. I'd go to work, drink until I passed out, and on the fifth day spend the weekends with her. We got engaged after a couple of months, and after a year and a half, we got married, but I was not happy and didn't know why. I had everything I wanted, a wife I loved and good people in my life, but I was just miserable. It never crossed my mind that drinking was a problem.

I'd drive home and say, "I don't want to drink." I'd intend to have one drink and always have another one. I was also trying to quit smoking. Whenever I quit smoking, I'd stop drinking. I was desperate to stop smoking, so I decided to quit forever. Then I had this idea never to drink again and haven't had a drink since.

I got hooked up with an online support group for smoking addiction. There are online AA meetings too. The smoking group had a section for people who also had other addictions. I talked to these people online a lot, and they all told me I should go to AA. The online smoking group showed the Just for Today daily reading, and I got involved with the discussions on the excerpt. I did this for years before I went to AA.

My wife got involved in an outpatient addiction program, and they told her to go to AA. She had a positive reaction from attending, so I wanted to go with her and find out why she had reacted so well.

I went to meetings in Plymouth and eventually got a sponsor. I also did the steps and worked through my resentments. Through working the steps, I had a spiritual awakening. I felt a connection with all the people at these meetings. I don't feel angry anymore and enjoy life.

Looking back, when do you think it was mostly out of control?

I was miserable throughout my drinking. In the beginning, I knew I was screwing up, but didn't think it was because of alcohol.

How are you able to not drink or use daily?

I am very involved with AA and have a sponsor who I see and call regularly. I'm engaged in my home group and help AA at the district level. I've memorized the Prayer of Saint Francis and try to remember to say it in my head when I need to.

What is your thought about medication-assisted treatment?

It's outside my expertise. I used Chantix to quit smoking, a prescription that was on a timeline, and it worked for me. As far as opiates, I don't know much about that.

Is there anything you want those struggling with addiction to know?

You're not alone.

Matt D.

Date of interview: 4/29/19
Sobriety date: 8/27/16, 2 years
Hometown: Berlin

When did you start drinking or using drugs, and how did it progress?

The first time I drank, I was 14 and hanging out with friends. I drank six beers, got drunk, and threw up. I was 90 pounds soaking wet. On my mother's side of the family, there was never any drinking going on. On my father's side, the adults always had a can of beer in their hands, no matter what they were doing.

My parents divorced when I was a baby. I was born with congenital heart disease, which meant I was born with a hole in my heart. My left pulmonary artery was about the size of a hair. Eighteen hours after I was born, I had to be taken by ambulance to Boston Children's Hospital. I lived my life with a bag packed under my bed, just in case of an emergency. My lungs collapsed a few times, and I would turn blue from lack of oxygen and have to go to the hospital. Today, the surgery I had only takes 45 minutes. In 1978, it was a lot longer.

I had 27 procedures, five open-heart surgeries, and 22 catheterizations to block the hole in my heart. A couple of times they operated on me, I died and was revived. Keeping me paralyzed for some time, they kept me still to get me back in for another surgery. I had two major open-heart surgeries in the same year, at the age of eight. The catheterizations they did went through the main artery in my leg up to my heart. They'd do a balloon dilation of the pulmonary artery to try and stretch it out.

My medical problems made childhood difficult. My parents were awesome through all of it. My mother and stepfather did the absolute best they could. They gave me the most typical childhood I could have. I played baseball, was in the Boy Scouts, went skiing, and was really into swimming. I didn't go to school full-time until fifth grade. I started out going to a private school and would only go half a day because I would get too tired. This lack of attendance put me far behind academically.

In high school, I couldn't keep up academically, couldn't keep up in sports, but I could keep up with drinking when I went to Curry College for one semester. This college is where I picked up my pot-smoking habit, which consisted of getting high every single day. After about a year or so of that, I tried cocaine, and shortly after that, Ecstasy became big. I got into that for a long time. Because of the way my heart was, I shied away from stimulants and started going more towards opiates. I had a 14 year on-and-off battle. I was using OxyContin every day for months, 80-100 mg. Then I moved to an apartment by myself and met some friends down the street who were sniffing heroin, so I did that for a little bit.

In my mid-20s I moved out of the apartment and didn't touch heroin for a long time. I got into another living situation and started using Percocet. Using this drug is where I fell in love. I could control Percocet to a point. I wasn't nodding off like I would with Oxys. I was still smoking pot and drinking too. My fiancé gave me an ultimatum. It was between her and the opiates, so I quit the opiates cold turkey.

A friend of ours lost their child and another friend OD'd and died alone on his kitchen floor. This is when I decided to shoot heroin. One night, by myself, I found it on the street, tried it, and loved it. I didn't do it the next day, did it the day after, didn't do it the next day, and then overdosed. I ended up in the hospital in a locked unit because I had made threats. When my mother came to see me, I had died, and she saw me after that. I saw the look on her face, and it reminded me of when she saw me go through heart surgery as a child. She felt as if she were going to lose me.

My mother called my therapist while I was in the hospital and asked him what she should do. He suggested she get me into detox. I went to detox at High Point in Plymouth, Massachusetts. When I went in, I was clean for two or three days, and they tried to put me on methadone. I told them no. I was there to get off everything, not be placed on something. The first three days, I didn't feel I belonged there. They told me I could leave after a week, or I could stay for the second week.

When I tried to decide whether I should start the next week, I remember walking outside and asking God to send me a sign and not a subtle sign. I said, "I need you to tell me." I went back inside and sat down. A kid I got along with pretty well came up to me. He knew I had the choice to either leave or stay. He said to me, "I don't know what it's worth, but I just thought that you've been doing good here, and you've helped out some of us. I think it would be perfect if you stayed for that second week," and he just walked away. I took that as my sign and stayed for the second week.

I read a lot of books about addiction while I was there, many books by musicians in recovery. Music is a big part of my life. I've played the drums since I was 11 and had been teaching myself guitar for the previous five years. My mother and stepfather always had music playing when I was a kid. I read the book *Slash* from Guns N' Roses. He is a significant part of my sobriety.

When I came out of High Point, I went to therapy twice a week for a couple of years. I still smoked weed but no drinking or other drugs. I would get filled with anxiety if I wasn't high. I smoked marijuana to deal with it. I couldn't be around a lot of people anymore without pot, and I wasn't honest about it with my therapist. Having this anxiety was unusual for me because I was in drama and on stage a lot growing up. I had never had this anxiety before. He knew fear was a problem for me, so he helped me get through it.

It got to the point where he said he didn't think I needed to come back. I was reading books about addiction the whole time I was in therapy. After I stopped seeing my therapist, I got into reading about musicians that had recovered from drug addictions and listened to their songs. Their methods of staying sober helped me and my recovery because I connected with them.

I read a book called *Scar Tissue* by Anthony Keates, the lead singer from Red Hot Chili Peppers. He started doing drugs at age six and was snorting cocaine and heroin with his father at age 12. He came out on top. My mindset for reading these books was to connect with the authors and find something that worked for them that may work for me, and I followed the same things.

Slash made an album about recovery that I would listen to, and it helped. I read his book six times and use some of his spiritual processes. I also read a book by the bass player from Guns N' Roses. I spend my time doing things to help with addiction and recovery.

Looking back, when do you think it was mostly out of control?

At the end of my drug use, it was the most out of control.

How are you able to not drink or use daily?

I came up here from Massachusetts to be away from all the drug use. It was hard for me to get away from the people I was friends with who smoked pot. Being in a different setting and being around sober people is helpful for me. I also work with people with addictions and don't allow myself to be a hypocrite. I don't want to go back to using and have something that controls me. I read books to help me in my recovery. I just finished *The Four Agreements* for the third time and am currently reading *The Power of Now*.

What is your thought about medication-assisted treatment?

If it is used properly and is a temporary situation, it can be helpful for some. It can be used to get you through withdrawals and get you to a point where you can become sober. It was intended to help people stop using and get help. You get to a spot where you need therapy to fix underlying issues. I don't think it's okay to use long-term.

Is there anything you want those struggling with addiction to know?

It's so much better on the other side. Getting high and chasing the drug all day long sucks. When you get sober, life still sucks at times. You're just able to deal with it and deal with it without using drugs or alcohol. Drugs make life worse. When you're sober, you get to enjoy the parts of life that don't suck. With an addiction you can't, you can only see the negative. What I mean by life sucks is that you still have to pay bills, you still have to be responsible, you still have to go to work, etc., but there are so many enjoyable aspects.

Maurine P.

Date of interview: 5/29/19
Sobriety date: 12/24/16, 2 years
Hometown: Nashua

When did you start drinking or using drugs, and how did it progress?

The first time I used was age 12. I drank a couple of beers. My dad's a beer drinker, and it was always in the fridge, so it was easy. I had two beers and didn't like it, but I kept drinking them anyway. The next time I used was in high school. I was 14 and started smoking pot. From day one, I was a daily pot smoker.

When I was between the ages 14 and 16, my parents went through a vicious divorce. My identical twin sister, who does not have this disease, and I were on an emotional rollercoaster because of the divorce. At age 14, I became withdrawn and depressed, so the doctor put me on anti-depressants. I was on them for 10 years.

I started taking the Xanax I got from my mom. She had Percocet and Xanax. I took both, and then started taking Adderall. By the time I was 18, I was a full-blown drug addict. I graduated from high school but couldn't go off to college, so I worked at a dead-end bar.

The bar is where I was introduced to crack. One of the bartenders sold crack and heroin. She also sold Percocet, which was my drug of choice at the time. When the Percocet was gone, she gave me heroin. I didn't know what I was taking. I just did it. I wanted to feel better. She's also the first person who taught me how to shoot heroin. I started IV heroin use, got addicted quickly, and went to treatment for the first time when I was 18. I was scared to death but thought rehab was going to cure me.

I went into rehab, and they told me that I'd be back because I didn't believe that I had a drinking problem. I went to a lot of treatment centers, IOPs, counselors, and therapy in general. I didn't want to believe I was an addict or an alcoholic because this would mean I would have to stop.

I went back to work at the dead-end bar. I couldn't get a job anywhere else and couldn't keep a job. I would steal money, including from my family's restaurant. At age 21, I stole a bunch of money from a bagel shop. This time was the worst in my life. I headed to Lawrence with a co-worker, and we picked up heroin. I got arrested with 50 grams of heroin. I got charged with stealing money from the bagel shop, all this on the same day. I had a moment where I knew this wasn't going to stop, an awakening.

One day, I was working at my family's beach restaurant, it was the middle of July, and my brother came up to me. I was sitting at the bar with a glass of wine, nodding off with the restaurant full of people. He said, "You can't be here." He's not an addict or an alcoholic. His heart broke. He told me I couldn't see his kids anymore either, my niece and nephew. I went back to my mother's house and sat on the couch. Then my mom said, "You can't be here." She told me I had to go somewhere. "You can't do this anymore." I felt as if my family had turned their backs on me.

This guy, who lives right across the street from my family's restaurant and who I've known my whole life, came to my house with another guy, Scott, who worked for Process Recovery. Scott said, "You're coming to Process Recovery in Hudson." My mom brought me there and gave me $100 for food. We pulled up to the building, and I thought, "Wow, this place is beautiful." I was there for 30 days and said, "That's it, I'm going home." My mom didn't agree.

I got into a relationship three months into my sobriety and got pregnant. My boyfriend couldn't stay sober for the life of him. He was in and out of treatment, overdosing every other day. I ended up having an abortion. It was super-emotional. I took all the pain killers the doctors gave me that day, and about a week later, I picked up heroin again. I got thrown out of the sober house and called my mom. I told her I relapsed and asked if I could come home. She said, "Yup, you've got a week." I kept using it when I got there.

I went out drinking on the 23rd of December, came home super, super drunk, came to the next morning, and found out one of my best friends had died. That day I looked in the mirror, and I couldn't cry. I didn't feel anything. I didn't want to be alive. A week later, I got back into the sober house. I went to an AA meeting the day I got there, and this girl came up to me and said she had a sponsor for me. I didn't know the sponsor at all. She was my age, had a kid, was two and a half years sober, and had just come back from Florida. She started sponsoring me.

I knew what the steps were, but I didn't know how you did them. I did everything my sponsor told me to do when she told me to do it, and I didn't ask questions. I didn't want to feel the way I was feeling anymore. I didn't want to hurt anybody anymore. She told me to give sobriety a try; your miserable life is right there waiting for you if you want it back. She told me not to get into a relationship. I didn't talk to any guys for the first seven months of my sobriety and went through the steps by my eighth month. The steps saved my life. My emotions hit me pretty hard when I stopped using. If I hadn't had other people to help, I wouldn't have been okay.

Step 1 was easy for me. My life was unmanageable, and I was powerless over alcohol and other drugs. Step 2 and 3 are about turning our will over to a power greater than ourselves. Every single morning, I would say, "God, please help me. Please help me." I kept it in the day.

I wrote a fourth step, which took me a couple of months to write. Then I started working on my defects. Lying was my most significant defect. It was so hard to cut that habit. Then came Step 9: amends. I made amends to everybody except five people, so that means about 150 people. I've been sober for almost two and a half years. Steps 10 and 11 are so important: writing inventory, prayer, and meditation. I want to say I meditate a lot. I don't. I've probably meditated six times in the past two and a half years. I have a hard time sitting there with myself. Step 12 is helping others achieve sobriety. I sponsor others and it helps my sobriety.

I'm in my family's life today, and they want to be around me. They come to me for advice. I see my niece and nephew every other day.

I'm able to pay bills, have a nice car, and have a great job. I work with groups out of New York, New Jersey, and Connecticut. It's crazy to think about how I have transformed in the past two and a half years. I honestly never thought I'd be okay in my own skin, or that I would be alive at this time.

I don't regret any of what has happened to me, because it taught me lessons about who I'm supposed to be, who I want to be and what I don't want to be. It gave me a way to see the world differently, a more beautiful aspect.

Looking back, when do you think it was mostly out of control?

The six to eight months before I got arrested with the heroin. I truly believe I couldn't control my use.

How are you able to not drink or use daily?

I get up, and I pray every day. I have to thank God every single day. I have five people I sponsor, three of them I talk to daily. It helps me to help another person.

I never try to get too far into the future. I try to keep it in the day; I just don't drink today, and the days add up.

I used to read the *Daily Reflections* from AA. I get up so quickly now and go. I go to meetings three to four times a week. I talk to my sponsor every day who has 25 years of sobriety.

What is your thought about medication-assisted treatment?

The 12 steps are awesome, but they don't solve all your issues. There are some things that you need to be pulled out of, deep depression, or other mental health issues. Taking care of your body and eating right also helps.

I took Suboxone for a short time, three months. I was on 8 mg a day and just picked up again after that. That is my experience. If Suboxone keeps somebody alive long enough to hear hope or a message that will help them find sobriety, I'm okay with it.

There should be a plan to get off Suboxone. People should have an end goal, a weaning off. I don't think anyone should be on it longer than a year. I know somebody that's been on methadone for five years, and the stuff it does to your body after long-term use is crazy. She still drinks. I think there's so much more to life. You're still clouded while you're on it.

Is there anything you want those struggling with addiction to know?

Your life isn't ruined. It's not over; it's just beginning. If I can do it, anybody can.

Melissa C.

Date of interview: 5/1/2019
Sobriety date: 10/25/93, 25 years
Hometown: Bedford

When did you start drinking or using drugs, and how did it progress?

I was 13 and living in Ohio. My friend's parents had a keg in the garage. There were four of us, and two of the guys drank way too much and ended up sick. I just drank about a six-pack and felt good. I liked it and wanted more, even though it was a bit traumatic with the boys being sick. We had to call their parents, but it didn't stop me.

When I got to high school, I would drink at least a 12-pack a night on weekends. I drank to get drunk, not the first time though. In ninth grade, I started having blackouts. I couldn't handle my alcohol. I was dating a senior, but the older kids wouldn't let me do the drugs they were doing, thank God! My alcoholism progressed through my high school years and I started to drink during the week, any opportunity I could. Like most teens, I didn't like to be at home, so my friends and I would drive around the county, find a beach or park, and get drunk. It started out fun; I thought everybody was drinking as much as I was.

My parents were pretty lenient and maybe preoccupied. I had curfew, kind of followed the rules, and was maintaining respectability with them. I was in musicals, president of my class, and kept up with cheerleading, but didn't want to do schoolwork. I also worked at an amusement park over the summer and lived there in a dorm. I worked a ton and partied a ton. That summer ramped up my drinking. I was hanging out with older people, had a fake ID, and was drinking in bars. I'd drink until like three in the morning and go to work at seven. I had terrible hangovers, but then I'd get out and do it again, every day. That summer, there were rarely days when we didn't drink. I hung out with people who drank as I did. If you didn't drink like me, I didn't want to know you. I also smoked pot but didn't love it; it would make me paranoid.

My parents decided to move to Michigan, and they wanted me to go with them. I wanted to stay, so my dad got me a job at his company. I now had a real job, an apartment, and my drinking got worse. I started hanging out with a couple of girls from a local bar, quit my good job, and started working in the bar full time. I was 19. The owner knew I was underage, but he let me drink anyway. I went to Florida for spring break, drank like a maniac, and blacked out every day. Then, I came back and worked in the bar.

I wanted to "get my life together," so I applied to college. I got myself in, signed up for classes, and moved in with my best friend. I got a job at a country club and at a bar as a bartender and was drinking a lot! Sometimes I would go to classes and sometimes not. I was hungover often, had a lot of shame about my behaviors, and didn't like myself much. There was rarely a day that I was sober, so I eventually stopped going to classes.

One of my friends was moving to Atlanta. Since I just had a breakup, I decided to go with her. I was very impulsive. I wanted to escape, take a geographical cure. We both got jobs right away; this was August of 1992. My drinking was terrible, but I was trying to control it at the time.

I got a job at a car dealership and got a new car. I wrecked it the first night I had it and got a DUI. It was in May of 1993 at three a.m. I was taking someone home and crashed into a parked car with people in it. I blacked out and woke up in jail. My friend bailed me out that morning, and I was drinking by noon that day.

I drank for six more months, during which I went in front of the judge for the accident. I had to go to DUI school, met a neighbor there, and went out drinking with him. I woke up the next day at four in the afternoon on the floor of my apartment, and I had this moment of clarity. I called a sober friend, cried, and said, "I can't do this anymore." She had been waiting for me and told me to call AA, so I did. The AA hotline told me about a meeting that night. Whoa, too soon, so I went the next day. I jumped in from there.

Looking back, when do you think it was mostly out of control?

The truth is it was out of control almost from the beginning. After about 14, anytime I drank, it was out of control.

How are you able to not drink or use daily?

I stay sober one day at a time. I try to remember to be teachable, curious, and honest. I rely on my recovery network for support to help me when I forget. I have to tell on myself continually and be as honest as I can. I let people call me on my stuff, and I'm always checking my ego.

What is your thought about medication-assisted treatment?

I think it can undoubtedly be useful for initial detox, but it is overprescribed. I don't believe it is a cure for addiction.

Is there anything you want those struggling with addiction to know?

There is hope! No matter what you did or what's been done to you, you don't have to live the way you are living. There's another way. Life gets better. It's not always easy, but it becomes manageable without substances.

Mike A.

Date of interview: 3/24/2019
Sobriety date: 6/7/87, 31 years
Hometown: Waterville Valley

When did you start drinking or using drugs, and how did it progress?

At age three, I would walk around taking sips of drinks at our family events. My uncle gave me drinks when he babysat so that I would pass out and he could have his way with his girlfriends. At age 12, on my first day of school, I walked to school, and these kids said, "Do you smoke?" And I said, "Sure." We smoked pot in the woods, and within a couple of months, I was smoking daily. It was fun, and I felt accepted. I felt like an outcast before that. I was a poor kid in an affluent town, and my parents bought the cheapest house in the city of Newton, Massachusetts.

By age 14, I got into drinking. Pot made me mellow, and alcohol made me crazy. LSD also came into my life. Someone would bring a can of Hi-C into school, drop a bunch of acid in it, and we'd drink it during the day. By the time I was 18, I had gotten away from the acid and gotten more into cocaine, pills, and shooting heroin. My drug use went on until I was 30. I owned night clubs, produced records, and had a lot of money.

I woke up when I was 30, and everything was gone. I was working in restaurants, waiting tables, and bartending. I'd wake up in the morning, throw up, and go back to work. I would come home from work and drink until I passed out. I drank over the bitterness of how the world treated me. I didn't realize it was my addiction that took me to these places.

In 1986, I was working the night shift at the IHOP as their manager. That's how I kept my self-respect: I could wear a tie. My disease allowed me to accept complete hopelessness. An old friend of mine looked me up and asked me to start a company, but he wanted me to stop drinking. I said, "What do you mean, before work?" He offered me a job as a vice president, marketing a healthcare company. I tried every day to stop drinking. I was making real efforts to find heroin or cocaine but just drank because alcohol wasn't hard to get.

I believe God entered my life at this time. Otherwise, everything I was using would have taken me out. I started working with this man and was doing great at my job. I was always able to overachieve, but he knew I wasn't at my potential. He was an older gentleman with 20 years of sobriety. One day, he took me out to lunch to talk to me. He asked if I was drinking, and I denied it. He called me a liar and sent me to rehab.

In rehab, I was the only guy in my group who was there for the first time. I realized I wasn't unique. I realized I was sick, not bad. I followed the instructions when I got out, like going to 12-step meetings. I found people who knew my name and wanted to see me. I felt like I belonged and have been sober ever since.

Looking back, when do you think it was mostly out of control?

I tried to stop in 1987. I thought I was giving it my full effort. I would tell myself I'm not drinking today and then get a beer. I would treasure that last drink in the bottle and do anything to keep it down, but I often threw up. I would cover my mouth so I wouldn't lose it if I gagged. I found relief instantly when the cashier handed the bottle to me at the liquor store.

How are you able to not drink or use daily?

I treat my illness as an illness. I follow the suggestions people in 12-step meetings give me and remain grateful. I don't bend to my addiction or my addiction will rule my life. I acknowledge I have an illness, and I'm not like everyone else, but I'm like every other addict.

What is your thought about medication-assisted treatment?

I don't know enough about it.

Is there anything you want those struggling with addiction to know?

You're not alone. You can get off the merry-go-round at any time. People are willing to help you.

<u>**M.M.**</u>

Date of interview: 5/31/2019
Sobriety date: 2/19/11, 8 years
Hometown: Undisclosed

When did you start drinking or using drugs, and how did it progress?

My father is a drug dealer. When he and my mother met, she was a prostitute and a runaway. He fell for her and saw that she was engrossed in the street life. He knew she wasn't going to make it and moved her to New Hampshire.

While I was growing up, there were raids and stabbings. My dad is a paranoid schizophrenic and had drug-induced psychosis. There was also a lot of psychological abuse. There was a lot of gang activity and I felt out of place with my background. I didn't want to be a part of this lifestyle. My grandfather was a heroin addict and passed away in our house on Christmas Eve.

My childhood was just a messed-up. I was a straight-A student and in all advanced classes, but I had the so-called "isms." I'm also gay. My lifestyle as a gay man is extremely challenging in conservative New Hampshire.

I had an emergency appendectomy at the age of 13, and they put me on drugs. I loved them. It was an instantaneous and significant feeling of comfort. My whole demeanor changed after taking them. Within a year, I was involved in juvenile probation and parole and became a chronic runaway. I dropped my advanced classes and started hanging out with a whole new set of friends.

I had easy access to substances and was using what usually only adults can get their hands on. I also learned how to doctor shop. At 15 years old, I got doctors to prescribe me six bars of Xanax a day. I loved it. I used alcohol and Xanax together for eight years in a row, was involved in a lot of criminal activity, and chronically overdosed. In the last few years of using it, I had seizures. I don't remember a lot of those eight years.

After high school, I lived in a drug house with family friends. I used OxyContin and a drug that had the effect of OxyContin and morphine mixed together, Oxymorphone. We called it Opana. I lived with someone who distributed it. I did anything I could to get my hands on it. I had no off switch, even if I knew it wasn't a good idea. It was a love relationship.

For the last two years, I was in college; I was failing. I would black out all the time and in the hospital for substantial amounts of time. Part of my game was to pawn this off as mental health issues and keep doing it. I took lots of psychiatric medication, because if you add alcohol and drugs, it amplifies the medication.

The drug house kicked me out because I was chronically overdosing and attracting negative attention. I was in and out of rehabs to avoid homelessness. Finally, I went to rehab, one I had been in and out of for a year a half before I got sober. I was having seizures but wanted a functional life. I would never admit it, but I had a lot of dreams and aspirations for my life.

It wasn't an active choice for me to get sober. It was a slow progression of willingness. I had to be willing to put two feet in the program. I couldn't just dabble with it, pick and choose what I wanted to learn. There's a solid line between fighting and not.

My seizures affected my brain, and it took a month to detox. I couldn't remember how to drive. I was so screwed up. People in AA took care of me.

Looking back, when do you think it was mostly out of control?

When I was using and having seizures, it was the most out of control.

How are you able to not drink or use daily?

I'm actively engaged in the 12-step program. I go to at least three meetings a week. At first, I went to one every day. I don't make my decisions regarding my sobriety. I base my program on what my sponsor advises. She's not a dictator; it's a partnership. I have five more people in my recovery who know my story, so I always have someone available. I make healthy choices, hike, have a schedule, and have appropriate coping skills.

I effectively processed all the traumas from my childhood. I found a healthy way to have that sit in my mind. My whole life includes a 12-step community. If I drink, it would be far more than picking up a substance. I would instantly lose all my friends, my career, etc. I've gained profound relationships with very healthy people who know appropriate boundaries.

What is your thought about medication-assisted treatment?

I didn't need it. It is a valid option in the beginning for some people, not alone, but with meetings and further treatment. Someone may need it if they have been using drugs for 40 years. It may be tough for them to stop abruptly. It is not useful for long-term treatment. I don't ever want someone trying to get sober in AA to feel uncomfortable to be at a meeting. If they are at a meeting, they might hear a message that makes them want to come off it.

Is there anything you want those struggling with addiction to know?

Don't think that how you feel today is how you will feel in a year. The good you feel in the first year, multiply that by one hundred, and that's where you can be. Don't sell yourself short, because it doesn't matter what your background is; you can be a healthy person in the world. You can have a healthy, well-adjusted life. I thought people would remember me for my actions before getting sober, but the reality is that people are too caught up in their own stuff. Give it five years, and you can walk down the street, and no one will remember who you were no matter what you've done in the past. This release of fear is far more comfortable than drinking or drugging, and it's far better.

Mona F.

269

Date of interview: 4/2/19
Sobriety date: 2/15/18, 1 year
Hometown: Berlin

When did you start drinking or using drugs, and how did it progress?

The first time I ever drank, I was 17 years old and was with my cousin and her fiancé. By the time I was 21, my life had gotten rocky. I was in all kinds of abusive relationships. I got married in September of 2008 when my daughter was three months old. My first marriage lasted four years. We didn't drink, and there were no drugs. I just got sick of the relationship and where it was going.

I got into a relationship with someone, and I was doing Vicodin here and there, but nothing major. That relationship ended because I lied to him about using. I had my son and now had two kids. Eventually, I ended up with someone else who never drank and drugged. I stayed with him for a little bit but finally broke up with him to be with the guy that got me hooked on my addiction.

I was in my 30s and thought everything was okay. One day, I realized my bathroom door was shut and didn't know why. I went in, and he was shooting heroin. That's when he told me he had been doing this all along. I had always told myself I would never shoot up. That day, I snorted a line of heroin and was immediately hooked. The next day I injected it. He did big shots, and I shot up as much as he did. I shot up every drug I ever did for the next two and a half years: Molly, crack, heroin, and other drugs.

I've overdosed three times and was Narcanned two or three times. I never went to the hospital for overdoses. We always kept Narcan in the house; we have had four people overdose there. One of them died. The guy I was with always did CPR to bring me back, so no one knew. I didn't want to go to the hospital out of fear of losing my kids or getting arrested.

One time, I quit heroin for a month but was taking my boyfriend's Suboxone. He would sell the Suboxone to get more drugs. There were always times when I wanted to quit, but my mind wasn't there yet. People were in and out of our house buying drugs. People were overdosing, and there were guns. My boyfriend became the next big drug dealer in town, and he didn't think he would get caught, but he did. I wasn't able to be there for my kids because of the drugs and drug-dealing activities. I lost my kids on February 6, 2018.

In the middle of February, the police raided our home. The house was surrounded, and the police were everywhere. They took us all out in handcuffs. I was released; my boyfriend is in state prison for 10 to 20 years. The police blocked off our road and stormed into our house at 6:30 in the morning. They confiscated over 90 grams of heroin and fentanyl as well as assault rifles and other weapons.

Since that day, I have been clean and sober, and I haven't touched a drug. Meetings help me. I've had unsupervised and supervised visits with my kids. I quit heroin cold turkey. I was sick on and off for two weeks and just spent time in bed. I started seeing a licensed alcohol and drug counselor and going to Narcotics Anonymous meetings daily.

Looking back, when do you think it was mostly out of control?

When I had two people overdose in my house and almost die.

How are you able to not drink or use daily?

I listen to music and talk to my kids daily. I spend time around the recovery center and go to two NA meetings a day.

What is your thought about medication-assisted treatment?

If it works for other people, then that's good. I chose not to use methadone or Suboxone to get sober because it would just be another addictive drug. If it works and it keeps people off more harmful drugs, then maybe it's okay.

Is there anything that you want those struggling with addiction to know?

If recovery works for other people, then it can work for you; 12-step programs work. Connect with a recovery center, and there you may find a family of people in recovery.

If anyone has kids, I advise you to choose your kids over drugs. I know friends who are in their 20s and can't put the needle down to have kids.

Nick B.

Date of interview: 4/17/2019
Sobriety date: 5/26/86, 32 Years
Hometown: Alexandria

When did you start drinking or using drugs, and how did it progress?

I was a sophomore in high school. My father was in the military and was in Vietnam. I was the oldest, and my mother couldn't control me. A friend of mine's brother had just gotten out of prison, so a few of us got some speed from him. I had never taken pills before. I had had alcohol maybe once or twice before this. We got the pills, got home, and one of the kids got caught with them.

I played sports and hadn't had any run-ins with the law. I started to drink when at the school dances. It slowly progressed until the middle of my sophomore year. That's when pills and pot happened. It went from me never skipping a single day to the last quarter of my sophomore year, attending school maybe five days. I don't know how I managed to pass that year, but I did. I never went back though. I was off and running. We'd go into the Boston Common, hang around, and smoke pot. We gathered money to start a little nest egg and start dealing drugs.

I was using speed and heroin as much as I could. By the time I was 17, I was using 10 bags of heroin a day. I moved out and got a room at the Salem YMCA. I lived there for about two months before they found my pound of marijuana and scales. They reported it to the police, and the police arrested me. That was my first drug bust. I got arrested, but the case was dismissed after a year. Heroin was more accessible to obtain than the pot in the Salem and Beverly area.

For the next 10 years, I was either in jail or on probation. I was getting arrested for things like breaking and entering, robberies, assault on a police officer, and drug charges. The longest time I was in jail was four years, the state prison. I just drank and drugged myself into the ground, but somehow, I knew I could do better in life. I had three different heroin arrests.

When I was doing sports, it was excellent; I was a record holder. I had a little exposure to AA and a couple of drug programs due to court orders. I had a drug and alcohol counselor while I was in prison, and sometimes the prisons would hold AA meetings. They would give you good time, and that was the incentive to go. It got you out of your cell and kept you busy. So that's where I got introduced to AA. I had a son at this point, and I wasn't much of a father, so that was a concern for me and may have helped me stop. I was also afraid I might hurt someone by the crazy things I was doing.

I finally realized I was paying a very high price to drink and use drugs, and it wasn't going to change unless I did. I began asking God for help and began trying to do the next right thing.

Looking back, when do you think it was mostly out of control?

273

It was always out of control.

How are you able to not drink or use daily?

I ask God for help and I try and do the right thing.

What is your thought about medication-assisted treatment?

I think many forms of trying to help are excellent. Everyone is in a different condition, so what is going to work for one person isn't going to work for the next. Some people may need a little crutch to go into the world and make changes, and then you can slowly take them off it.

Is there anything you want those struggling with addiction to know?

You don't have to struggle. If you go to meetings, you will hear things that will make sense. At first it didn't make sense to me, but it eventually did.

<u>**Nick W,**</u>

Date of interview: 4/25/19
Sobriety date: 8/9/14, 4 years
Hometown: Concord

When did you start drinking or using drugs, and how did it progress?

I was 14 when I had my first drink. I had 10 shots of all different things. The first shot felt good and I wanted more. I also tried marijuana at that time, after tennis practice in a friend's car. I found them both, and they both felt incredible.

Throughout high school, I used drugs whenever I could. It wasn't every day, but when I did it, I went all out. Then I started stealing alcohol from my parents and other people's fridges in the neighborhood when they weren't home. During my junior and senior year, I was smoking weed every day and experimented with OxyContin my senior year.

When I went to college, I blacked out at orientation. The first weekend there, I got dosed with acid and ended up in a psych ward. They told me I was bipolar, so I believed them. They started me on Lithium at 18 years old. They wanted to kick me out of school after all of this, but I ended up staying and made it work. Now, I was drinking and taking Lithium.

For the next seven years, I drank and took opiates, stimulants, and hallucinogens. During all this time, I was in and out of four psych wards and five rehabs and taking many different psych meds prescribed by doctors. Doctors gave me Ritalin, Valium, Depakote, Seroquel, Lithium, and others. Always various cocktails.

Then I started getting into spirituality. I wanted to see natural cures for what I thought I had, which was bipolar disorder. Looking for a natural remedy was a pretty intense experience. My parents are both dentists and didn't believe in natural cures. I hated being on medication. After going to my sixth rehab, I wanted not to use this time. I had four months sober and went to meetings every day, but I was miserable and isolating, and eventually relapsed. My parents found out and kicked me out of their lives completely.

Getting kicked out was the best thing that ever happened to me. I fell to my lowest level ever. I was couch surfing and got kicked out of those places for stealing. I was 24, drinking, using opiates and stimulants, and getting paranoid about everything. I finally asked my parents for help and got into another rehab. That was the last time I used drugs.

I was in detox for 14 days, and a nurse said, "You know you don't have to keep messing up." This simple statement shifted my attitude. I started listening to the counselors and doing what they asked me to do. Everything they offered, I did it. I got involved in astrology and loved it. I started to see a way to look forward. I realized I could make my music and teach.

I was able to finish my master's degree in education. I got involved in an Emmy Award-winning play at my college. I was able to bring my rap music into schools with an anti-bullying message. Today I teach astrology, meditation, the law of attraction, the 12 Steps, and spirituality at Avenues Recovery in Concord, New Hampshire. I'm allowed to be myself at work. My plans for the future are to be a thought leader, have my own YouTube channel, and rap. I want to explain things to people with my music.

Looking back, when do you think it was mostly out of control?

At age 22, I was dealing with some shady characters and eating other people's methadone. I was smoking crack and doing all kinds of other crazy stuff.

How are you able to not drink or use daily?

I never stop growing spiritually. I believe spirituality is the solution. Members of 12-step groups tell you it's all about spiritual growth. I never stop connecting with my higher power. This morning I woke up, meditated for 30 minutes, said three affirmations, worked on my voice for 15 minutes in the shower, did yoga for 20 minutes, and went for a walk for 30 minutes. Every day I'm on a mission, and I don't feel as if I'm working hard. I'm lit up from the inside to do these things. I found my spiritual essence and feed that every day.

What is your thought about medication-assisted treatment?

If medication is the best thing that's going to work for a person, I say go for it. For me, it's just another drug.

Is there anything you want those struggling with addiction to know?

Ask for help and get to detox. Don't think about surviving, think about thriving. If you're trying to get by, it's not going to be fun. When you start to create a life you truly love, you won't want to go back.

Paul D.

Date of interview: 4/24/19
Sobriety date: 9/3/07, 11 years
Hometown: Newmarket

When did you start drinking or using drugs, and how did it progress?

The first time I drank I was 19 and at UNH. A high school classmate, who was also attending UNH, and I ended up at a house party. I drank and blacked out. I guess my behavior was obnoxious, and I woke up deathly sick. For a couple of years after that, I couldn't even stomach the smell and had no interest in any alcohol.

By the time I was 21, that feeling had passed. I dropped out of UNH and had an apartment with my best friend, who had just come back from the Army. We drank together, but it wasn't out of control yet. We would go out two to three times a week and have two to three beers each time. I would buy a six-pack every two weeks and sit on the back porch on a weekend afternoon and drink the six-pack between the two of us. Eventually, my friend ended up moving away to do something else with his life.

By the time I was 25, all my high school friends were spread out, which left me without any friends. I decided to go to bars a couple of times a week to meet new friends. There was a music venue, and I liked acoustic music. I met a woman at the bar. We got married and had three kids. I also developed a group of friends by going there. My wife and I were both looking for someone who could complete the other, and we fit together really well, just not in a healthy way. We would go to family picnics, have cookouts, and drink plenty of beer. By the end of the day, we were intoxicated. Eventually, we got divorced, and I went back to school in Boston.

The commute to Boston was too much, so I moved there. After class, several of us would go out to the bar, and we held parties every couple of months. At some point, I started to bring beer back to the apartment. That's when it began to affect my performance in school, and I stalled as far as school was concerned. My dad had a bypass operation that wasn't entirely successful, and he couldn't do anything around the house as far as maintenance goes, so I moved back in with my parents in NH.

The drinking stayed the same when I first moved in. I had a job and started to do side jobs on Saturdays. I'd buy a six-pack on my way home when I worked on the side jobs. That would last me a week at that time. It went from drinking every other day or so to every day. It went from two bottles to three, to four, to five, and eventually, it was a six-pack every day. That went on for about three to four years, and throughout all of this, I was deeply depressed.

One Friday night, I bought a box of 12 beers and thought I would be okay until Sunday evening, and that wasn't the case. By Saturday night, those 12 beers were gone, and I'd have to get more beer. At this point, I was 52, and one Sunday evening after drinking all weekend, I was standing at my workbench thinking about all the people who had wronged me or hurt me, and it felt as though all those things had just happened right then. I exploded into rage.

I picked up all these beer bottles I kept in a big trash can and threw them, one at a time, at the woodstove across the shop until they were all broken. After that, I picked up a hammer and started beating on my workbench. I remember yelling as loud as I could, "I'm insane. I don't care that I'm insane."

After I calmed down, I went back into the house and told my mother that I needed help. She called the emergency room, and I spoke to someone on the phone for a while. I was still drunk at the time and threatened my ex-wife's life. I eventually went to bed, woke up the next day, and called in sick to work. I had a list of counselors and can't remember why but I called three of the names on the list. One called me back, so I made an appointment. I still drank and I didn't stop instantly. I was very resistant to going to AA. I met with the counselor every week though. This was in April 2002.

In September 2003, I stopped. I knew I had to. I didn't want to. Somewhere in 2003, it went from not wanting to quit drinking to wanting to be sober. I started by cutting out my drinking days pretty much one at a time. Eventually, I was able to cut it out altogether. I realized that I had been hungover for about four to five years straight.

Sometime around 2004, I changed jobs and went to a company Christmas party at a restaurant. I ordered a pint of beer and didn't drink again after that for another three to four months, but then went into a convenience store and bought a couple of beers. Another month later I bought more, and it progressed to where I was eventually drinking a couple of times a week again.

I got caught in early 2007 by my girlfriend, and she left me. After that, I decided to go to AA meetings in my town. I had my last drink on Labor Day of 2007. I do think that relapse was beneficial in the long run because it pointed out that it could happen if I am not vigilant in my sobriety.

Looking back, when do you think it was mostly out of control?

It was the most out of control over the last three to four years of drinking.

How are you able to not drink or use daily?

I prepare myself when I know there will be beer or wine at a family event or cookout by reminding myself that there will be alcohol and drinking. I articulate to myself the intention to be sober and say no if offered a drink. I do the same before grocery shopping, and I avoid the beer and wine aisle if possible.

The closest Market Basket has their nuts in the wine aisle, so reminding myself beforehand that I want to be sober is essential. I don't go out to bars anymore because I don't trust myself to go alone and not drink. I also meditate for 30 to 40 minutes every morning.

What is your thought about medication-assisted treatment?

From what I've heard and read, it can help people. I heard it does not help everyone. My doctor prescribed an anti-depressant, and I took it for several years. The side effects were terrible, so I stopped taking it.

Is there anything you want those struggling with addiction to know?

Although alcohol momentarily makes things feel okay, it only keeps you in the same rut and makes things worse. Once you can unhook yourself from the cycle, it gets better. I spent years and years depressed. Talking to a counselor can help you feel better. The things I was feeling sad about then are still in my life, the problems that I had are still there, but I feel happy anyway.

Drinking kept me stuck.

<u>Paul L.</u>

Date of interview: 5/27/19
Sobriety date: 5/5/05, 14 years
Hometown: Bristol

When did you start drinking or using drugs, and how did it progress?

It wasn't unusual when I was growing up in the 1950s and 1960s for parents or grandparents to give kids a sip of their highball or beer. I was 13 when I made my first decision to take a drink with friends in the neighborhood. We took liquor from our parents' cabinets, mixed it all, and drank it. I was off and running after that. I liked the way it made me feel and how it made me feel closer to my friends, a bonding experience.

I experimented with marijuana, hash, and smoking opium in high school. In my sophomore year, I tore my meniscus while on the varsity wrestling team, so the doctor gave me Demerol. I yelled and screamed to have more. As I was exiting the hospital, I was in withdrawal and they sent me home with an unlimited supply of codeine. When that ran out, I used marijuana, hash, pills, and alcohol daily and often multiple times a day.

At 15 and 6'6" tall, I was able to buy alcohol by dressing in an old raincoat, fake glasses, and using an ID I stole from my gym teacher. I used every single day until my friends and I were drinking in the high school parking lot and throwing the beer cans out the window, which landed me in detention. My dad picked me up, and I remember how disappointed he was.

I met my current wife, Wendy, in detention. She had done the one thing wrong she'd ever done in her life: she had skipped school and

Chem-Free Sobriety

wound up in detention. At her request, I stopped drinking and drugging for some time. In my senior year, I didn't drink or drug, and my grades went up enough to go to college. My reading and comprehension had gotten pretty poor from drinking and smoking pot every day; Wendy helped me with this.

During college, my dad died. It turned my life upside down. Wendy and I had planned to get married and almost postponed the wedding. My mom took my dad's death poorly; she had suffered from mental health issues before, but it kicked into high gear after his death. After she attacked my brother with a kitchen knife, I had her committed. This was not her first violent act. She was prone to hitting us, and when I was four, she tried to snuff me out with a pillow. I never dealt with this traumatic abuse and would drink, do drugs, or work obsessively to hide the insecurity of feeling worthless because my mother would have preferred to suffocate me. Twelve years after my father's passing, my mother took her own life. Shortly after that, Wendy's dad passed away from cancer, and her mom had a stroke. This stress affected us tremendously. I had no tools to deal with it.

When our daughter was born, we went back to church weekly, and I managed to stop drinking and doing drugs for five years. Then, in the late 1970s, I started my own software business and also began work on a master's degree in business. I drank a gin and tonic at a business lunch, and shortly after, my drinking was out of control again. Still, I managed to build the business to over 80 staff and 400 customers. I was on a mission to make as much financial success happen before I turned 40. I figured I was destined to die in my 40s, just like my father.

With a perceived death cloud over my head and unresolved trauma, my drinking and drug use came back at a whole new level. The jackpots and the consequences got worse. I started having physical problems and got hooked on opiates after going through a few surgeries. I had been chewing opiate tabs as if they were Altoids. It was nonstop, trying to cover up the symptoms. I had many trips to the doctors with new ailments and pains to keep me supplied. There was a lot of drinking during the day for business, then taking Ambien to sleep. I took Provigil in the morning to wake up, Xanax during the day to cut the anxiety, and opiates to reduce the pain. I overdosed once in NYC with a combination of psych meds and alcohol.

It all came to a head when Wendy said, "Either fix this now, or I'm leaving." Faced with the fact that I would be losing my family, I left Rhode Island and came to New Hampshire for three months. I never went to a treatment center, detox, or anything else, other than to my counselor of 20 years. I went to my usual bar in Bridgewater, but it was closed, so I called the Alcoholics Anonymous 800 number, and they helped me get to my first AA meeting. I met my sponsor there and he saved my life.

The next night, I went to a drinking hole by Lake Winnipesauke, and it also happened to be closed. I decided to go to my second AA meeting, and my sponsor was there too. Our relationship was airtight from that point on. I achieved sobriety through his help with the 12 Steps of AA. After a year, I got pretty cocky, went on vacation, and got loaded every day. I had relapse after relapse.

Finally, in 2005, I set a date to quit. It was the date my son got married. I've been in recovery ever since. That means I have not found it necessary to get loaded or high since. I have had surgeries, including an excruciating back fusion, but with transparency and the support of my surgeon and wife, I used fewer meds than prescribed and weaned off as soon as possible.

Looking back, when do you think it was mostly out of control?

In my junior year of high school and my late 40s, it was the most out of control.

How are you able to not drink or use daily?

I pray, meditate, work my program daily, and attend AA meetings. After six years of staying sober, I got into martial arts and involved in Kuntao Ju-Jitsu. I'm now a fourth-degree black belt and teacher. My anxiety and depression are less when I'm physically active, eat well, use holistic stress management tools, and get healthy sleep.

Once I got off all the psych meds, I focused on healthy habits. I work out, take nutritional supplements, and handle stress appropriately. I read inspirational material every day and throughout the day through social media. I'm always looking for that gem that I can repost, something that is going to touch me or somebody else. I work and live the 12 Steps in my life. I consider it a way of life. I try my best to make amends quickly. I also went to counseling. I dropped the medication-driven psychiatry. Most of all, I stay connected to my family and try to make living amends to them daily.

I helped set up a non-profit residential treatment center as the incorporating chairman, Webster Place in Franklin. I've purchased and launched a couple of sober houses in Northfield. We all have talent, and mine is at a business or board level. Recently, I got involved with The Chris Herron Project as an investor and board member. I've only focused on recovery investments since 2005. I am associated with technology that helps people in recovery stay connected with a support system. I'm involved with the recovery community and find it rewarding to help expand recovery capacity and create new recovery tools.

What is your thought about medication-assisted treatment?

Medication-assisted treatment is appropriate for a short time. MAT is supposed to be used as assistance, not permanent. Too often, people end up on high doses, and it becomes challenging to titrate off. Psychiatrists layer psych meds to treat marijuana psychosis, thereby making people more psychotic. Some people shuffle, drool, and become nonfunctional on some forms of MAT.

Holistic doctors can get people off psych meds and MAT. We need to treat people holistically. A whole-person approach to recovery is successful. I still have a lot of back pain and neuropathy. I manage it without pain meds. I keep active, stay hydrated, take supplements, and keep my weight down. I sleep well and listen to what the pain is telling me. This process helps me decide to rest, get a massage, or have an acupuncture treatment.

Is there anything you want people struggling with addiction to know?

Recovery is possible, and it doesn't require having to be on medication. Do not live in a silo of either 12 Steps or medication-assisted treatment or any other one thing. It's not just your sponsor; it's not only the 12-step program, Smart Recovery, your counselor, or keeping busy at the gym. It's everything: sleep, nutrition, controlling stress, exercise, human connection, help others, prayer, mindfulness, and family. Try using Zen philosophy, Yoga, Reiki, or acupuncture. Look at the whole picture.

Peter A.

Date of interview: 6/3/2019
Sobriety date: 10/02/00, 18 years
Hometown: Hopkinton

When did you start drinking or using drugs, and how did it progress?

The first time I used, I was 14. I grew up in Allentown, Pennsylvania, and was on a sledding hill with my friends. We found a six-pack outside a college dormitory. We shared it, and I remember feeling warm and feeling bad, like bad was good. It was exciting, but I knew it was something we weren't supposed to be doing. Next was at a family wedding, and I drank some of a mixed drink. I didn't get wasted those first times, but my use evolved. In ninth grade, I went to parties at hotels where we would get a room and drink beer. In tenth grade, I went to a boarding school, but it wasn't too far from home, so I still hung around with my public-school friends.

Boarding school exposed me to little parental supervision and a whole lot of people who enjoyed experimenting with drugs and alcohol. I was a daily pot smoker during high school and experimented a little with psychedelics. I also had my first blackout as a junior in high school. Blacking out only scared me to the extent that I was worried someone would catch me and I'd get kicked out. When I realized I hadn't gotten caught, I started to feel invincible and drank more than just on weekends. I was drinking hard alcohol on a fairly regular basis and loved it. My grades were okay, and I was the captain of the soccer team. I graduated, and the partying just continued.

I knew I would go to college because everyone from boarding school goes to college. I picked a college based on how much fun I could have. What followed was a transition to alcoholism, codependent thinking, and terrifying years where blackouts were the norm. I got put on academic probation my first semester and ended up taking classes in the summer to make up for the zeros.

Sophomore year I decided to finish school and take courses a little more seriously. I still drank every day but did my homework. I needed to drink or smoke pot or do something to go to sleep at night. A few times in high school and college, I tried cocaine. I knew I was an alcoholic, and those nights I added cocaine to the equation was a good time, but the next day was horrendous. I

286

didn't mess with it after this and didn't have people around that were doing it.

I finished college in four years and moved to Colorado with one of my buddies. Someone we went to boarding school with was going to school in Boulder, Colorado. We ran out there and got a job, drank daily, worked, and smoked pot. I was cruising through life and wasn't happy. I moved back to the east coast because my younger brother was dealing with my parents' divorce on his own. He and I moved in together with some friends. I was not a great example for my brother. We stayed in the house together, and I had a couple of random jobs. I lived in many different places over the next two years. I did the same thing everywhere I went; I worked in a restaurant, drank, smoked weed, and was miserable.

I was getting close to my bottom and knew I couldn't survive on my own. I was drinking daily and had to find people to help me. I met my first wife at a restaurant I worked at; she was a waitress there. We moved to Santa Barbara, California, in February of 2000. My friend, who I had run out to Colorado with, now lived in Santa Barbara. We established residency there, and she finished school. I worked at a restaurant and knew the relationship wasn't going to last if I continued down the path I was on.

Many people started asking why I drank so much. I would drink a six-pack a day and smoke weed to be able to sleep. When I needed or wanted more, which was most of the time, I would hide the empties, so my girlfriend wouldn't know I was drinking more than a six-pack. I tried to stick to beer since hard liquor always made me black out, but I would end up breaking this rule so I could let go and drink the way I wanted to.

Labor Day weekend of 2000, the bartender of the restaurant had a Labor Day party. The restaurant closed and everyone went to his house. I drank two bottles of wine by myself, took Ecstasy, and smoked pot. It felt great at first, as if I were walking on air, but then it got scary. I ended up falling into a kid's tub and broke the soap dish off the side of the shower wall. I had a massive bruise on my back after that. I realized I was too old to be drinking like this anymore. I wasn't going anywhere. People around me were getting help, so I did a few sessions with an energy healer. He tricked me into reading chapter five of the AA Big Book, how the 12-step program works. He then told me I should go to a meeting, and I joined the program.

September 21 was my first sobriety date. I stopped doing everything suggested to maintain sobriety, and after two and a half weeks, I had a glass of wine. Every part of me wanted more, but I only had that one and went to a meeting the next day and told everyone about my experience. I always say I am so grateful for that glass of wine because it brought me into sobriety. It was my last drink, and it felt terrible.

Looking back, when do you think it was mostly out of control?

Ages 22 to 27 were DARK. They were a mix of regular blackouts, failed relationships, moving a lot, choosing to buy alcohol instead of paying rent, not being in touch with my family, and during the few sober hours, feeling like a complete failure. The only thing I could do to deal with that feeling was to drink or get high.

How are you able to not drink or use daily?

I make a list of what I need to do and use my calendar to organize things. I have two children who are 10 and 12. I think about what they need. I think about my commitments at work. I am mindful of what food I put in my body. I make sure I get enough sun and fresh air. I'm aware of how much media I consume. I apologize when I screw up and figure out how to do things differently the next time. I also read spiritual material, philosophy, and short stories.

What is your thought about medication-assisted treatment?

I have mixed feelings about it. I want people to have access to different ways of getting well, but I think people have to be very careful. People use substances irresponsibly. There has to be an end game to physicians prescribing medication. I don't like the approach of people thinking that they need to be on a medically assisted program long-term. There needs to be a plan in place to get someone to a baseline and then transition to psychotherapy and meditation or whatever may be necessary.

Is there anything you want those struggling with addiction to know?

You're not alone. You're not using any drug or in any situation that people haven't been in before. People in recovery have experienced all kinds of trauma. There's no excuse for treating yourself the way you are by abusing substances. Give sobriety a shot.

If you've ever wondered if you're an alcoholic or drug addict before, then you may be.

Peter M.

Date of interview: 4/19/19
Sobriety date: 5/11/08, 10 years
Hometown: Concord

When did you start drinking or using drugs, and how did it progress?

I was in sixth grade and with a group of neighborhood kids. They asked if I wanted a beer. I was picked on and bullied for not using drugs or alcohol in school, so I thought I would try it. I felt some connection. I felt like I fit in.

Transitioning into high school, I went from a private Catholic high school to a public school. I started smoking weed and drinking more. During my sophomore year came the introduction of prescription drugs and Ecstasy. I tried Ecstasy for the first time and before graduating from high school, I was a heroin addict.

Everyone thought my drug use was out of control and that I needed help, except me. I was 16 years old and doing heroin in the bathroom on the back of a toilet before one of my classes. From this day on, I became a daily user. If I couldn't get heroin, I would take whatever I could. I shared a needle with a guy who told me he had HIV because I needed to get what I needed.

I didn't start getting help until I was 21. My parents showed up at my work and said they couldn't be in my life anymore, and that I needed help. A few days later, I went to an inpatient treatment center, Serenity Place. From there, I went to the Farnum Center and had a great experience. They didn't do the three principles then, it was AA. The day I graduated, all the graduates went out and got drunk together.

I stayed away from heroin for two to three months, got a job in Connecticut, and drove all over the country building cell phone towers and got drunk on the weekends. One night I ended up using again. I didn't think I had a problem with alcohol at this point, just drugs. I ended up in treatment again after this, back to Serenity Place.

One day my parents took me up to a secluded house in the woods and left me there for two weeks so that I wouldn't use. Two months later, I attempted suicide. I had written a suicide note, telling my parents I didn't know how I could ever beat this thing and that they were incredible parents. Then I injected all the drugs I had. The next morning, I woke up at my parents' house. They hadn't seen the note. I then went to Phoenix House in Keene, detoxed, and stayed there for 76 days. I finally realized I couldn't use alcohol or drugs.

Looking back, when do you think it was mostly out of control?

When I was living on my own, it was the most out of control. When lived at home, even though I was using, I was kept in check by my parents. I lived alone, and it was complete chaos. I was up all night, going on runs, getting arrested, and committing crimes.

How are you able to not drink or use daily?

I place my recovery first over everything. Everything in life is a zero, being a husband, father, brother, etc. My recovery is the number one most important thing to me. So, after number one come the zeroes. An unquantified number. Without the number one first, it would be just zero, nothing. You lose if you don't stay sober.

I have a foundation and a routine. When things don't go my way, it never comes to mind that substances or alcohol could help. Early on in sobriety, I established new principles. There is a lot of praying, meditation, and a high level of caring for other people. I have a purpose and a lot of goals. My goals are about others.

What is your thought about medication-assisted treatment?

There are multiple paths to sobriety; mine is complete abstinence. There is a shift toward medication treatment with big pharma connected. They don't want to pay for abstinence recovery because it doesn't serve their bottom lines. I don't think medication is for someone to get on and be on for the rest of their lives. If I went to a methadone clinic, I don't think I would be able to get off it because I know how debilitating it can be.

Is there anything you want those struggling with addiction to know?

There is help, and we don't all recover, but we all can. Just try. Who you surround yourself with is extremely important. You are the average of the five people you spend the most time with.

Peter O.

Date of interview: 5/29/19
Sobriety date: 8/23/11, 7 years
Hometown: Bristol

When did you start drinking or using drugs, and how did it progress?

The first time I picked up a drink I was 10 years old. I'd finished mowing the grass and decided I was old enough to have a drink. My dad had a keg in the refrigerator in the basement. I got one of the frozen glasses from the freezer and poured myself a beer. I didn't care for the taste, but I liked that it was cold and bubbly.

The first time I ever got drunk was when I was 15 years old. I was babysitting for my brothers. My parents had gone out, and I decided to get into my dad's liquor cabinet. I took four juice glasses and poured a few fingers of different liquor in each glass: bourbon, scotch, gin, and vodka. I drank each one down in short order and went into a blackout. The next day, I was sick, and my brothers told me about some of my bizarre behavior. I didn't drink very much until I was in the Navy; there was a lot of marijuana use in high school though.

After graduating from high school, I joined the Navy. I was 18 when I went to boot camp. I met a girl from Connecticut while I was in submarine school and ended up marrying her at 19. She liked to drink, so I began to drink more often with her. We occasionally smoked pot as well. I would do shots at night and drink beer. I started waking up and feeling like I could not go to school and function. That's when I learned I could take a drink in the morning and make myself feel better enough to go to school and work. After completing my training, the Navy stationed me on a submarine in Hawaii. Hawaii is where I got introduced to cocaine. I loved it. I drank, used cocaine, and smoked pot. All this use was recreational and within my budget.

I was honorably discharged from the Navy and got a job testing electrical systems on new submarines. A few years later, I got a job with a Navy R&D facility. In December 1993, my organization was raising money for charity at Christmas time by putting on breakfast on a Monday morning. I volunteered to cook but had a bender of a weekend and showed up with a hangover. I should have called in sick but went to work anyway. An older co-worker who sat close to me shook his head and said, "Jesus Christ, Pete." I suspect he could smell the alcohol coming out of my pores. The gig was up. I called the personnel manager and said, "I think I might have a problem with alcohol." She told me to look in the yellow pages for help and I ended up in an aftercare program. I went for three months and stayed sober for three and a half years. During those three and a half years, I went through a divorce with my first wife. Both of us had our problems. It was a reverse situation: I ended up with the house and kids.

I started dating a co-worker and married her; she is my current wife. My life got good. I was now with a person who was more of my background—college-educated, with a good job, and responsible. I started drinking again on our honeymoon. I thought, "It's my honeymoon, and I'm entitled to drink." I didn't get into any trouble with alcohol on the cruise ship. We had drinks on three of four different evenings, nothing terrible happened, and I never picked up a drug after my first period of sobriety.

A few years into our marriage, I was having lots of bender weekends and was waking up in the middle of the night drinking. The truth is that I was drinking when I wasn't sleeping. My wife was going to Al-Anon, which made me angry. When she went to Al-Anon, I drank more with a vengeance. I didn't go to work on one particular Monday, and my wife had had it. She came home from work and was frustrated with me. I went into a blackout, fell several times in my bedroom, hit my head on her dresser, and cut it open in an awful way. I knocked over her armoire and broke a figurine that meant a lot to her. I also bled severely on the carpet and the bed. She came home to this nightmare—I was passed out—and was very frightened and immediately called an ambulance.

When I came to, there were ambulance people, fire department people, and police in my bedroom. We live on a cul-de-sac with 11 homes in the neighborhood. The fire truck, the ambulance, and police car were out front with their emergency lights on. To say that the situation had my neighbors' attention was an understatement. The first responders were telling me that I needed to go to the hospital. I was telling them "I'm not going to the hospital and get out of my house." The police officer said, "Look, if you don't go to the hospital with the ambulance personnel, I'm going to put you in handcuffs and take you myself." I told him he couldn't put me in handcuffs because I was in my own house and it's not illegal to be drunk in your own home. I then told them to leave. At that moment, I wanted a drink more than anything else. It was clear in my head that if I went to the hospital, I wasn't going to get the alcohol I needed so desperately.

I did not want my neighbors to see me leave my house in handcuffs, so I went out on the gurney with the ambulance crew. The next day I came to realize the gravity of the situation. I had been on a three-day bender and had split my head open, causing an embarrassing situation for my wife and me. It had been a shit show. I stayed sober for just under a year after this episode, going to one or two AA meetings per week.

We purchased a new home in New Hampshire on a beautiful lake. We were out on the deck one Saturday afternoon. Our neighbors were all outside on their porches having happy hour, and I said to my wife, "I'm miserable. These people are having fun, and I'm not." My wife said, "I can tell when you've had too much to drink, so if you just listen to me and stop drinking when I say you've had enough, I wouldn't care if you drank a couple of beers or a couple of glasses of wine." I replied, "Honey, I can do that." I was off to the races for another eight years of alcoholic drinking.

In August of 2011, I had some vacation time coming. I came to New Hampshire for a long weekend and put together six days of drinking. I had been drinking around the clock and had to stop to go back to work. I could not stop drinking, and it scared me. I blew Monday off. On Tuesday, I was in no condition to go to work. I pleaded with my wife not to go to work. I was afraid if she left me alone, I would start drinking again. I told her I would call a friend of mine from AA and get back to meetings. She stayed home, and I called my friend. He came over and called a cardiologist who's in the program. He came over, took my blood pressure, and told me I should go to detox. I was afraid of how it might affect my government clearance, so I stayed home, detoxed myself, and started going to AA meetings again and have stayed sober ever since.

Looking back, when do you think it was mostly out of control?

Anytime I picked up the first drink.

How are you able to not drink or use daily?

I hit my knees in the morning and say the following prayer: God, thank you for keeping me sober yesterday. Please keep me away from a drink today. Please remove the obsession for a drink today. I pray to you for the knowledge of your will and the power to carry that out. Please grant me patience, tolerance, kindness, and understanding so that I may be a better human being, a better friend, a better husband, a better father, a better brother, and a better son. Please guide my thoughts, words, and actions. God, please remove all my shortcomings. Thank you for my sobriety, thank you for the gift of life, and thank you for my wife, children, grandchildren, family, and friends. Thank You for my career and all the blessings you have put into my life. God, please show me how I can help another human being today. I pray that you watch over my family and friends. For those who are sick and suffering, I pray that you offer them comfort and peace. I pray to you through your Son and my Savior, Jesus Christ. Please make me an instrument of your peace. Amen.

I typically attend four meetings a week and stay active in my program. I talk to my sponsor regularly and work the 12 Steps of Recovery. I say yes to service work, take people to meetings, and speak with other alcoholics. I take suggestions; it helps me remain sober a day at a time.

What is your thought about medication-assisted treatment?

My older daughter struggled with using heroin. She was in a methadone program, where she was getting treatment every morning, and changed to Suboxone after that. She graduated from high school, and we got her into a phlebotomy training program. She was able to get a job. Her life got better, and now she's a mother of two. She still drinks, and I'm a little worried about her, given our family history.

Speaking for myself, I believe that alcohol use sets off a physical compulsion, a mental obsession, and a spiritual malady. AA has taught me to use abstinence, prayer, meetings, and a program to stay sober a day at a time.

Is there anything you want those struggling with addiction to know?

It gets worse, and it can kill you. You're not yourself. You don't think of other people. It makes you sick and everybody around you sick with worry and angst. We put the other people in our lives through emotional hell. It's just not fair.

Phil R.

Date of interview: 2/1/19
Sobriety date: 4/8/02, 16 years
Hometown: Bristol

When did you start drinking or using drugs, and how did it progress?

My earliest memories of alcohol were watching my parents have fun and laugh while having their parties. I always wanted to be a part of that kind of fun. I associated alcohol as being a rite of passage to adulthood. It wasn't until age 15 that I acted upon it.

I worked at a golf course as a pro shop employee with older people. After work one day, I played in a softball game with them, and one of the players gave me a six-pack. I drank the whole thing. I got so drunk and didn't think I would ever get that high again for the rest of my life. For the next 26 years, I drank to try to achieve that high.

Through high school, I could only drink when it was available and got drunk on occasions in the summers. Between my parents' supervision and being involved in sports, I kept from using alcohol during the school season. In the summer, I worked at the golf course, and there was less parental supervision and more access to alcohol. The older folks I worked with bought me a beer, and I would bring it to my friends, and we'd drink. It made me popular and took away my shyness.

I went to college in upstate New York and was no longer under parental supervision. I had a lot of freedom, which allowed me to make my own decisions. I drank mostly on weekends and drank to get drunk. I wasn't studying the way I should have been, so my grades suffered. This type of drinking continued until my junior year when I was asked to leave the college. It was a wakeup call for me, but I didn't think alcohol was the problem. I felt I needed to straighten my life out, so I joined the Marine Corps. It helped me manage my drinking for a little while. I was able to go back to college a year later and graduate.

A year after graduating from college, my sister died suddenly in an accident. Losing her impacted my family and me significantly. I took a long look at my life and knew I was going down the wrong path. I felt terrible for my parents. I wanted to become the best person I could be to fill the void that was left from the loss of my sister. My change involved quitting drinking and getting in good shape. I was lifting weights, running daily, and eating a healthy diet. However, I felt angry all the time, even though I wasn't drinking.

After three months of not drinking, I was out in Arizona for training and experiencing this intense anger. I knew what would resolve it, so I decided to buy a six-pack and go back to my barracks and drink. I cracked open one of the beers and drank it down. Immediately, I felt so much better. At this point, I needed alcohol to keep me sane, and I was off and running. I believed drinking would keep me sane and anger free.

I was back to regularly drinking on weekends and occasionally during the week. I met a girl at the golf club and married her two years later. We lived near the golf course for five years and made plans to move to Vermont. We had two children who needed to finish the school year, so I moved to Vermont first for three months before she and the kids joined me. During that time, my drinking progressed from weekends to every day. It started with a couple of beers a day, but it progressed to a 12-pack a day.

When my wife moved up, I began to hide my drinking. The beer was not giving me the buzz I needed, so I began to drink hard liquor. At first, I would drink it at night after work but then that wasn't enough, so I drank it in the morning before work. Then I drank at work. My drinking progressed to 24 hours a day. I thought no one knew.

At age 41, I stopped drinking because of an intervention at work. Someone reported me being drunk to my boss and I was given a ride home. At the time, I didn't know why. I asked the driver, and he said, "Because you're drunk." That was the first time I knew others knew I was drinking.

My wife freaked out and called everyone in both our families. The treasurer of the club came over to talk about what happened. He said, "You just need to take it easy, not drink so much." My parents were in a little denial and wanted my wife to deal with me. My boss said, "Take a couple of days off and then come back and talk." I took the weekend off, reluctantly. I knew I needed help but was afraid the anger would come back if I quit drinking.

My wife gave me the name of someone in Alcoholics Anonymous, and I threw it away. Through her work, I was able to get an interview with the Starting Now Program at the Brattleboro Retreat. My only experience with drunks was when they wouldn't show up for work and I would send them home. I would shun drunks in general and look down on them. They were the trench-coat people. I didn't belong with them. I was the drunk who could show up for work. I had a total misconception of what a drunk is.

I realized I needed help. I had three kids and a wife now. My life was not good because of my drinking, nor was my health. When I went to get life insurance, my test showed my liver enzymes were high, which likely was caused by alcohol abuse. I had to pay four times the standard premium because of this. I was 60 pounds overweight and knew I needed to change.

I began the Starting Now program in and went four days a week for 10 weeks. They required us to go to AA three days a week. It was a wicked learning curve right off the bat. I had no experience at all with understanding alcoholism, addiction, and what it does to you mentally.

Over the past 16 years, my life has changed in almost every way. I no longer have the urge to drink. I go to AA regularly. I believe in a power greater than myself and have become honest in all my affairs. The changes I made by not drinking and working the 12 Steps have given me a life second to none. Today, my view of life is not narrowing; it is expanding.

Looking back, when do you think it was mostly out of control?

The last three years of my drinking were the most out of control. I wanted and needed to drink.

How are you able to not drink or use daily?

I know that I have the disease of alcoholism. It helps me understand that I can't drink. Also, because I went through an intensive outpatient program that taught me about addiction, I learned I needed to consider living life in balance. It taught me what my irrational behaviors are and gave me a plan for daily living, which includes AA.

What is your thought about medication-assisted treatment?

Medication wasn't offered to me because I didn't have any

withdrawals. I am totally against it and would try every other means first.

Is there anything you want those struggling with addiction to know?

There is an answer. You have to be willing to change. Be open-minded and have a willingness to try suggestions.

Piers K.

Date of interview: 4/26/19
Sobriety date: 9/16/94, 24 years
Hometown: Effingham

When did you start drinking or using drugs, and how did it progress?

I was 11 when I started smoking pot. At first, it was irregularly and then whenever I could. After age 13, I was smoking daily. I also started drinking on weekends and sometimes after school. I would drink at least a six pack and sometimes hard liquor. I was a heavy drinker right out of the gate. We got older people to buy the booze for us and found dealers to give us pot. I was in Washington, DC, until I was 13 and then in Farmington, Maine.

Maine is where my use progressed. At 15, I used cocaine, LSD, and PCP. I was drinking more and by age 20 I started freebasing cocaine. I freebased a few times a year in fairly epic binges. My drinking increased after I was of legal age to buy, drinking more and more. Eventually, I was closing the bar four nights a week and smoking pot all the time. I was also doing the weekend warrior stuff with the cocaine.

I started fooling around with crystal meth and heroin when I was 29. Crystal meth was irregular. When I started using heroin in 1993, I caught the habit and used it every day. For the last two years of my using, I was an IV heroin user. I was using heroin and dealing marijuana. I was getting ready, believe it or not, to go into graduate school for comparative religion and was a pretty functional marijuana dealer.

I had a lot of things going on, and it all blew up because of heroin use. It was the grunge era, so I'm a veteran of that. I moved to Olympia and then to Seattle, Washington, in 1983. I finished school, went to Evergreen State College, sold weed, and bummed around. I graduated and moved towards going into graduate school. My use got out of hand; I was using heroin all day, every day. It didn't change from that.

I got clean in 1994. I was going to get a $14,000 financial aid check, and I didn't think I'd live through it, so I decided to kick it and hold myself up in a motel room. A few things happened. I was drinking and doing benzos to kick heroin. I got on the phone and did a little dialing while intoxicated, which I never did. These calls led to my parents finding out and they did an intervention on me, and I went to St. Mary's Hospital in Lewiston, Maine. I was there for 27 days. It was seven days of detox and 20 days of residential treatment.

I was always spiritually hungry. I knew I needed spirituality but couldn't find it. In May of 1995, the weekend I got sober, I met Don Pritts. That's when I started the 12 Steps, and spirituality began in my life. Before this, I was only going to meetings and counseling. I was sober but miserable. Pritts was a 12-step master. He has had an inordinate influence on the world of recovery, from Native American reservations to prisons to Soviet Russia. He was remarkable. I make a considerable distinction between steps and AA. People who do the steps are a small subculture within AA, a tiny minority.

I recovered. I don't have a mental obsession with doing drugs anymore, which is what the Big Book promises. When I got past the amends, it cleared. I don't even think about using drugs. I don't think about being an addict. I needed to be abstinent to grow spiritually. I can't be in recovery if I'm not abstinent. You need to grow along spiritual lines, not just be abstinent. Abstinence and medication-free, that's the gold standard. Maybe not everybody can achieve it, but it's the gold standard. Thousands of people have made it.

Looking back, when do you think it was mostly out of control?

When I was shooting heroin. That was the last two years of my using. In those two years, it just got more and more out of control.

How are you able to not drink or use daily?

I'm just engaged in the lifestyle. I practice yoga, meditate, and try to help people. I have a non-profit in the Maine State Prison system, where we teach guys to be yoga teachers. I have a good life.

What is your thought about medication-assisted treatment?

I was in a methadone program. I used drugs every day while I was on it and didn't miss a day. There is a place for harm reduction strategies, and it's not treatment. Historically, we've only treated opiates with opiates. Heroin was marketed as a non-addictive alternative to morphine in 1898. The Nazis invented methadone to make up for shortages of morphine on the battlefield. It sat on the shelf until 1971, and then we had methadone clinics.

Suboxone is many times stronger than heroin, so withdrawal symptoms are worse. If you feel you need that, understand that it's harm reduction. The problem with harm reduction in the United States is that we are not like Europe, where they have all kinds of wraparound services. In Europe, you can go to treatment, transfer to housing, be placed in a job, and receive an education. It's a real harm reduction program. Here, we're moving towards you taking Suboxone in a homeless shelter, and the taxpayers get to pay for it.

Not one of our 50 clients would say they believe medication-assisted treatment works. We have people who come to our treatment center to get off Suboxone. We also see clients that are telling us the only opioid they ever abused was Suboxone. There's so much Suboxone on the streets, people are using it as a drug of abuse and catching habits.

Is there anything you want those struggling with addiction to know?

Abstinence-based recovery is possible, and addiction is not a chronically relapsing condition. It happens, but it doesn't have to. People have been recovering from addiction for 85 years. It's an unbroken chain. People going into recovery need to be aware that they are worth more sick than well to certain interests. Addicts are worth more to big pharma, the treatment industry, the prison industrial complex, and a few other players.

Rebecca S.

Date of interview: 6/10/19
Sobriety date: 12/2/17, 1 year
Hometown: Hillsboro

When did you start drinking or using drugs, and how did it progress?

The first time I ever drank was my 14th birthday. I drank liquor in my parents' liquor cabinet. I had some girls over for a party, and we thought it would be fun to try it. I took a shot, and that was it. I felt excited, happy, and physically warm inside. It was almost as if

I had come alive for the first time. I drank a few times at that age and went to a couple of parties, maybe once a month. I would never drink just a drink. I drank to feel out of control, excited, and the life of the party. It changed when I was closer to 16. I started to drink every other weekend. I got into a relationship with someone who was smoking weed and drinking a lot. I joined in with what he was doing. I would be smoking, drinking, or both, but not every weekend.

After I graduated from high school, I went to college. I was still with this guy who had introduced me to all the different party drugs: Cocaine, MDMA, shrooms, etc. During my first year of college, I was smoking weed every day and drinking twice a week. I've struggled with mental illness since high school, diagnosed with borderline personality disorder. Using drugs took away the pain of feeling.

After the first year of college, I went home and started seeing someone else who had a cocaine addiction. I was doing cocaine three to four times a week and then it went to almost every day. I quickly got addicted. I went back to school the following year thinking that I just needed space and would be fine, but that wasn't the case. I found my dealers in Toronto at college and started using drugs by myself. I got through the semester, and it didn't affect my grades that much, but I fell apart when I got back home for Christmas break. I spent every day with the guy I was dating, and we did cocaine every day.

I first realized I had a problem on Christmas Day. I woke up and used cocaine. I couldn't eat my Christmas dinner because I was so high. I went back to school in January, was there for two weeks, and then had a complete breakdown. I told my parents I needed to take time off from school because my mental illness was terrible. It was more about drugs. I moved back home and in with the guy I was seeing. I was there all the time, and it wasn't working. We smoked weed, drank, and used cocaine every day for four months.

I had two different rock bottoms. One rock bottom was in May of 2017. I wasn't showering or getting out of bed. I was barely eating. All I would do is sleep all day while he went to work. I'd wake up, and we would both use all night. It was disgusting. We isolated ourselves from the world outside. I didn't want this life, so I went to a therapist, and she told me she thought I should break up with him and he was unhealthy for me. I took her advice and broke up with him. I thought when I did, my drug addiction would go away. I thought he was the source of my problems.

I got my own connections and started using it with my friends. I had the drug lifestyle I wanted and was partying a lot. Two months after I broke up with this guy, I told my parents I had a problem with drugs. What caused me to tell them was that my little brother started experimenting with weed and alcohol. I was so scared for him. I did not want him to go down the path I had. I knew I couldn't work or go to school if I was using drugs. I couldn't get out of bed. Thinking of him going down that path just made me have to tell them. They were amazing and so supportive. They told me they would get me help, loved me, and were in this with me.

They booked a rehab for me in the middle of October. I had the date, and that was the day I was going to stop using drugs. From August to October was the worst time of my life. I wanted to get all the partying in that I could before I stopped. I started stealing from my family and my friends. I started sleeping with a guy in exchange for drugs. It was a dark time. I remember my mom telling me later that she didn't know if I was going to make it to rehab. I got into several car crashes and didn't remember them until I saw the dents in the car. The last weekend before I went to rehab was Thanksgiving in Canada, and it was horrible. I used so much cocaine I couldn't speak. I couldn't do anything except keep using drugs. My whole family was there. It was just awful.

On a Monday, my mom brought me to rehab and dropped me off and I went through detox. I felt amazing because I was now free. I just slept and ate for a week straight. It was a 30-day rehab in Ontario, Canada. I met a guy there and we started a relationship about two weeks into the program. When the rehab found out, they kicked me out. My parents were devastated. I had to sign a contract with them for me to come home. It included me going to another rehab that was longer than a month. That's when we found His Mansion. I ended up relapsing after being home a month. I made a lot of bad choices in that month, watching movies with people using drugs in them, hanging out with the wrong people, etc. I relapsed that one time and hated it. I felt the same way I had right before I went to rehab. Every time I think about using, I think of that weekend.

Looking back, when do you think it was mostly out of control?

The two months after going to my first rehab, it was the most out of control.

How are you able to not drink or use daily?

My relationship with God is the reason I'm able to stay clean. Having a safe environment has been helpful to me. I have a daily routine. I get up and go to sleep at the same time. I eat three meals a day and make sure I have a quiet time every day. I have people I check in with every day. I read the *Bible* and my devotional book every day. I have to be aware of how I'm feeling and keep my thoughts in check, which took a lot of training. If I see something that's triggering me to use, I tell someone I trust. I talk to my mentor and my friends if I can't handle thoughts on my own. I never let these thoughts go unchecked.

What is your thought about medication-assisted treatment?

If you need to use something to stay safe while you're getting clean, it can be helpful for a short period. I think it's a crutch though. People don't get to experience the fullness of sobriety and a life without drugs if they're forever taking a replacement drug. It's a useful harm reduction technique, but they're missing out on the joy of being sober and experiencing a full range of emotions. Suboxone or methadone keep you from experiencing emotions. It keeps you a slave to your addiction.

Is there anything you want those struggling with addiction to know?

Getting clean is a choice. It's not just going to happen. You didn't just fall into addiction. You're not just going to fall out of it. You have to work to be in recovery actively, and you have to want it. Once you make the hard choice to go through the steps, life is better than you could ever imagine. It's so much better than before you were using or while you were using drugs. It's a new chapter that brings you the life you've been trying to find with drugs.

Regina B.

Date of interview: 2/4/19
Sobriety date: 2/7/96, 22 years
Hometown: Campton

When did you start using drinking or using drugs, and how did it progress?

At age two my family told me I used to ingest cough syrup and alcohol. By age 13, I started having a little independence with a couple of friends outside of the home. We would get together and drink. I had a cousin who was my first source of alcohol. When I had access to it, usually with friends, I would get marijuana. I would drink or use it when I had access. In hindsight, I knew it was about looking okay and feeling okay. I could not feel a connection either with myself or other people. For me to connect with others, the solution was to drink. I was very isolated within my family, and I only knew what I could see. Alcohol use was a coping mechanism for us. It was normal to drink; that's what you do.

Truthfully, I experienced the effects of alcohol the first time I drank. It often created a loss of control. By age 28, I began the pattern of my desire to not drink, believing I could have one drink, and then experiencing over-consumption daily. I drank in isolation and secret. This loss of control frightened me. It revealed the truth that I was an alcoholic. Living two extremes of life is exhausting, and it was, ever so slowly, killing me from the inside out.

Looking back, when do you think it was mostly out of control?

In the military, I married a physically and psychologically abusive man. I was alone and fleeing for my life. The military wasn't the support I needed.

How are you able to not drink or use daily?

I receive help daily. It is no longer a tortuous, uncertain, and frightening endeavor. Instead, it's a conscious blessing to live as fully as possible. This fullness includes living in these truths: I live with alcoholism, and I am not my disease. Each day is an opportunity to learn about how the disease can benefit or hinder my opportunities. Recovery means being fully human and helping others do the same. My disease and humanity are founded in the spiritual principles and practices, including the 12 Steps and 12 Traditions. I continue to seek help and work at the underlying suffering. Before sobriety, I sought relief through alcohol and other forms of dysfunctional coping. Today, I live!

What is your thought about medication-assisted treatment?

My addiction is set up to kick in through other influences, such as medications. These medications continue the vicious cycle of addiction. My detoxification was a natural consequence of my using, and it remains an experience treasured. It helps me understand how horrifically the disease of addiction affects my body, mind, and soul. Feeling the path back to healing was, in part, a deterrent to relapse. The pain of physical sobriety gave me clarity and desire for wanting to remain sober.

Today, I desire to feel the experiences of being human and alive. I experience my internal self without the need to anesthetize. Medication-assisted treatment only prolongs suffering. The path on which I live today includes a spiritual means, meditation, supporting others in recovery, therapy, diet, exercise, healthy relationships, and other forms of care to create my wholeness. MAT is a crutch that can become enabling and crippling to the wellness of being whole, especially to those with addiction.

Is there anything you want those struggling with addiction to know?

You are worth saving. You have value. No matter what you have done and what you tell yourself, you can overcome and heal. There are many of us out there like you. You are not the worst of the worst. Your shame, guilt, remorse, anxiety, depression, suicidal thoughts, and all the other internal torment has a place among us; we are the courageous ones. We do understand you, welcome you, and hope that you too will be so daring to reach out and work toward your vision and journey.

Richard D

Date of interview: 6/8/19
Sobriety date: 3/18/03, 16 years
Hometown: Bridgewater

When did you start drinking or using drugs, and how did it progress?

I was in the seventh grade in Medford, Massachusetts. I stole liquor out of the family cabinet. My friend and I took a little from each of the bottles so my parents wouldn't know. We poured it into a Coke bottle and went out to the truck graveyard in West Medford. We got pretty hammered. We both blacked out and didn't know how we got home.

The next day I felt like crap and drank sporadically after that. I had a taste for it and liked the way it made me think. It would often be on my mind. My drinking progressed when I hung around individuals who drank as I did. There was a distance though. I was a sports guy, and my family told me to stay away from those guys, but I wanted to fit in.

I went to Bridgton Academy in Maine, a college prep school. My father had gone there for football years before. He thought it was a good idea to send me there. It was all men in the woods of Maine. That's where my drinking started to escalate. There wasn't too much trouble at that point, but I began to get obsessed with alcohol. It was weekend parties, fun, and no real consequences. Not until I went to college.

I went to New England College in Henniker, New Hampshire. I lived on campus. We could come and go as we pleased. My parents weren't around, and there were no curfews. Many of my friends dropped out of school at the end of the first semester. They just flunked out of school. Somehow, I was able to maintain myself and get through college, but I had a lot of blackouts.

I was always able to justify my excessive drinking. The night before graduation, we were at a big party at Pat's Peak. When a cop came by the next day at 7:30 a.m., we were still there. He said, "You guys need to go home." Unfortunately, on the way home, a couple of my buddies got killed in a car accident. I started to see the consequences of our drinking, but we just carried on. We drank; that's how we processed our sorrow. It became a tool.

The consequences continued to mount up: protective custody, DWI's, car crashes, destroyed relationships, angry parents, and disgusted employees. I trudged through and justified it all. That dragged on for years. Then it all came to a crashing halt. I was living here in New Hampshire and drinking at a local bar as I always did. I came home one night with a couple of people from a local bar. I blacked out, waved a gun around, and fired it a few times. The SWAT team showed up, and I woke up in Grafton County Jail. I was in a suicide cell in my underwear. I had no idea why. The guy who came to my house that night said I was going to kill myself and maybe kill him. Drinking can make you dangerously insane. It was like rolling the dice with me when I drank. I didn't know what was going to happen. I can't drink in safety.

I woke up in jail on a plastic mattress, toilet paper roll for a pillow, toilet in the middle of the floor, and a camera on the ceiling. It was just crazy. I thought to myself, "What am I doing here?" There was also a stainless-steel polished piece of metal on the wall for a mirror. It had knuckle marks and scratches on it. I remember looking at myself in the mirror, trying to grasp what had happened. It was like looking at a funhouse mirror; my face was distorted. I was horrified. I didn't know how I got there or what happened. I was able to bail myself out with a credit card for $10,000.

Monday morning at the Plymouth Court House, the judge looked around for the Sheriff to bring in the guy who had committed the crime. The judge asked, "Where is the guy?" I said, "I'm right here." I wore a suit and just didn't fit the narrative of who they expected. I couldn't even say anything because I didn't remember anything. I knew it was time to change.

My first AA meeting was in Ashland on a Monday night. I met a great person, Tammy, who was standing at the door. I walked up to her and said, "Is this the AA meeting?" She said, "I don't know; I was going to ask you." It was her first meeting too. I'll never forget hearing: If nothing changes, nothing changes. I felt at home. It was the strangest feeling in the world, and I wanted to go back. That was it. I wanted to change, and I needed to change. Everything is better. I don't feel impending doom anymore. I have less anxiety, and my health is better. My thinking is clear, and I'm available. It's a fascinating transition.

I was laid off during the recession in 2009. This was the catalyst to move me forward. I never looked back. After I left my job, I went to school again and now work in the addiction profession. I don't need anything to enhance, improve, reduce, or manage symptoms of anxiety or stress. I thought I could never do this on my own. I go to meetings, listen to other people's stories, and hear how they stay sober. It just takes time.

You have to be willing to live a different life and do the next right thing. I walk around and say to myself, "Is this the right thing to do?" I had anxiety when I first got sober, so I asked my doctor if I could have something to take the edge off. My doctor said, "Like what?" I said, "Something like Valium." He said, "Rich, you know what you're suffering from? You're suffering from early recovery." And I'm like "What the...?" But it made a lot of sense and having someone say that to me put it into perspective. Some other doctor might have just given me the Valium, and who knows where I might have wound up.

Looking back, when do you think it was mostly out of control?

At the end of my drinking, it was the most out of control.

How are you able to not drink or use daily?

I get up, have some coffee, sit at the table, and reflect. I do a meditation with an insight timer app on my phone. At the end of each day, I do a reflection of what I did that day. If I did something that wasn't right, I take corrective action. I try to keep my side of the street clean. I keep it simple. I still go to meetings, sometimes five a week.

The key for me is vigilance. I need to remember my illness. If I get away from like-minded people in recovery, AA meetings, or my routine, I start to think that maybe I was unduly alarmed about my alcoholism. I might think that perhaps I wasn't that bad or maybe I can drink. I have a built-in forgetter. I'll start romancing the good times drinking and forget about all the bad shit. I might not remember the consequences and begin to think about needing immediate relief, sacrificing the future for the present. If I play the tape of the past all the way through, it's a shit show. That's the whole crux of the problem, forgetting how bad it was.

What is your thought about medication-assisted treatment?

The medication blocks your thought processing. It's a Band-Aid. If somebody's on medically assisted treatment, they're just substituting one drug for another. They're managing feelings and emotions with prescribed medication. They never work on the problem. Addiction is usually a symptom of something else that's going on. The issue never gets addressed. They have to address feelings of unease, restlessness, irritability, discontent, insecurity, fear, anxiety, or whatever. They can do it. There's evidence. I see people with multiple years of sobriety that are doing fine.

MAT may work with someone who chronically relapses. I knew a man who was addicted to heroin and could not stop. Suboxone helped him get off the merry-go-round long enough to get back on his feet. Hopefully, he'll get off it soon. My concern is, what happens five or 10 years down the road? Do we have hundreds of thousands of people on Suboxone in this country? Are people driving around on opiates? What happens if someone taking Suboxone gets delayed at the airport and misses their dose? Are we kicking the can down the road?

Is there anything you want those struggling with addiction to know?

There is a solution. As bad as things might seem and as much as one thinks they might need alcohol or a drug to exist, it is possible to get off the shit. You can unwind and retrain the brain. If you can stay away from it for a while, you can adjust the automatic thought processes.

Robert M.

Date of interview: 5/15/19
Sobriety date: 7/19/15, 3 years
Hometown: Derry

When did you start drinking or using drugs, and how did it progress?

I was 12 when I found a bottle of whiskey in a cabinet. I drank a small glass of it and got pretty drunk. When I took that drink, I remember feeling the world was okay. I became happier than I had ever known. I grew up in a home that wasn't conducive to self-esteem, so I developed sensitive feelings, which I sought to escape with alcohol. I began to drink anytime I could. Sometimes a week or a month would go by, and then I'd go to the cabinet and drink.

I hung out with a group of boys who drank. They'd bring alcohol from their house; we'd mix it all together and called it jungle juice. We'd pass it around, and each of us would take a drink. There was a period where, if alcohol wasn't available, we'd sniff glue. The glue high made us drunk-like for about 15 minutes. At some point, they put an additive in the glue that made it smell horrible. That's when sniffing glue faded out, and the drug phase came in.

I started to experiment with drugs, although alcohol was always my drug of choice. I took LSD, barbiturates, mescaline, and cocaine. My favorite was barbiturates, when I could get them. One night at a party, I bought 50 pills. I don't remember any of it, but the story is that I kept taking the pills and drinking wine, taking the pills, and drinking wine. I fell on the floor, passed out, and was coughing up powder. I woke up in the hospital strapped to a bed. It wasn't a suicide attempt; it was the compulsion to drink or use drugs. I couldn't stop once I started.

That experience shut down my barbiturate use. I was still drinking though. I began to experience terrible blackouts by the age of 16. One day, I woke up in another state and had no idea how I got there. I stayed overnight in jail cells, not knowing why I was there. DWI's followed. I also became very violent when I drank.

In 1975, I detoxed. In detox, I experienced my first AA meeting. I left that detox, went back to work, and started taking Antabuse. Eventually, I drank on them. It wasn't an enjoyable experience. My family thought it was too dangerous for me to keep taking Antabuse and said I should probably stop. I immediately felt relief because I wanted to drink.

I had periods of long-term sobriety. One time, I had a year, and another time six years and then I became active in weightlifting but ruptured a couple of disks in my back. I was six years sober then drank for a day. I was doing great at work and weightlifting. When I got this injury, I felt terrible about myself and was in chronic pain. I thought, "What's the use? I might as well drink," and injured my back even more. I was trying to push myself to do things that I shouldn't. I was sober again for seven years and went through a troublesome divorce, one I did not want. The stress from divorce and chronic pain caused me to drink again. All the while, I was in psychotherapy.

Another time, I ended up going to a concert with a group of people who kept offering me drinks. After refusing them at least eight times, I thought, "I've been sober this long, I could probably have a few drinks and be fine." That was not the case. I don't remember the concert. I do remember opening my eyes and being in a jail cell. I started pounding on the door, asking why I was there, and the officer said, "You were just drunk." I was devastated. How could this possibly happen again? How could my mind be so sick to think I could take one drink?

I don't have thoughts of drinking anymore. I know any of my blackouts could have resulted in death. I don't know why I sit in this chair today. I do know there is something that runs this world. I'm not a religious person, but I believe there is a spiritual force in this world that is available to us. The trick is, we have to make ourselves available to receive it. If we're not available to accept it, and we're not able to grasp that we have a new life, then devastation can happen to any one of us. We have this malady if we pick up that first drink or drug.

Looking back, when do you think it was mostly out of control?

It's amazing I survived my teenage years.

How are you able to not drink or use daily?

I live my life one day at a time and try not to experience regrets from the past, although sometimes they creep in. I do not project myself into the future and I try to be of service to others. I have empathy and compassion for those I serve. I try to put whatever time I have left, at 65 years old, into helping others recognize that they can recover. I get up in the morning, look out my window, and realize there is an entire universe wanting to teach me goodness. I go to AA meetings often and read the *Twenty-Four*

Hours a Day book daily. I read Buddhist spiritual literature and recognize that every single thing that ever happened in my life brought me to this moment. I don't have to take a drink or a drug to quell any physical pain or mental anguish.

What is your thought about medication-assisted treatment?

I haven't had any experience with heroin or other drugs that are popular today. I believe short-term medication may be beneficial within weeks of detox. I don't think anyone should be on any long-term medical treatment to remain abstinent from their drug of choice. They need to try and figure out what their soul is. When medicated, we are not going to get to the bottom of who we are and what our purpose is. It is only by getting to the bottom of ourselves that we can obtain any lasting sobriety. When we put addictive medication into our bodies to change us, it results in a progressive and fatal illness.

Is there anything you want those struggling with addiction to know?

Know love. At a certain point in our lives, we have to self-nurture and stop blaming. We have to realize that we are offered Grace in recovery. It's up to us to till the soil and receive it. Once you receive it, you can't keep it unless you pass it on to the next person. There's not a pill in the world that can do that.

<u>Robert W.</u>

Date of interview: 5/2/2019
Sobriety date: 3/17/10, 9 years
Hometown: Bedford

When did you start drinking or using drugs, and how did it progress?

I was in eighth grade. My friends and I got alcohol from my

parents' liquor cabinet. We were daring and defiant. My parents got divorced when I was young. My mother was an alcoholic at the time, but I don't think I knew it. I knew my parents' marriage broke up for some reason, but I didn't know why. Their divorce is not what I wanted. I thought I came from an ideal situation. I was 10 when they got divorced and noticed I started to care less about things after that. I was mad and didn't have the tools to cope with situations. We didn't have great guidance for dealing with emotions. Our family went from this beautiful little nest to this very different thing.

After my parents broke up, my mother felt more comfortable drinking the way she wanted. We kids got caught in the crossfire of the divorce. I felt uprooted, humiliated, and embarrassed, and now had to go to a different school. I drank to block it all out. I remember thinking, "Well, if I can't count on them, I can't count on anyone." I never let anyone get close to me, looked out for myself, and put walls up.

I was drinking as an anti-establishment statement. This is what kids do, right, rebel? When I was 13, I drank on weekends regularly. When I graduated from high school, I was 17 and turned 18 that summer. My friends and I drank and smoked pot, mostly on weekends. There were times when we drank and smoked marijuana at school too. It all seemed so innocent to me. At 19, I was a challenging kid, and I was drinking and driving. People were trying to get through to me, but I was not receptive.

Eventually, I moved to Vail, Colorado, and got a job at a ski area and worked in sales. I went from making $250 a week in New Hampshire working for my dad to $800 a week in Colorado. Our rent was super low in Colorado, so there was a lot of money left over. Even though I was making good money, I came back to New Hampshire. I went to work for a ski area here as a social director. At 23, I moved back to Vail, Colorado, with a guy I met at the ski area. We found a place living with four other people. I got my job back where I was before and worked hard.

We were day drinking by now, and at the end of the day, we'd smoke pot and drink wine on Vail Mountain. We'd be the last ones down the mountain. I was drinking, smoking pot, and snorting cocaine. I knew I wanted more for myself, and at age 24, I came back to New Hampshire. I took my insurance license exam and passed. In December of 1984, my mother died of cirrhosis of the liver because of her alcoholism. She was only 51 years old. It was an awful thing to go through.

Shortly after that, I met up with a girl in the summer of 1985, who I had previously briefly dated, and we got married. I was still drinking and raising hell. She put her foot down, which was probably a good thing. I went to work and for the next 15 years applied myself. At this time, I was drinking socially, perhaps too much on occasion, but I wouldn't say alcoholically.

In my 40s, I was drinking pretty heavily. I was faithful for the first 18 years of my marriage and then a little less so for the last two. I felt terrible about it but drank more heavily to relieve those feelings. My wife and I separated after 19 years of marriage in 2004. She was trying to push me to get help, but I refused. I hadn't gotten a DUI, which I thank God for now because I had driven drunk hundreds of times, hundreds. As my marriage dissolved, I remember thinking, "I can do what I want now. I'm finally going to have freedom again," which is all nonsense. She eventually said she didn't want to be married anymore and filed the paperwork. Somehow this made me feel as if I were a victim.

In 2005, I was living in my house with a friend who was also bad news. We were drinking and raising hell. It was an awful situation. I started a relationship with a woman, and we rented a house together. I knew I was still drinking too much. There was an instance where I was supposed to pick up her daughter from kindergarten. She called me, and I was passed out.

When I got there, there were no other cars and no other kids, just her and the teacher. The little girl said to me, "Were you taking a nap?" I didn't care if I let myself down or other adults, but this little girl was different. I remember thinking this wasn't okay. I finally agreed I needed to do something, which started me getting better.

In 2006, I went through detox for five days and stayed sober for six months. It was a great beginning for me. I got a keen insight into how insane I was. The rehab taught us about cross-addiction, but I didn't buy into it. I thought I only had a drinking problem, not a drug problem.

I decided to go to AA. I thought this was logical and very well thought out. Someone at the country club I'm a member of asked me if I could still do cocaine, even though I couldn't drink. I said, "Of course I can." I did some, and we played golf. I felt a little more connected after that, but it didn't take long until I developed an obsession with using drugs. It went horrifically downhill after this.

Thankfully I never shot up, but I was in drug dens buying large quantities of cocaine and was a regular user. I was using at least an ounce a week, if not more. I was starting to get strung out, spending tens of thousands of dollars. I never drank again after detox, but my cocaine use went on for two and a half years. In the last few months of it, I was entirely owned by the stuff. All logic was gone; my relationship was deteriorating. I was doing crazy things. I was completely broken and knew I needed to do something.

I had no idea the level of pride and ego that played a role in me trying to get help. I didn't want to go back in for help because I was afraid about what people would think of me. I realize now it takes an incredible amount of courage to get help. I started to go to meetings every day. If someone asks me if I can drink, I say, "Of course I can. I choose not to." I don't want to drink or use anymore. I have been given the gift of sobriety and get to help people recover from this disease.

My mother couldn't get sober. I know she saw what it was doing to her kids, but she couldn't figure out how to stop drinking. I'm sad my mom didn't have the chance to be sober. Because of my experience with her, I get to help families today. I'm a child of an alcoholic and have had counseling to deal with it. My experience is helpful to others. For this, I am grateful.

Looking back, when do you think it was mostly out of control?

Around 43 or 44, it was the most out of control.

How are you able to not drink or use daily?

I go to meetings almost every day. I read literature, and I'm involved in AA. I sponsor people and have a sponsor. I also follow the 12-step program of recovery pretty closely.

What is your thought about medication-assisted treatment?

I'm uncomfortable about it. It helps some, but I've also seen people stay on it for years, and I can't understand this. If you say it is better than using, maybe it's a good idea. I don't know why you can't address why you use, so you don't need to use anything. If there are underlying issues, psychological or emotional, the person should receive counseling. I know a lot of people who have been on medication for a very long time, and it doesn't seem to be the solution.

Is there anything you want those struggling with addiction to

know?

There is hope. Using drugs feels so hopeless. You feel lost and desperate, so you stay in the problem. You don't have to use drugs, and others will help you achieve recovery.

Ronnie O.

Date of interview: 3/24/19
Sobriety date: 8/20/11, 7 years
Hometown: Plymouth

When did you start drinking or using drugs?

At age eight I was on a family camping trip. My oldest sister found whiskey in the freezer and offered me a drink so that I wouldn't tell. I don't remember too much after that. My mother came in and wanted to know what happened, and I ran out of the camper. I blacked out and didn't remember much. I remembered parts of it and didn't drink for a long time after that.

When I was 10, I smoked my first cigarette. My sister gave me a cigarette because she wanted to make sure I didn't rat on her. I continued to smoke off and on. By age 12, I started buying cigarettes for myself. I would tell the store I was buying them for my mom and got hooked on them by age 15. I also started drinking alcohol. I drank at parties and would have beers occasionally alone later on. I began hanging out with people who drank and smoked cigarettes. I smoked pot for the first time. I figured it must be good because everyone else was smoking it. Plymouth had a head shop downtown, and I would purchase marble bowls and started smoking it by myself.

By age 15, I ran away to Colorado with a group of friends. I got my first job working at Jack in the Box and stayed for six months. The people I went with smoked a lot of pot. I returned home and went back to school to graduate. I got my driver's license and attended a lot of parties. I continued to drink, smoke cigarettes, and occasionally smoke weed. I also experimented with acid and cocaine. Heroin was not around then.

When I was 17, a girlfriend used to come by and pick me up. We would snort cocaine, and I did acid for the first time with her. When I was 18, I had a bad trip on acid. I took a whole one and went to a party. I had terrible thoughts and visions. I went home and couldn't fall asleep for hours. At three or four a.m., death came over me, and I woke up. I looked in the mirror and was white as a ghost. I told myself I would never do acid again. However, six months later, I took a quarter hit. That was the last time I used acid. I drank and occasionally used pot. I didn't like marijuana that much. I would go for years without smoking it, and then I would smoke it on occasion.

My drinking progressed. I had to drink more to get the same effect. I got my first DUI at age 21. I moved away, got married, pregnant, and stopped drinking and using. Within a year after my daughter was born, I went back to drinking a couple of times a month. By age 31, I got introduced to people who used cocaine. I'd buy an eight ball, and it would last a week or so. It got to the point where I couldn't afford it, and it was interfering with my work. The supplier moved, and I couldn't get it anymore.

I continued to drink to suppress the feelings of my marriage failing. I had to go into hiding because my husband said he was going to kill himself or me if I left him. He told me I would never see my daughter again unless I went back to him. I moved back to New Hampshire and got a restraining order. During all this, I was drinking to deal with my emotions. He fought for custody, and we went through a three-and-a-half-year divorce. During this time, I got caught for driving under the influence and went to High Point rehab in Plymouth, Massachusetts. I gave up custody to him to stop the fighting, and the court case ended.

I couldn't remain abstinent. At age 37, I went into Friendship House in Bethlehem, New Hampshire. They taught me about Alcoholics Anonymous and hooked me up with a sponsor before I left. The following day, I met my sponsor at a meeting. Without having the support of a sponsor showing me the way, I wouldn't have been able to remain abstinent.

For the next eight years, I went to AA meetings and talked with my sponsor. During this time, I met a man and had two more children with him. He was in the military and went on a couple of tours. At the same time, my sponsor stopped being my sponsor, and I stopped going to AA. When my boyfriend came back from his last tour, I thought it would be okay to have a glass of wine. The next week I had another glass of wine. One thing led to another, and I drank heavily for a couple more years.

In 2011, I went to rehab again for two weeks. This time, I went to Webster Place in Franklin, New Hampshire and got myself back on track. I have been sober ever since.

Looking back, when do you think it was out of control?

There were so many red flags along the way. My father was an alcoholic and I grew up thinking of drinking was a rite of passage to adulthood. I needed to know subconsciously I had a problem. After my divorce was final and the monkey was off my back, all I had left was me and my alcoholism. Now, it had to do with me changing. It took my sponsor, the support of family, building a sober network, and AA to find a new way of life. Things slowly came together.

How are you able to not drink or use daily?

I have the support of family, friends, a sober network, and a relationship with my higher power. I haven't found it necessary to drink or use it since 2011.

What is your thought about medication-assisted treatment?

I am conflicted! When I stopped using, I felt like crap and had difficulty dealing with life on life's terms. I wanted so desperately to feel okay. I sought out help for the emotions I was going through. Doctors thought I had depression/anxiety and prescribed different medications, but nothing helped fix me. Looking back, I just needed time to heal and repair the damage, and there was no quick fix. If I had been offered a prescription to make me feel as if I were still using, I would have taken it and would not be where I am today. I am grateful they didn't have medication to make it all go away. I believe our bodies are resilient and will repair themselves if allowed.

MAT is not allowing individuals to go through the process of repairing themselves. I think it can help get them through the withdrawals and change the behavior from using. However, I do not believe it should be used for long-term treatment and replace the individual's drug of choice.

Is there anything you want those struggling with addiction to know?

There is a way out. Find someone to help you locate your inner strength. Don't listen to your disease telling you, "You can't live without me," because you can! Don't give up until the miracle happens.

<u>**Russell B.**</u>

Date of interview: 4/26/2019
Sobriety date: 7/8/09, 9 years
Hometown: West Ossipee

When did you start drinking or using drugs, and how did it progress?

I was 16 years old, and it was a minimal amount of alcohol. I was on a trip to Scandinavia with the youth orchestra I was playing in and drank one beer. This experience was very profound for me because it washed away all my fears and inhibitions. Up to that point, I had never used drugs or drank alcohol. I was against it because I had an older brother who had addiction issues. When I took that first drink, I decided there was nothing wrong with it. My drinking progressed to drinking on the weekends and went from one to three or four beers.

I started smoking marijuana at the end of high school, and when I went to college, I was drinking and smoking pot every day. It wasn't too excessive and was usually at night. By the time I was 22, it crept into earlier and earlier in the day and led to me skipping class to do it. When I went to graduate school out in Arizona, I couldn't go very long during the day without picking up a substance. I stopped going to classes and stopped taking care of my responsibilities. It wasn't a luxury anymore; it was something I needed to do to get by. When I wasn't drinking or getting high, I felt uncomfortable.

My use escalated to the point where I would wake up in the night and drink. In 2000, I got into AA and managed not to drink, and I stayed sober for six years. I had some excellent recovery during that time but never felt comfortable in my own skin. I was severely depressed and had a lot of anxiety, so I relapsed and started drinking again. At this time, I discovered cocaine, and shortly after that, crack cocaine. Then came IV cocaine and opiate use.

In a short period of time, I fell off the face of the Earth. I was living in Worcester, Massachusetts, and I held up in a cheap hotel room for weeks on end using drugs. My family didn't know where

I was or whether I was dead or alive. After six years of sobriety, it got much worse when I picked up again. I cycled in and out of a few detoxes during the next year and a half.

Finally, in 2008, I ended up in an excellent abstinence-based treatment center in Plymouth, New Hampshire and went to sober living for three months after that. I relapsed in sober living, so I went back to treatment in Plymouth for a couple of weeks. Then I went back to sober living and relapsed again. I had a tough time getting sober the second time around. I got a third chance, and this time something clicked for me and I've been sober ever since.

Reflecting on the difference from the first time I got sober to the time I finally stopped—the first time I did the step work. In the third step, the book talks about surrendering to a higher power, and getting in touch with my ideas about the way I wanted my life to look. The first time I surrendered to a degree but not fully. My family changed after I relapsed a couple of times. They had had it and said they didn't want any contact with me until I had been sober for a significant period. My parents' tough love, coupled with the help and direction of my sponsor, put me in a place where I decided to surrender to this thing called recovery ultimately. I didn't know what my life was going to look like, but I couldn't keep living the way I had been living.

After six months of living at a sober house, I became the house manager, which meant I was the sponsor of every person who came into the house. I got thrown into this cycle of helping people recover. Eventually, I went to graduate school and became a mental health counselor. Helping other people solidified my recovery, and my life went in a different direction.

Looking back, when do you think it was the mostly out of control?

There was out-of-control sober, which I think is essential for me to say because a lot of people think sober means "I'm okay if I don't drink or do drugs." At the end of my first six years of sobriety, I could not even get out of bed in the morning. I couldn't show up for life. I was sober, and my life was out of control.

Then there was out-of-control high and the absolute chaos of being on IV crack cocaine drug benders for weeks. The only thing I did from one moment to the next was try to get more drugs to keep the bender going. Any period of sobriety within that period was so excruciatingly painful.

How are you able to not drink or use daily?

I've done all 12 Steps and have made all possible amends that I can. I continue to practice Steps 10, 11, and 12 and sponsor people. I also try to live an honest life and attend meetings regularly. On top of all of this, I have a yoga practice and eat healthily.

What is your thought about medication-assisted treatment?

I never took methadone or Suboxone. I went into an abstinence-based treatment center, and that's what I know. As a person in recovery and as a clinician, I think it can be dangerous for people. If you try to get off either of these substances, they are equally hard, if not worse, to get off than heroin. Prescribers are telling people they need to be on these medications long-term. I don't think it's a long-term solution.

It worries me how much of a push there is on medication for people in recovery. It feels unnatural to accept something into your body that has an opiate in it, something that alters your state of mind. There are so many people in my clinical practice, and those I sponsor, who have tried it and failed miserably. They used drugs while on it and also sold it.

I think it can be used for harm reduction and for a short period to help stabilize someone. It doesn't provide the type of recovery I've come to know. Medication shouldn't be the first entry into recovery for most people. People need to know they can live a sober and happy life without the use of any substances.

Is there anything you want those struggling with addiction to know?

You absolutely can get sober and have a great life. You don't have to struggle every day, trying to figure out when and how you're going to use drugs. Many people get sober from working the 12 Steps correctly. Big Book step study meetings help with this process.

Ruth C.

Date of interview: 3/20/2019
Sobriety date: 5/15/87, 31 years
Hometown: Laconia

When did you start drinking or using drugs, and how did it progress?

I drank after age 18. This was common at the time. I never used drugs. My son said he knew something was wrong with me when he was only four years old. He's an adult now. He remembers having to stay at a friend's house because Mommy was "sick." That was in 1969 and 1970.

At the end of my drinking, I was taken into protective custody and put in the ICU for two weeks because of the effects it had caused on my body. The nurses said I was a miracle patient. They didn't expect me to make a full recovery and thought I would end up in a nursing home. The drastic effect alcohol had on my life is why I needed total abstinence in my recovery.

Looking back, when do you think it was mostly out of control?

At the end of my drinking, it was the most out of control.

How are you able to not drink or use daily?

Sobriety is a lifestyle. Staying sober is a lot easier now. In the beginning, I sponsored a lot of women, helped with interventions, went to AA meetings, and annual recovery events. As I got older, life changed. My "group" and I still stay in contact, but other things have filled my days.

What is your thought about medication-assisted treatment?

I can only speak about alcohol. There is a drug that causes you to get sick if you drink. I did not want to have anything to do with that or any intoxicants.

Is there anything you want those struggling with addiction to know?

If you are an alcoholic and think you can drink, at some point, it is going to catch up with you. Either your life will fall apart, you will not live the full experience you could be living, or your internal organs and body will probably give out and you will prematurely die. You'll have denial, and you'll incorrectly blame it on something else. Society promotes moderation. If you can take alcohol or leave it once in a while, you might be fine. Otherwise, consider giving abstinence a chance and see how it compares. You might find a whole new world and a much more fulfilling life.

<u>Ryan G.</u>

Date of interview: 4/6/19
Sobriety date: 7/08, 10 years
Hometown: Merrimack

When did you start drinking or using drugs, and how did it progress?

I was 10 years old and stole my parents' alcohol. I don't know where I got the idea of drinking something to change the way I feel. After I started smoking marijuana, it quickly graduated to smoking daily. By the age of 13, I had progressed to drinking three times a week. At age 14, I started experimenting with designer drugs, stimulants, and pills. I'd smoke marijuana daily and binge drink on the weekend.

By age 16, I would travel to music festivals and would be around a bunch of Grateful Dead people, but I would wear a polo shirt. I didn't even like their music at first. I was there for the drugs. By the time I was 17, I was using inhalants three times a week and under the influence seven days a week. I had experienced withdrawal symptoms from alcohol twice by then.

I woke up one morning and was no longer welcome in my parents' house. I glorified living the street life until I woke up one morning with half my face paralyzed. Like a real badass, I called my mom, who is a nurse. She told me to come over and saw the paralysis. She and my dad looked nervous and asked me to stay the night. At 10:00 p.m., it felt as if someone were hitting me in the head with a hammer and my muscles had locked up. I was vomiting and blacked out. The next thing I knew, I woke up in the emergency room.

I got shuttled to Boston Children's because they thought I had a cancerous tumor on my brain. They ran some tests and needed to do an emergency biopsy. The doctor asked if I drank. I said, "Of course not." Then he asked if I did drugs, and I told them, "Absolutely not." They stopped and said, "Look, you must tell us because we need to know for anesthesia. You're going in for a precise surgery, and you'll be awake but not with it. If your body is resistant to any inebriating effects, it can affect the anesthesia." I still didn't tell them about my alcohol and drug use. I felt all of it.

After the surgery, I was put on OxyContin 180s and loved them. I abused them right away. After they stopped prescribing them, I graduated to heroin. One night, I sniffed heroin and combined it with benzodiazepines. I was out cold for 24 hours and woke up in full-blown withdrawal. I couldn't get anything up my nose to relieve the symptoms. I vowed I would never use needles but asked a friend to show me how. At 18 years old, I became an IV heroin addict.

I went to my first treatment that year and proceeded to go to four others. I went to numerous 12-Step meetings but was never motivated to stop. I was arrested multiple times and incarcerated. Addiction is the only illness that tells you, "You don't have a disease." I became a person who didn't even resemble myself. I contracted Hepatitis C and was pretty convinced I had HIV. I was surprised when I found out I didn't. I tested positive for Hepatitis C after two and a half years of sobriety. I was a mess physically and had the early stage of kidney failure. I was dying.

I disappointed everybody in my life, and my family excommunicated me. One night I attempted to take my own life and woke up with my father over me. He told me he knew I had lied and was on the run from my probation officers (PO). I felt a calm surrender, even though I was in a lot of trouble. I walked into my PO's office and turned myself in. He had recently petitioned the court to have my maximum sentence imposed and send me to five years in prison. I told him I was ready to go. He went out back to grab the handcuffs, and another guy came out. It was the court counselor. He said, "Ryan, we've been watching you come in and out of here since you were 17, and you've tried to stop using multiple times. Why don't you give this one last shot?" We walked over to Keystone Hall, and he told me I would go to treatment and then aftercare.

I asked a guy at Keystone for help. This guy demonstrated a fundamental principle of abstinence-based recovery: he showed up for free to help me. He started to read about what was wrong with me. He read the AA literature and explained it to me in a way that made sense. He said I was mentally and bodily sick, and my disconnection from spirituality was causing my restlessness, irritability, and discontentment. This guy told me I was sick, and there was a solution. He said I needed to get well, and I would stop hurting myself and others.

I was in detox for 45 days. My dad drove me to Southeastern New Hampshire Services in Dover and dropped me off. I had two trash bags with all my blood-stained clothes. I was there for 90 days. It was the best program I ever went to for treatment. After rehab, I went to six months of a highly structured halfway house program. I aggressively worked the 12 Steps and had a revolutionary change in my attitude.

My parents showed up for family day and I was shocked. At first, all the families would come, and mine wouldn't. My father taught me a valuable lesson. The amount of pain I had put him and my mom through was causing the separation between him and me. He told the group that this was the seventh or eighth time he'd been to family counseling, and he didn't have high hopes for me, and they shouldn't either. Everybody just shrank. I looked at my father and thought to myself, "I can't believe this is what I did to him." It was a realization. I couldn't believe I had done this to them.

My father and I made amends to each other, sitting on two paint buckets in an apartment he owned. I rattled off the list of stuff I had done to him, and he chuckled and said, "Well, I'm thrilled we just did this again. You know, Ryan, I'll tell you what sucked. When I went out on a Sunday morning to get the paper, you were sleeping in my basement like a bum, and you had been arrested two nights before. Your face was on the front page as the Heroin Kingpin of New Hampshire. I look up, and all my neighbors are looking at me because they're looking at the same article—that hurt. Secondly, I laid next to my wife and watched her get physically ill, to the point where I didn't even know if she was going to make it. You forced me to do that night after night. I had to lay there and try to console her. That hurt too. Lastly, you know what hurts? You stole the only option I ever had for having a relationship with my youngest son. You're never going to give me that back. You can't heal time." I said, "How do we get the books to balance? Can we ever do that?" He then said, "Your mother has more hope now than she ever has. If you cannot use for a consistent period, we can at least get neutral. We're not good, but we're not bad."

My dad called me the day after my fifth sober anniversary and said, "I'm so sorry. I forgot about your anniversary." I said, "It's just one day." He got angry and said, "It's not just a day. It was the most important day that's ever happened in our family. I told you that you could never make this right. I need you to know that I forgave you a long time ago. I've never been prouder of any of my kids than I am of you." I always wanted to connect with my father and never could, because I'd get in the way. I finally removed everything between us through the recovery.

I have a child now, and my parents are crazy over him. They help us with him. Watching my dad connect with my son on a level that we were always trying to communicate on is something. This experience is what abstinence and recovery gave me.

Looking back, when do you think it was mostly out of control?

When I was 26, I'd been shooting up for a long time. My negative behavior and circumstances in my life progressed. The illness is progressive, and what I had to do to keep using escalated. What was not okay yesterday all of a sudden became okay. You couldn't lower the bar any lower than it got for me.

How are you able to not drink or use daily?

I have a daily meditation habit and participate in 12-step recovery. I work on my health and fitness regularly and have a certification in ancestral health with Paleolithic Diets. These practices have a positive effect on my body and mind. I feel connected spiritually and exercise in my free time. I hike the White Mountains, travel, and try to be a decent human being. I try to remain on the path of what's right and not get lost in external things. I focus on the internal stuff.

What is your thought about medication-assisted treatment?

If someone doesn't want to be abstinent, but they also don't want to do fentanyl, a MAT program may be suitable. If you don't treat the underlying condition, they're going to continue to behave the way addicts do. The right abstinence provider is equally appropriate. Prescribing things to people in a blanket manner is crazy. If somebody says MAT is all they're willing to do, that's all they're willing to do. That's better than somebody being dead.

Telling somebody you're going to be on medication-assisted treatment for the rest of your life or this is as good as it gets isn't true. Your whole limbic system is never able to heal or respond appropriately while being dosed daily with Suboxone. The actual healing process, just from a physical standpoint, doesn't take place until you remove the outside substances from the brain.

Is there anything you want those struggling with addiction to know?

Start by admitting there's a problem and seek help. There is help available for people regardless of resources.

Sandy H.

Date of interview: 4/15/19
Sobriety date: 1/20/88, 31 years
Hometown: Plymouth

When did you start drinking or using drugs, and how did it progress?

I was 18 years old. I got married to a man who liked to drink. He drank, went out, and had fun. That's when I started to drink. Before that, I never drank in any consistent way. My marriage was not very good; he would beat me. It was a struggle. I came from a home of abuse. The apple doesn't fall too far from the tree. He abused me the same way my family had. When he and I worked, I'd come home and sneak drinks. I would make vodka and orange juice or rum and Coke—a lot of sweet, heavy beverages. I used to love Golden Dreams, Grasshoppers, and Sombreros. Then I would replace the alcohol in the bottle with water so that he wouldn't know I had taken some.

I got pregnant shortly after marrying him, and then another child, and another. My husband had many severe seizures from drinking, where he would go wild like an animal. It was a tough life; I wanted to keep my family together, so I went through a lot. I would drink when he wasn't around and when my kids were sleeping. He'd have these wild seizures, and he'd leave for two or three days. He would become another person during his seizures. Drinking was my out and I loved it. I also loved to smoke cigarettes. I loved to have a cigarette in my hand and loved to eat. All my emotions went into my addictions. I'm a food addict, alcoholic, and drug addict.

When I weighed 230 pounds, I went to my doctor. He prescribed me black beauties to lose weight. These pills were all the rage back in my day. I'd start on one tablet a day and did that for a week. Then I went to two pills a day. Soon after that, I'd take one in the morning, one in the afternoon, and one at night. Then I'd take them all day, half of one here, half of one there. I'd come home from work wired, clean house, put the kids to bed, and drink. I thought my role in life was to be with this crazy man. He would go out and do this and that, then come home and find a piece of dirt on the floor and beat the hell out of me for it. It was a lot for a woman with four children to go through. I was determined to stay with this man and did it by using drugs, black beauties, alcohol, and food.

At one point, I had three different prescriptions from three different drug stores. This drug use went on for 30 years. I was drinking maybe three times a week and taking black beauties. I was in a lot of pain, and I tried to hide it. I tried to be everything to everybody. I'd do anything you wanted. I'd take care of you, but I never took care of myself.

My husband died during a violent seizure while threatening to kill me and everybody in the house. Just like that, he died. I didn't know who I was or what I wanted to be. For six months, I just drank and ate and drank and ate, and worked. One morning I washed my face and looked in the mirror and said to myself, "Who are you?" I didn't know what my name was or what my favorite color was. I didn't know what I wanted to be when I grew up. I didn't know anything about this person in the mirror.

Someone I knew heard about this program called Overeaters Anonymous (OA). She said they have this program that people go to and lose weight. I had not thought of alcoholism. I needed to lose weight. I walked into an OA program in Norward, Massachusetts, and surer than hell, there was this banner hanging down that had the 12 Steps on it. I looked around, and we were the fattest people in there. People remember me too; my hair was all scraggly.

I heard someone speak. She did the things I did; she would sneak food and sit with a whole gallon of ice cream and eat it. They mentioned addiction. I never knew what addiction was before this. The woman who spoke said her name, and she was an addict, and this is why she ate the way she did. They talked about God and a higher power. They said to go to at least two meetings. I came home and went through the cabinets and cleaned them out. I got a sponsor who was 10 years younger than me. She told me to call her every day and get down on my knees every day and ask God to give me strength. I called her every day. She brought God into my life.

I ask God every day to guide and help me through the day to stay abstinent. My whole life has changed. I have no fear anymore. The only thing that keeps me strong is my meetings and my Lord Jesus Christ. He picked me up into the light. I found Him in the 12-step program of recovery.

Looking back, when do you think it was mostly out of control?

The whole 30 years during my marriage, it was out of control. My husband would go out and drink all night, and I would drink at home. I'd sometimes put my kids to bed unwashed. I was all screwed up. I didn't know what I didn't know.

How are you able to not drink or use daily?

I pray daily and take God with me everywhere. I struggle more with food than alcohol. You have to eat food. You don't have to drink alcohol. I gave up sugar and flour. I don't physically get to meetings as much anymore. I have a couple of people I sponsor, and we do the steps together. I'm very involved with the steps and the Big Book. I think everybody could use the 12-step program.

What is your thought about medication-assisted treatment?

Being an addict, I only take a vitamin pill. I have a heart condition, and they wanted to put me on medicine; I said, "No." They tried to put me on blood pressure medication; I said, "No." I asked if I had to be on it, and he said, "No." When I came back to him a month later, my blood pressure was lower. I could have been on the medication for a year. The day you tell me I have to or I'm going to die, I'll take medicine. If you're telling me to try a pill, I don't think so. I'm not an advocate for anyone who's addicted. You need to do it yourself, and with God's help, you can. You only have to do it one day, just today. Anybody can do it for one day. There are many stories where people stopped doing drugs or alcohol. They struggled but were able to stop drinking or using.

Is there anything you want those struggling with addiction to know?

There is hope and a place to go. There is a 12-step program of recovery, and it's only an hour a day. The most crucial factor is that God will help you. He's with you 24 hours a day. Nothing tastes, smells, or drinks as good as abstinence feels. Hang in there, wait, wait, and watch the miracles happen.

<u>Shelley R.</u>

Date of interview: 3/22/19
Sobriety date: 10/25/89, 29 years
Hometown: Holderness

When did you start drinking or using drugs, and how did it progress?

Age 13. I tried marijuana first, and then I got into my stepfather's wine cellar. I just needed to get rid of the feelings I was feeling. I suffered from PTSD after a traumatic event in my life. I was present when my father ran over a six-month-old baby. After this, his alcoholism escalated, and he got into a car accident. He went into a coma for 18 months and eventually died. From age 16 to 18 were my worst years.

I went to a boarding high school in Rhode Island and was very depressed. I then lived in Spain for a year when I was 17 because I was about to get kicked out of high school. In Spain, I found LSD, hash, and alcohol. During this time, I had suicidal thoughts. I was living in a city and was leaving my dorm at night to walk down to a bar. When I came back to Rhode Island for my junior year, I got involved in risky behavior. One time I was in a blackout and woke up with a man on top of me. I was 17, and he was a 20-year-old thug. He raped me.

When I went to a college in Oregon, I got on a ski team and began training. All of a sudden, there was a lot more structure. One night at a party, we had access to alcohol, cocaine, and LSD. I was found face down in the mud that night. I could have died. My junior year of college, I went to Spain again. I hooked up with some blue-collar workers who were anti-American. They felt their culture was invaded by multiculturism. I slept with a Spanish guy right before I left and got pregnant. Shortly after that, I had an abortion and was feeling very depressed, so I decided to go to a counselor.

After I graduated from Boston University, I moved to Aspen, Colorado. I had to look at what I was good at, skiing and partying. I got a job as a nanny, which was short-lived. They left, and I stayed at their condo complex. I got shit-faced one night, took the keys to their condo, trashed it, and convinced them not to press charges.

I moved into a one-bedroom apartment with three other people. I was no longer able to keep food down. I would eat lunch and 10 minutes later have to throw it up. I then got a college-educated boyfriend, and we ended up living together. He was my first love. He was from Brooklyn, New York, and a hard worker. That kept me on the straight and narrow for a little bit, but then he dumped me.

Then a woman from Colorado wanted to start a bakery with me in Connecticut. I accepted the offer and we worked 14 to 16-hour days, at least six days a week. One time I made six wedding cakes in one day, it was overwhelming. I switched addictions from alcohol to work. My ex-boss, a raging alcoholic and my ex-boyfriend, came to Connecticut and managed the business for us. We got married and bought a home together.

My hangovers were lasting two to three days long and I started craving alcohol in the morning. I was always an athlete, and my body didn't like what I was doing to it. I eventually moved out of our home and went to therapy. The counselor asked me the 20 questions to determine if I was an alcoholic and told me to go to Alcoholics Anonymous.

I got dressed up as if I were going to church and went to my first AA meeting. It was a bunch of people from New York. One guy stood up to speak who had been to Ryker's Island. I identified with his story because he was talking about feelings. It hooked me. I started to go to a lot of meetings at this club. I found a bunch of girlfriends; we went to sober dances, and I liked it.

I went to Boston for law school and was dedicated entirely to therapy for my PTSD, which I experienced as a result of the incident with my father.

Looking back, when do you think it was mostly out of control?

It was between the ages of 16 and 26.

How are you able to not drink or use daily?

I'm outside every day walking with my dog. I meditate, do yoga, and talk to my friends. I also speak with my God.

What is your thought about medication-assisted treatment?

I think it's useful for some people. I worked in a methadone clinic, and there are varying degrees of recovery. Some people just need not to feel or not overdose. I don't have an opinion on long-term treatment. I was on an anti-depressant for my first 10 years of sobriety. Even in sobriety, I made poor choices for my emotional health, and medication assisted me.

Is there anything you want those struggling with addiction to know?

It's hard work, but it's so worth it. We are all different, and we are entirely unique. Whatever works for you, do that.

Steve I.

Date of interview: 6/4/19
Sobriety date: 1/14/04, 15 years
Hometown: Loudon

When did you start drinking or using drugs, and how did it progress?

Age 18. I grew up in a small town and had a great childhood. I had everything I could ask for growing up. My father bought a few businesses and was expanding. He owned parts of, or entirely, five different companies. I never realized we were well off because he wore work clothes all the time. All my friend's families wore suits. We had an inground pool and a camp on Winnipesaukee, but inside I just felt less than others.

I had two older brothers and a younger sister and brother. My sister passed away when she was 19 of a brain aneurysm; that was a bit rough. There was very little alcohol in the house, except on special occasions. I saw my father drunk once or twice while growing up. I never touched alcohol until I was 18. When I was a senior in high school, the drinking age was 18. It was legal for me to buy booze, but I didn't. Sports were important to me. I was the captain of the track team and ran track in the spring. I didn't drink in high school at all.

I went to college at Southern New Hampshire University for accounting. I was always good with numbers. In my first year of college, I drank quite a bit and decided college was not my thing. I left after the first year. My father paid for it all and wanted me to return the money to him by working in his office. By the time I was 20, I was running the office. I did payroll, accounts receivable, and accounts payable. I thought it was great. I had power and enjoyed it.

Then I started going up to our camp on Winnipesaukee and met some girls. At our camp is when the partying really started. I had my first blackout at a girl's house. I was drinking 151 rum and Coke and ended up in a blackout. I woke up the next morning and didn't know where I was or what was going on. The drinking calmed down after that. I'd only drink on weekends. I also had a progression with dating girls. I would date a girl, use her for a while, and when things got too serious, I left.

I met my wife on a blind date. I'd just broken up with a girl, and she'd just broken up with a guy. We went on a date and hit it off right away. We drank and partied the same. Three months after we met, we were out partying at a club, and the next morning I called her up and said, "Did I ask you what I think I asked you?" She said, "Yup." Then I asked, "Did you say what I think you said?" She said, "Yup," and we were engaged. Nine months later, we were married and are still married.

We had a five-year plan. We would party for five years and then settle down and have a family. Three months after we were married, she was pregnant. That was the end of the five-year plan. We had our daughter while we were both working full-time. Life was good. We were living in an apartment in Concord and ended up building a house in Loudon. There were no real jackpots yet.

We ended up buying a campground from my father. We started running the campground and were building it up. The campground got bigger and more stressful, but we weren't drinking, because we had a business. Even in the winter, we didn't drink much because we were raising our two daughters. Then we started to drink during business hours. She progressed quite a bit, and in 1998, she went to rehab. After she got out of rehab, we decided to drink in moderation. A year later, she was in another program. She couldn't help run the business. I didn't have the capability of running it without her, so we sold the campground. I could drink now because I didn't have to work. She was always at meetings and I drank daily. My wife was going to meetings and I was going downhill quickly.

One morning, I woke up and saw my daughter looking in my bedroom. She had a look of disgust. I laid there and tried to put myself together for work and thought, "What the hell happened to me?" I told my wife I thought I needed to go to AA and went on a Friday night in Concord. I went to that meeting every Friday. I never opened a book and compared myself to everybody. I thought I hadn't done that, or that, or that. I never got a DWI, lost anything, and I'd done well for myself financially. I gave myself six months, then gave up the ship. I didn't need AA anymore. I had it under control, and I was all better.

A week later, I decided to see how good I was. I bought a pint of rum, and it lasted a week, so I went to the liquor store and bought a fifth. That lasted a couple of weeks. I thought I was okay and bought another fifth, and it lasted another couple of weeks. Then I bought a half gallon. That lasted a couple of weeks, and the next one lasted a week. Then I bought two half-gallons and a fifth of brandy, and the progression was right there.

Six months later, I was lying in bed, trying to gather myself together, and I look up, and there was my daughter again. She had that same look of disgust. I was drinking when I didn't want to drink. Realizing I didn't have control of my drinking was when I knew I had a problem. I started going to two to three meetings a week.

I met a guy in AA, who played golf on Sunday mornings. I like golf. I was told to show up at 6:30 Sunday morning to play golf with a group of guys in recovery. Playing golf with people in recovery was the hook that kept me in recovery. It showed me that I could have fun. I wanted to play golf with these guys. I asked one of the guys to be my sponsor. A year later, I went through an AWOL, an intense 12-step study, with him. I got into the steps and started realizing why I was drinking. I got beyond the compulsion to drink. It was lifted right off me.

I started understanding who I am and made amends to my daughters. We have a great relationship now and they both live in the same town as we do. I have six grandchildren, and they've never seen me drink. Life is perfect. I couldn't ask for anything more. I can't say that I'll never drink again. I don't want to think that far ahead. I don't want to drink right now and won't today. It's just not part of my life.

Looking back, when do you think it was mostly out of control?

I was in AA and went back out. I thought I was cured and could drink. That's when I hit my bottom. I learned not to compare myself with anybody else. Others may have done things I haven't done but that only means I haven't done them yet.

How are you able to not drink or use daily?

My wife's in the program, so we talk. I read the AA *Daily Reflections* every day. I have a Big Book on my Kindle and read the Big Book once in a while. I pray, but I've never really gotten into a habit of doing it every day. I associate with a lot of people in long-term recovery in AA.

What is your thought about medication-assisted treatment?

If you're weaning off methadone, it's got to be a four to six-week process, not years. Not for the rest of your life. That's just another crutch—just another addiction.

When I was sober for three or four years, the doctor gave me 45 Percocets after surgery. I'd been in a few car accidents and had a lot of aches and pains, nagging injuries. I was playing in a golf tournament and decided to take one. Oh my God, I felt great, no pain at all, nothing. I played well and won the competition without pain. I had never played golf without pain. I went home, took the pills, and dumped them down the toilet. I said to myself, "Anything that can make me feel that good, I wouldn't be able to control." It made me feel too good. I just got rid of them. I knew I couldn't handle having them around.

Is there anything you want those struggling with addiction to know?

You're not alone. This disease affects everybody. You have not done anything that anybody else in the program hasn't already done. You haven't been anywhere that somebody else hasn't been. We're everywhere.

<u>Susan B.</u>

Date of interview: 4/15/19
Sobriety date: 8/10/83, 35 years
Hometown: Silver Lake

When did you start drinking or using drugs, and how did it progress?

I was three years old. My father left his beer on the floor, and my sister and I would drink it. We loved it. When I was in high school, I tried other alcohol, like gin. I never drank an average amount. One time, I was walking home from a friend's house after drinking, threw up, and wet my pants. This was my first drunk experience. I thought this was how it was supposed to be. I would smoke weed once a week and did some LSD. Occasionally, I'd have rum and Coke at a school dance.

I became a full-blown alcoholic when I was 22. I got married at 18, and a year later was pregnant and nursing. After I got divorced, there was no stopping me. At 23, the drugs went away a little bit. However, I used Valium to get over the shakes and hangovers. I got a prescription, my mother had a prescription, and our two neighbors had prescriptions. Between all of us, we kept ourselves supplied. My brother-in-law introduced me to Dilaudid and heroin, so I became addicted to these as well.

Now and again, I would have an overdose from Valium and alcohol. I remember the overdoses because of the violent throwing up. Eventually, I weaned myself off them and got pregnant again. After having my second baby, I had my wisdom teeth out and was prescribed opiates. I had a significant tolerance to opiates. The pills they gave me were not doing enough, so the more pills and booze I could have, the better I was. At this point, I was 26 and just a mess. By the time I was 28, my third child was born. I just went to town for about a year. I couldn't stop drinking and using pills. That scared me to pieces. It was the worst feeling because I'd always been able to stop before.

I told my sister that I thought we should all go to AA. My mother did an intervention at a center in Acton, Massachusetts. There was a guy who asked who wanted to go to rehab, and I raised my hand. I had the insurance to cover it, but no one to watch my kids for 30 days. My family knew I was a mess and in need of help, but they could not step up at the time. I went to AA and was able to hear certain things, but I still couldn't stop drinking. At this point, I was still in denial about the withdrawals and felt hopeless.

My second husband got a job right near Beech Hill Rehab. I went up there all the time to meetings. I wasn't an inpatient, but I was at meetings three times a week. I had access to all the people who worked there. It was almost as if I were in rehab. I ended up getting a sponsor, and the first thing she taught me was how to meditate. I did it for 30 minutes while she watched my kids, and I've been doing it ever since. It never occurred to me that I would be on a spiritual journey. I couldn't even imagine it possible. I gained all of this by going to AA and becoming sober.

Looking back, when do you think it was mostly out of control?

When I was 27, I couldn't stop. I would drink or do anything you put in front of me and didn't care. There was no awareness of caring about consequences or what I was doing to myself physically, spiritually, or emotionally.

How are you able to not drink or use daily?

I pray a lot, meditate, and remain grateful. A grateful addict or alcoholic will not touch a drink. I learned to be grateful for whatever I have.

What is your thought about medication-assisted treatment?

I'm torn because I've known people where medication-assisted treatment helped in the short term. I also know you can recover without it. What I see happening is they get Suboxone and take it with a bunch of other prescriptions. There's got to be a point where people understand that a pill or chemical is not the answer to a spiritual hole. It's not going to fill you. It's just going to maintain you, almost as if you're in limbo.

Is there anything you want those struggling with addiction to know?

No matter how you feel, if you ask for help, you'll get help. You can get help from the God of your understanding and from people who are also on the recovery journey.

There is nothing in a chemical anymore for us. If you can hang in there and believe that no matter how uncomfortable you are, peace and serenity can be yours. Ask for help. You deserve it, even if you don't think you do.

<u>Taylor B.</u>

Date of interview: 5/1/2019
Sobriety date: 11/29/16, 2 years
Hometown: Wolfeboro

When did you start drinking or using drugs, and how did it progress?

When I was 13, I drank and smoked weed. I took a bottle of Malibu Rum out of my mom's liquor cabinet and drank it with my friends. I got so drunk and hated it. I threw up and got the spins. After that, I couldn't wait to do it again. My mom wasn't around much, so I was forced to grow up fast. She worked two jobs, 60 hours a week. On the weekends, she would be out with her friends, and would throw house parties.

In eighth grade, I was dating a guy who was two years older and a drug dealer. By the time I was in high school, I was a daily drinker. I'd drink before or after school; it didn't matter. I didn't do high school social events unless I was drunk or high. I couldn't do anything sober because I was so uncomfortable with myself. I've always had a sense of not belonging. Not feeling like I belong may stem from being sexually molested for the more significant part of my adolescent years. I didn't come clean about it until I was 14 and told one of my best friends and then finally my mom. I struggled a lot because of this. I acted out in many ways, sleeping with men, cheating on my boyfriend, and seeking validation.

Freshman year, I smoked weed and drank alcohol. Sophomore year, drugs came into the picture. When I found Ecstasy, I was in love. High school was a blur. In my junior year in North Carolina, I got introduced to Xanax. I was blacking out from taking Xanax and drinking alcohol. I don't remember most of my time there. We moved home in my senior year, and I was in love with a guy who was five years older than I was. It was my best friend's older brother. The summer before senior year, I took a step back from the party scene because I was driving up to Concord every weekend to see him. We told his sister, and even after she said she was okay with it, he decided he couldn't be with me because of the age difference. We broke up, and I was a mess.

I was seeking outside validation from drugs, men, and even women. I was so depressed. I was going to college parties on the weekends as a senior in high school, and people were talking about Percocet and other opiates. After a couple of months, I tried Percocet. I hated it at first. One of my best friends told me I took too much, so I tried half of one, loved it, and got hooked. I convinced myself it was just a weekend thing and I wouldn't do it during school, and I didn't.

After I graduated from high school, my best friend's brother and I got back together briefly. I was so happy, but by the end of the summer, he told me he was in love with someone else and broke up with me. I have never been so heartbroken in my life. I left there and went to my friend's house, and we did Percocet all night. The next day, my friend had a bag of heroin. He convinced me Percocet was legal heroin. He told me heroin was cheaper and stronger. Eventually, I got drunk, and the fear of doing heroin left me, so I did my first line. It turned into a three-year run. Heroin did for me what I couldn't do for myself. It gave me a sense of love and security. It was welcoming, enjoyable, and exciting at first.

I went to college at Johnson & Wales in Providence and experienced withdrawals for the first time. I detoxed myself at school, and it was miserable. Right before my sophomore year, I moved home and got together with an ex who was selling dope. When I went back to school, I didn't even make it to Thanksgiving break before breaking down. I told my mom I had a problem and was doing opiates. She picked me up, detoxed me at home, drug tested me once a week, and told me I needed to get a job since I had just dropped out of college. I thought drugs were my problem; I never thought I was the problem. I would go to a bar, drink, and order shots. I was substituting dope with alcohol, and was also addicted to Suboxone, justifying it by telling myself that Suboxone was better than heroin.

I was drinking like a fish and substituting alcohol for drugs. Then I was introduced to crack and meth. I overdosed for the first time and was left in a cold shower, probably to die. No one I was with called 911. I totaled my car, got an insurance settlement, and used that money to get drugs. I was scheduled to go to NHTI and didn't go to classes. I enrolled to get a student loan check and got it. I was living in a crack house, taking Xanax, and snorting dope every day. I was dying. One day, I ran into a friend who didn't even recognize me. She reached out to my mom and told her I didn't look well and should go to treatment. My mom tricked me into coming home and brought me to my first treatment center, Phoenix House, in Keene. I learned so much about myself, and how addiction is an everything problem, not just a heroin problem. I am an addict and an alcoholic.

After treatment, I went to a sober house in Portland, Maine. I thought the people there were in far worse shape than I was; they did things I had never done. Eventually, I got kicked out of there for talking to men and moved into a less restrictive house down the street. I didn't have any accountability. I didn't have to do step work or go to meetings. I picked up my 90-day chip, came home to the girls at the sober house, and told them I wanted to shoot up. I told them I couldn't be done using until I tried it. One of the girls shot me up with cocaine for the first time, and I loved it. I tricked my ex-boyfriend into helping me shoot up heroin for the first time as well. The next three months were terrible. I overdosed six times and lived in a bedbug-infested apartment. It was the lowest I've ever been, physically, emotionally, and spiritually. I hit a whole new bottom.

I thought I could never be normal again. The next day my mom called and asked me to come home and go to treatment. I went back, detoxed myself, and used drugs with my ex-boyfriend for another week. We decided we couldn't detox on our own and went to a detox center together. Three days after being there, my ex-boyfriend packed his stuff and told me we were leaving. The nurse cried and gave me Narcan kits as she tried to get me to stay.

We moved to Waltham, Massachusetts, and I overdosed three times in one week. My ex-boyfriend had to use Narcan on me three times. Finally, he told me he couldn't get high with me anymore because I was going to kill myself. For him to say that to me, I realized things were terrible. I called my mom, went home, and told her I had been shooting up for months. The devastation in her eyes broke me. I believed wholeheartedly I wouldn't use anymore.

The next morning, she went to work, and I was so dope sick. I was texting everyone, and finally, my drug dealer answered. He came and got me high. I did a line and didn't even remember doing it. The next thing I knew, I woke up on the floor; there were EMTs and cops swarming around me. I had a drill in my bone marrow on my shoulder. I tried to sit up, and they were pumping me with Narcan. I was blue. The EMT told me I was gone for 11 minutes and they didn't think they would be able to revive me. The drill was the last option. I was emotional in the hospital and couldn't stop crying. I couldn't comprehend what had just happened.

It was a miracle I didn't have brain or nerve damage after being gone for so long. If it weren't for the drill being new and the EMTs having it on hand, I wouldn't be here today. They tried Narcan to revive me four times. Being so close to death was the scare I needed. When I got out of the hospital, I was reborn. I woke up a different person, got a Vivitrol shot, and went to meetings. I took all the suggestions and found my crowd of people in AA. I think there's more long-term recovery in AA.

Eventually, I met my current boyfriend, and we now have a child and a dog together. My son is my world. I have the most supportive and loving group of people in my life today. The opportunities that have come my way since I've been sober are just insane. I would have never pictured my life ending up as well as it has now. It will always get better. My life today is seriously a blessing. I can't even describe how grateful I am today.

Looking back, when do you think it was mostly out of control?

It was the most out of control in the end when I started shooting up.

How are you able to not drink or use daily?

I use prayer, meditation, my network, my community, and my son.

My son is a huge motivator not to use. I also have a love for myself. I've learned that if I love myself, then I'm not going to hurt myself.

What is your thought about medication-assisted treatment?

I was against it at first but being in the program this long and seeing firsthand what it can do for some people who use it correctly, instead of staying on it for years, has made me believe it can work. I don't think people should be on Suboxone or methadone for more than a year. It's not necessary.

Is there anything you want those struggling with addiction to know?

It gets better. No matter how dark it seems, there is always light.

Thomas E.

Date of interview: 5/16/19
Sobriety date: 1/6/10, 9 years
Hometown: Laconia

When did you start drinking or using drugs, and how did it progress?

I was in high school and 15 years old. Everyone was smoking reefer and I wanted to try it. I couldn't even tell you why. It was the '60s, sunglasses, berets, and poetry. It's what beatniks did, so I tried it. I didn't smoke cigarettes or drink. I got as high as a rocket, got off right away. That's been the blessing and the curse of my drug use. I got off on everything I did, which is why I did it and did it again. It wasn't every day, because I couldn't get it every day. I wasn't much of a party guy anyway. I was just this sweet little church kid. My mother would tell you, if she were still alive, I was a wonderful boy until I went to college.

College was the start of my secret life. When I'd go to parties, I'd find an empty beer can and walk around with it all night, so everyone thought I was drinking. I could blend in. The world opened up in college, traditional drugs, and things like dipping Pall-Mall cigarettes in paregoric and then smoking them.

I started drinking my freshman year in college and smoking reefer whenever I could. By my junior year, I snorted heroin and loved it. The best high I've ever had. I also knew that anything I enjoyed this much was potentially dangerous. Then it was cocaine, and then all the hallucinogens. I was doing acid and peyote. I'd fast for three days, go into the wilderness, do peyote for three days, and try to see the holy man.

The '80s gave me cocaine, which was God's way of telling me I had too much money. I was still doing heroin and had friends who could get anything. They could get you toasted on a pantry full of drugs on any given night. I relied on heroin. I was diagnosed with severe arthritis when I was 21, so I've been on anti-inflammatory medication my entire adult life. I had a doctor for 33 years who started prescribing opioids for the pain because it was the best pain relief.

I began with Percodan, which was Oxycodone mixed with aspirin. Then Percocet came out, which was Oxycodone combined with acetaminophen. I told my doctor it wasn't touching my arthritis pain. He then gave me steroid injections in my lower back. I tried other regimens to keep my thoughts away from just the pain medication. Back then, they just said give him more, give him more, until I fell to the floor. When I was on OxyContin, that was it. It allowed me to do heroin. Depending on how much I picked up and how often my ex-wife was going to horse shows and taking the kids, I'd be home on a three-day run. In the beginning, I didn't shoot up; I smoked and snorted everything. I did speedballs, cocaine, heroin, and started buying bundles in New York. I knew I had way too much heroin around. I could use it or not use it.

I stopped drinking for 19 years when I was in my clinical practice. I'd do a Tommy two-week test. Anything I enjoyed, I'd stop for two weeks to see if I had an issue physically or mentally, and if there was, I didn't do it again. Heroin was still around, but I managed it. I was just so two-faced and dishonest.

I had this whole other life. I had two other wives; the first I spent three years with, the second was a year, and she was 10 years younger. The last one was a keeper. We'd get high together but not on heroin. She didn't know I was doing heroin. I had five kids, all with the same person, only two were birth children. Three we adopted. My two oldest boys were brothers; we adopted them first. It was a huge job making sure no one found out I was using dope.

One night, I was at a business meeting where I was speaking. I went into the bar before the meeting. The guy I was with ordered a Grey Goose on the rocks with a twist, and he turned to me and said, "Tom, what are you going to have?" And I just said, "I'll have the same." It was my first drink in 19 years. Those 19 years I was using heroin, I didn't need to drink. It just got in the way. The next thing you know, I'm drinking handles of cheap vodka.

The moment of clarity came while I was meditating. A woman I was trying to help said some glorious things about the help I provided her. I heard the same kind of thing from other people and always was an empath, always wanted to help. Part of my practice is compassion. It is the essence of Buddhism. What I realized is if people say this and I'm high half the time, what would it be like if I devoted all my attention to clarity? I could use my time to benefit all sorts of pains. That's when I started my recovery. I never did heroin again. I weaned myself off opioids. I stopped drinking or doing all other drugs.

My Buddhism practice is strong. It allowed me to survive the death of one of my grandchildren, my son a year ago, and my parents. I've had significant moments of witnessing death in the streets and car accidents as a medic, but my practice has always been there for me. It centers me and allows my heart a chance to grieve. I'm human and I can be me.

Looking back, when do you think it was mostly out of control?

When I first started doing heroin until 2009, when I stopped. I lost my soul because I had two lives. In Buddhism, we call it duality. It's not serenity at all.

How are you able to not drink or use daily?

I meditate for two hours a day. I'm a monk. I've committed to 227 vows: I'm not supposed to sleep in a high bed, show you my knees, have tattoos, or wear cologne. I'm not a secret dope fiend anymore. I don't have to worry about what I say, covering my tracks, or letting anybody see my phone. I moved into the Riverbank House in July and I'm available for the Riverbank House community. I told all my children and my friends as much as they wanted to know about my past. I go to a lot of Heroin Anonymous and Young People's Meetings. I don't go to meetings because I'm afraid I'll relapse. Relapse does not have a place in my life. I go because while I'm here talking with you, my addiction is in the other room doing push-ups. It's just waiting for a moment to step in.

What is your thought about medication-assisted treatment?

I'm an abstinence-based guy. MAT is a bridge and may be useful to some. Nobody is saying no anymore. Harm reduction is harm. You're still using.

Is there anything you want those struggling with addiction to

know?

There is hope. When it seems hopeless, look in the mirror. You're still alive; you still have a family, no matter what's happened. There's an opportunity for you to care, be kind to yourself and to be truly awake. Recovery programs have helped millions of people; they're free and available everywhere. Smart recovery is also possible.

Thoreau said, "Every man has to carry his hide to the tanner." There are a lot of people to help you on your journey. People will walk alongside you, but you have to make the journey. They walk alongside you as spiritual friends, but you'll have to set the pace.

Recovery is inside your heart's center.

Tom G.

Date of interview: 5/14/19
Sobriety date: 5/12/06, 13 years
Hometown: Littleton

When did you start drinking or using drugs, and how did it progress?

I was 12 years old and living in Connecticut. It was at a wedding where a family member was getting married. No one was paying attention. My cousins and I were running from table to table drinking whatever we could. I got drunk, and no one seemed to care. I don't know if they thought it was just this one time, but no one stopped me. I loved the buzz. There was something inside me that enjoyed the feeling of euphoria.

The next time I drank, I was 14. I was with some kids from school. Someone found a way to get a couple of six packs of beer and asked me if I wanted one, so I took it. Again, I got drunk. I can't remember how many I had, maybe around five beers. My dad was coming to pick me up that night, and nothing terrible happened. I didn't get in trouble. If my father knew, he didn't mention anything.

After that night, I felt as if I fit in and had friends. I couldn't wait to do it again. I thought, wow, this is awesome. This alcohol thing makes me feel good. I can go out, socialize, have fun, and nothing terrible happens. A couple of weeks later, on a Friday night, I found a way to get alcohol. I was starting to actually look for it. There were ways to get it because the drinking age was 18, and we knew someone who was 18. I tried to get it every weekend but only got it two or three times a month. My illness slowly progressed, and I didn't even notice.

By the time I finished high school, I was drinking every weekend. There wasn't a weekend that went by that I wasn't drinking. By my senior year, I was drinking on weekdays too. Sometimes I skipped school and drank all day. There were a half a dozen days where we blew off school to hang out with friends and drink.

I went off to college in Vermont. I made my decision to go there based on alcohol; the drinking age was 18. In Connecticut it had changed to 21. Once I was in college, my drinking picked up. I did well in the first semester but drank weekends and most days of the week. Eventually, it turned into an everyday thing for me. I was drinking anything I could get my hands on, mostly beer. Hard liquor was involved sometimes, always something cheap. It wasn't uncommon for me to take exams or write papers while I was high. My grades were affected by it all.

After college, my drinking continued to get worse. When I drank, it was always to the point of getting drunk. I was blacking out and passing out. I was also smoking pot any chance I could.

I moved back to Connecticut and lived with my parents for a

while. People were concerned and started to talk to me about my drinking. My parents spoke to me about going out every night. Friends also tried talking to me about it. I was drinking hard. I didn't want to give up partying and be responsible.

I decided I was going to quit drinking for a little while and managed to stop for about two and a half months. I wouldn't say I was sober because I smoked marijuana the whole time. I didn't try and seek out recovery; I just wanted to shut people up. On the day I stopped, I planned the day I would start again. I went back to Vermont for the weekend to be with my college friends and picked up right where I left off.

I spent a couple more years at home, and then my brother was going up to Vermont. I wanted to get away, so I went up there with him. At this time, I was 24 years old and couch surfing. Winter was coming; we got jobs at a ski area, and my drinking was off the charts. I was drinking every day, and every time I drank, I was blacking out and passing out. I got a job as a snowmaker. The first day on the job, when the shift ended, the guys said they had a keg over in the maintenance shop. Everyone there partied, even my bosses would drink with us. I was drinking with these guys every day after work. I was going into work hungover the next morning or still drunk. I always managed to keep a job though. I had to support myself.

I was driving to work one day after leaving the bar and got a DWI. I don't know how I didn't kill anyone. I don't remember driving, and I don't remember leaving the bar. Someone called the police. I fell asleep while driving, crossed the road, and smashed into a brick wall near a store. I totaled the car and got arrested.

Going through the process of trying to get my license back started to wake me up a bit, but not enough to quit drinking. The DUI agency made me go to an AA meeting and write a paper about it. I listened and tried to pay attention. I managed to go to that meeting sober, then walked right out of the meeting and into a bar. The meeting put the thought into my head that if I ever did feel like I had a problem, I had a place to go. At 26 years old, I had no intention of stopping drinking. I went right back into my old habits, and I tried to control it and couldn't. I drank every night for another few years.

In the summer of 1999, I got another DWI. I was leaving the same bar. Now I knew things needed to change. I knew I needed to quit. That night I knew I was done drinking. The thought got into my head that if I didn't stop drinking, I was going to kill myself or someone else. I didn't care too much about myself, but the thought of killing someone else stopped me. That thought stuck with me, and I stopped drinking. I thought that if I just put the alcohol down, then everything would get better. I didn't know marijuana was a problem, so I continued to smoke it.

I didn't have to go to court for the DWI. Although I was arrested, the court dropped the charges. I guess the police never turned in their paperwork. For the next six years, I smoked weed, not even thinking about recovery. I eventually quit marijuana. I was getting more physically active, going to the gym, and starting to run. I just decided to stop. I got to a point where it wasn't doing anything for me anymore.

I ended up in a relationship with a girl who was struggling with alcoholism. She went into AA and relapsed, so things were rough with us. I also had a friend at work who was in AA, so I started to open up to him about my struggles. He told me to go to AA and to see what it does for me. After two weeks, I went. I didn't want to ask for help. I was trying to stay sober on my own and couldn't figure it out. I didn't know what else to do, so I went to AA.

Life today is so much different. I know how to deal with life and back then I couldn't.

Looking back, when do you think it was mostly out of control?

The three years between the first DWI to the second DWI, when I was trying to control it.

How are you able to not drink or use daily?

I stay active in my recovery process. I am always in touch with a higher power; it helps me stay calm and gives me inside strength to move through things. It helps me know that it will be okay one way or the other. I still go to meetings to be reminded of what I need to be doing daily. It also reminds me of what life will be like if I ever pick up a drink again. It's where all my friends are.

What is your thought about medication-assisted treatment?

I am not for it. I am in recovery and work with a lot of people, both personally and professionally. I see it doing more harm than good. The percentage of people who use the medication the way they are supposed to is small. The others are either abusing it or relapsing. I see too many people on it for too long. They are too afraid to get off it because of possible relapse or withdrawals, so they choose to stay on it forever. The people that do get off it, typically need to get into detox to do it. We give a drug to get off a drug and then have to detox them from that drug? It doesn't add up and only prolongs real recovery.

Is there anything you want those struggling with addiction to know?

There are ways to recover. Go to self-help groups, seek out counseling, sober houses, and intensive outpatient programs. There is a way to get and stay sober without having to use any chemicals. Find whatever works for you.

Tracy S.

Date of interview: 4/29/2019
Sobriety date: 10/26/01, 17 years
Hometown: Woodstock

When did you start drinking or using drugs, and how did it progress?

I was 14 and drank wine out of a plastic cup; I wanted to be a lady. I drank the whole bottle and was throwing up by the end of the night. One night, I made out with three different guys. This was not something I did when I was not drinking. The next day my friend reminded me of what had happened, and I remember that pit of a feeling in my stomach.

In the beginning, it was just here and there and a drink or two. I used to be upset because I would see other people drinking more, and I'd have two, and I'd get buzzed. I started smoking pot at about the same time. In high school, we moved up here from Lynn, Massachusetts, and I was drinking on weekends. I started drinking to get drunk, and I always did things I regretted when I was drunk. I smoked pot and started using cocaine too. I used mescaline and acid a couple of times. I think I tried everything once. My babysitter gave me my first hit of mescaline when I was 15.

My drinking and using progressed after graduating from high school. I didn't go to college, but I would party at colleges on the weekends. When I was 19, I moved to San Diego. My use took off out there. I got into using crystal meth and got a DWI when I was 21. At this time, I got sober for a year and went to a 12-step program, but I wasn't sure I had a problem. The first night that I drank again, I wrote in my journal; I'm not an alcoholic, this is awesome because I can have one drink. Not long after that, I was back at it. From age 22 to 24, I used cocaine, crystal meth, and drank. One year I used crystal meth every day straight.

My friends and I started a company while using crystal meth. I used to cut out the shoulder pads on my clothes when we were traveling on airplanes and put crystal meth in them. I needed the meth to keep up with the business. It was go, go, go.

After my parents' house burnt down, I came back to New Hampshire. I was 25. I started working, met somebody who did drugs, and got right back into cocaine again. That relationship lasted about a year. By the time I was 26, I was drinking daily and started taking pills: Percocet and OxyContin. In the beginning, I was taking them one to three times a week, just for a good time. Then it turned into one a day. I wanted more, but it was hard to get.

Abusing opiates was just starting to get big. I ended up moving back to Lynn, Massachusetts, and that's where my drug use took off again. I was doing OxyContin and cocaine, sometimes together. It lasted a year and a half. I drank and took pills all the time. I just wanted a way out from feeling empty inside.

On October 25, 2001, I popped an Oxy at eight a.m., went to Concord, and ended up in a bar. I popped another Oxy and was flying high. I had to get back home because I was babysitting for my nephew, who was 12 at the time. I flew back from Concord, high as a kite, and picked him up at school. I bought a bottle of wine and took him to celebrate at a bar. I continued to drink while I had him there. Luckily, the bartender called my sister-in-law to come to get him. I blacked out that night. The next morning, I woke up, and I was just done. My sister-in-law came over—she is a wonderful person—and told me she was so disappointed in me. Those words crushed me. I just said to myself, "I can't do this anymore."

Looking back, when do you think it was mostly out of control?

California, because of the crystal meth. The pills were also magic to me. That high was so amazing. However, I had to take more and more to keep that high. I could have been dead at any point.

How are you able to not drink or use daily?

I live in recovery and help people. I work in the recovery profession, so recovery is around me a lot. I go to a lot of meetings, once or twice a week, and I meditate. The more I meditate, the better it is for me. My connection to God is huge.

My husband is in recovery as well. I believe we have a good foundation at home, and we practice our principles. I stay close to a lot of sober people and I work out with a group of ladies who want more out of life.

What is your thought about medication-assisted treatment?

I've tried to think it might be useful for some people, and I want to believe that it can be, but what I've seen is that it's not working. Those who are on medication are not finding a way to live life without anything in their system, so how can that be sober? How can that be experiencing life in on life's terms? People are afraid to get off substances. They can do it without anything.

Is there anything you want those struggling with addiction to know?

I want them to know they can stop drinking or using. There is hope if you give yourself that chance. I don't know the magic words, but I want them to know that they can do it. You have to want it. Some days are hard, and things happen. Stay, though. By just not drinking or drugging, one day at a time, you can live this life better. You have no idea what's in store for you. Give yourself that chance.

<u>**Vanessa B.**</u>

Date of interview: 5/24/19
Sobriety date: 11/7/05, 13 years
Hometown: Lebanon

When did you start drinking or using drugs, and how did it progress?

I was 12 years old, and it was pot. There might have been a sip of booze before then, but it wasn't enough to put me in an altered state. Once I discovered an altered state, I liked to be in it. My brother and I both enjoyed the altered state; he too is a recovering addict. We grew up in Raymond, New Hampshire, which became the drug capital of the state. There were a lot of hard drugs around. From when I was 14 on, we did crazy stuff. I remember having PCP on a joint and thought I could fly. I almost went up to the roof of my friend's house to demonstrate I could fly.

I started dating a drug dealer and eventually married him at age 17, which was convenient. We sold cocaine, so there was a lot of free coke. Ages 17 through 19 were my cocaine years. I didn't weigh very much, because I didn't eat very much. When I was 20, I wasn't feeling happy in my marriage and decided that a cocaine life wasn't really for me. I had my dalliances and started to drink heavily. I put on some weight because of drinking. I drank to get obliterated as I had a tremendous feeling of emptiness. I was searching for something to fill up a space within me.

I ended up getting back with my husband, and we moved to a different town. I thought children would make a difference for me, so I got pregnant. I was using right up to the moment I discovered I was pregnant and then, boom—everything shut off. I had two children, no alcohol, no drugs, no nothing. These children were my entire life and still are.

I went for six years only drinking a glass of wine or a mixed drink now and again. I had no compulsion to use but still felt an emptiness within and wasn't happy in my marriage. I went back to work full time, earlier than I should have. I worked in a pharmacy, so there were drugs at my disposal. I dabbled in them a fair amount but would still classify them all as "recreational."

I had a sudden life change when I met a woman and fell in love. She was cuckoo crazy and thank God I didn't end up with her permanently. I left home and moved to where I am now to continue working at the pharmacy. The whole transition from being with men and then being with women was not easy for me. I didn't know what I was doing, I was baffled, my family was mad at me, and I felt miserable. I started to buy larger bottles of less expensive wine so that I could drink more. Cocaine came back in, a lot of alcohol, pot, and then the pills.

I took Percocet once in a while in the earlier days. When that and other opiates stopped being available, I went to the Fioricet. When I took enough, the effect of the butalbital was quite nice. I got prescriptions for a while, but to support the habit, I got it right at work. It was available on the shelves; no one realized you could get so high on it. I was 32 when everything hit the fan, and my life became unmanageable.

There was a guy in a 12-step program who worked in the back room of the pharmacy, the supply guy. He didn't drink and was in recovery. He would talk to me about recovery from time to time. I went to some NA meetings but still struggled, and my partners changed, which was extremely emotional. I wasn't healthy and was never with healthy people.

At some point, I decided to go to Quitting Time, which is an outpatient program over in Wilder, Vermont. I went willingly, but my attitude in the group had me seriously dragging my heels. Before I was to start the program, I had my last two beers. I remember saying, "I'm going to be bored for the rest of my life if I can't use." Using always accentuated something good and decreased the pain of something terrible. It was still useful at good and adverse events. It was a big part of my life.

Eventually, a switch happened in my mind, thanks to a good LADC at Quitting Time. I went to AA and NA meetings, got a sponsor, and learned a lot. I relapsed once at six months clean but was honest about it. Since then, I haven't looked back. I go to meetings, and I'm committed to recovery. Things have indeed changed; my life today is so blessed.

Looking back, when do you think it was mostly out of control?

When I was 32, my pill use was horrible. I couldn't stop. My life was unmanageable. I would wake up every morning and say I'm not going to take those pills off the shelf. I could not control picking them up and ingesting them. I was a basket case.

How are you able to not drink or use daily?

It's the 12-step program that saved my life. I stay connected to people in recovery and go to one meeting a week for professionals. If I get squirrelly or there's a life event that's upsetting, I will go to AA or NA. The 12 Steps are a guidebook for life. I also connect with my Higher Power and practice the 10th step daily.

What is your thought about medication-assisted treatment?

I worked in a clinic that prescribed Suboxone. Quitting cold turkey is difficult for some, and I've seen people suffer from it. It is kind of magic what taking a dose of Suboxone will do to the symptoms of diarrhea, sweats, and shaking. Some people want to get off heroin. They realize that their lives have become unmanageable and don't want to be on something for the rest of their lives.

Some people want to take another drug—a legal drug—there's no question about that. Some people have a co-occurring disorder and may be on it for the rest of their lives. That's harm reduction. They're not using heroin, and they're together enough not to harm themselves or others. I've seen it work, so I have to go by my experience. If you'd asked me before I ran a treatment clinic, I would have said no way, you're taking one drug and replacing it with another.

The Vivitrol shot is another option. It's crazy that it costs so much.

Is there anything you want those struggling with addiction to know?

Put your best self forward. You can become a better person in recovery. Develop a conscious contact with a Higher Power and connect with this Power. You may find this out in nature, by running in the woods, or riding a bike. Go to meetings and build a community support network.

Zachary B.

Date of interview: 6/7/2019
Sobriety date: 6/30/13, 5 years
Hometown: Hooksett

When did you start drinking or using drugs, and how did it progress?

I was eight years old and living in Maine. I was getting into mischief and had a lot of room to roam around because we lived on a large farm. Then we moved to Rochester, New Hampshire, and the first time I got drunk was a year later at a wedding. I was drinking other people's drinks on the table when they weren't looking. I didn't get caught, so there were no repercussions. I didn't get sick or black out.

I've always been short and would get picked on for it in sixth and seventh grade. I remember always wanting to fit in. I started skateboarding at the public library with a group of older kids and got validation from them because I was a good skateboarder. One day, I was in a treehouse, and a friend pulled out some weed, and we smoked it. I ran through the woods, laughing, and had a good time. Everything changed when I went to high school and had a lot of friends. I went to a private high school and played sports: hockey and football. Life was good. I was the only one in my freshman class who used drugs. I was considered the bad boy. In my sophomore year, everyone was doing it. My drug use wasn't affecting anything yet.

When I was 15, my friend, whose father had terminal cancer, stole some of his father's OxyContin and asked if I wanted some. He sold it to me for $15, and I did it that night. I got super sick because I did almost all of it. I thought opiates were not for me. However, it opened the door for me to try other drugs. I was doing Percocets and random pills during school. I smoked weed every day and drank on the weekends.

In my junior year, I got in trouble at school for being high at a school dance and got suspended. My parents had me talk to a psychiatrist who thought I might have ADD or ADHD and prescribed Adderall. My life drastically improved on Adderall for a short time. I was a straight A student on Adderall with minimum effort. However, I abused Adderall very quickly. I started sniffing it and told my doctor it was wearing off in the middle of the day. Within three months, I was taking 90 mg a day. I barely ate and wouldn't sleep. My friends and I would sniff it on the weekends, stay up, smoke weed, and drive around.

After graduating from high school, I went to Plymouth State University with my best friend. I made it for three semesters, got put on academic probation, and gave up. Friends at Plymouth introduced me to cocaine and Ecstasy. The big thing for me was cocaine and alcohol. People around me could do it, turn it off, go to school, and get their stuff done; I could not. When I came home, I was a mess. I told my parents I had been doing cocaine for the first three semesters. They put me in substance abuse counseling and tried to push residential treatment on me, which I was very good at avoiding.

At 20 years old, I enrolled in the University of New Hampshire. I had a steady job and was still drinking. I ran into a friend, and we decided to get some cocaine. We went to buy it off my friend's uncle, and he cooked us up some crack. I took my first hit and thought it was the greatest thing I'd ever done.

I smoked crack every day after that. I stopped showing up to work, and within a month, I started shooting it. Within a month, I was shooting cocaine and heroin. I stopped going to UNH and was a full-blown heroin addict. I was one of those users who didn't sleep. I was using seven grams of crack a day, shooting up four to five times a day. It was a 24/7 cycle. I stayed up for 22 days one time. You need a lot of drugs to do that. I was hallucinating all the time.

When I was 22, my dad picked me up after I hadn't been talking to him for a long time. I hadn't showered in days, was on the run, and had been arrested for my first narcotics possession. He picked me up and brought me to treatment. It was a 30-day program on Cape Cod. I walked out after three days and was shooting cocaine again.

My buddy took me under his wing and taught me the ins and outs of being a junkie. At age 23, I overdosed. I remember being in the back of an ambulance and gasping for air. They brought me to the same hospital where my dad and mother worked. When they brought me in, I had aspirated so much of my fluid that I had aspiration pneumonia. I was hooked up to a ventilator for three days and was in the intensive care unit for another seven days. I remember physicians and counselors coming by to talk to me about treatment, and I told them I was okay. I walked out of that hospital, shot dope for three days, and disappeared again.

I had another warrant out for my arrest and decided to go to the methadone clinic. I got on methadone and showed up at court. I started working a regular job and saving a significant amount of money. I was shooting a ton of cocaine while I was on methadone. When my friend's probation officer came over one afternoon, we had needles all over the place. We both got picked up that day, and I ended up going to jail for six months on a probation violation. I was only on 70 mg of methadone at the time, and it took 33 days to detox. I didn't sleep, and I would sweat through two sets of clothes a day. I would never have gotten off methadone had I not gone to jail. I am grateful for this. In minimum security, I was eligible for work release. I would work until four and then get dope. I was bringing dope into the jail and left the jail with a significant dope habit.

One night in 2011, I decided I couldn't do it anymore. I showed up at my parents' house, went down into the basement with a gallon of whiskey, and drank myself stupid for two weeks to detox. After that, I started going to the Suboxone clinic and didn't use other drugs for 11 months. I never went and got psychological help. The underlying issues were causing me to use, but the Suboxone took care of my cravings for other opiates. I started working, paying bills, and having relationships with my family. It was an enjoyable year.

Then I got bored. I started doing crack again, shooting dope, and selling my Suboxone. My parents began to notice a change. I was arrested in Lawrence on my birthday on my way to pick up drugs. I didn't show up to court and went on another year-long tear. I got heavy into bath salts and shooting them up.

My brother-in-law knew I had a warrant out for my arrest and said he would drive me to turn myself in. He drove me there at two a.m., and I turned myself in. I was smoking spice and doing other drugs while I was in jail. However, I did start to pray and convinced my parents to bail me out. They allowed me to stay in the basement of their new house as long as I got into a program, so I did. In August of 2012, I was walking home from a new job, saw some guys looking into cars to break in, and said to them, "Hey, let's go do some drugs." I didn't even know them and went with them to shoot cocaine. At Christmas Eve dinner, I nodded off into my soup bowl.

In March, I experienced the worst detox ever. My parents tried to get me into treatment, but they finally kicked me out and put me up in a lodge in Manchester where people went to get high. I went on an absolute bender. In the third week of June 2013, I was in the hotel, looked around at the people, the situation I had put myself in, and something came over me. I was now the guy who was showing the younger kids how to shoot up. I realized I had enough. I grabbed this kid's cellphone, called my mom, and told her I would go to whatever treatment she wanted me to. I just wanted help. She said, "I'll pick you up right now." I had to have one last score, so I had her pick me up the next morning after I shot my last bag.

My mother made me call Teen Challenge. She and my father said I needed to be in Teen Challenge within a week. They gave me a week to get my physical and TB tests in order, and I was supposed to detox that week, but I left every day and got high. I went into Teen Challenge the following Monday and stayed for 15 months. I did 11 months after that as an intern, and then they offered me a full-time job. I have been here for six years and manage academic life. I finished college on May 16th of this year. I'm taking the MCATS and planning to go to medical school. I've always wanted to help people and genuinely think I was meant to do this. Drug use is not an option for me today.

Looking back, when do you think it was mostly out of control?

The worst of it was from when I was 19 years old until I was 27. There was no fluctuation in how bad it was.

How are you able to not drink or use daily?

I have support from God first. I read the *Bible* every day, pray, and have people in my life who are counselors. I have an incredible support network that ministers and mentors me. The other aspect of it is service. My job here provides an excellent platform for me to serve all the time with people who are walking the same path I have. We serve the homeless and try to figure out diverse ways to help people. I exercise, run, and lift weights. I read self-help books and literature to help me become a better person: Dale Carnegie, *Dysfunctions of a Team*, and *Life-applicable Skills*. I meditate as well.

What is your thought about medication-assisted treatment?

Medication has its place in treatment. I believe there are a lot of great doctors who want to help people.

Is there anything you want those struggling with addiction to know?

It's never over; you can always get clean. I've seen the worst of the worst, and their lives change through recovery. It's still possible.

PART 3

Providing Cairns for Others

Cairns are stacks of rocks hikers leave on a mountain trail to keep others from getting lost. Just as hikers help each other, people in recovery need to leave a trail of solutions for those who want to abstain from substances. Speak up when it comes to laws and rules regarding addiction. It is imperative that our local, state, and federal representatives hear from people who do not use addictive chemicals in recovery.

We must influence political parties to make the right decisions for those who suffer from a SUD. Just as you vote for an elected official or spend time as a jury member, you can help people in positions of power understand recovery and make changes happen within our government system. They work for us, and many do care about what we think, so don't hesitate to provide information. They need to hear from us, whether it is through a legislator reading this book, or from you directly.

Like hikers leaving cairns, let's leave the legacy of our lived experience for legislators, so others will have a chance at abstinence-based recovery. Use the stories you have read and the following compilation of data to bring about change.

Anonymous I

You will never stop this crisis until you send financial help directly to the people who are suffering. Use a bottom-up approach, and you may get this addiction crisis under control. Giving millions of dollars to agencies who have money is not the answer. Give it directly to the clients, homeless shelters, case managers, therapists, and recovery coaches. Have an accountability person in charge of making sure money is spent correctly.

Anonymous II

Twenty years from now, we'll have the discussion we had in the '90s about over-prescribing pain medication. We'll discuss how we pushed MAT and how subdued the nation is with another pharmacologic pill that takes the life out of people. Suboxone takes away desires and the ability to be a human being. It blocks you from feeling the emotions required for the human experience. Put money into abstinence-based programming and subsidize abstinence-based sober living.

Anonymous III

Get educated more on addiction. Shaming people into stopping isn't working. Look at the way drugs are coming into the country and change that. Look at how medication-assisted treatment is either helping or hurting. Keep track of people staying on medication or being taken off. Fully inform people about the medicines before giving it to them, instead of just giving it to them. Look at what's working and what isn't for the sake of our children and grandchildren. Learn from those that have walked the path of recovery.

Abraham S.

The war on drugs doesn't work. It's like cutting off the head to cure the headache. America imprisons more people than any other country in the world, any other country in the history of the world. We have more prisoners in custody than China does right now. More prisons are built in this country every year than universities. The war on drugs is how you get elected to Congress or office. From 1980 to 2010 were to be the years we were hard on drugs on both sides of the aisle, but here we are. Sheriff's departments, police departments, task forces, FBI, and DEA, they all run on this idea that they need more money to fight the war on drugs, and if they don't have a budget that exceeds last year's budget then their budget will be cut, and no department head wants their budget cut. My brother is a cop, and one time he walked into a meeting in the morning, and the sergeant said, "I want each one of you to write and execute a search warrant by the end of today." Decriminalize all drugs. Invest in treatment. Work to battle drug addiction rather than incarceration for non-violent offenders.

Adam S.

Stop pumping money into the police and the correctional industry. That's where all the money is going. We cannot lock this problem away. The success rate comes with recovery; recovery is where the money is needed. Recovery is the solution. We can't keep locking these people away; you just become a better criminal. There's no rehabilitation in jail. Don't get me wrong, the police deserve what they need, but signing bills into law that give all the money to correctional institutions isn't the way to go. Combine corrections with recovery; this is what's starting to work.

Albert L.

This NPR story will help lawmakers understand: A woman police officer came across a young woman in a parking lot who was drugged up. Instead of interrogating her or arresting her, she said, "Can I help you?" This woman had lost everything, and she was near death from all the drugs she was on. The woman said to her, "No, I think I'm beyond help." The police officer, instead of arresting her, gave her a business card, and said, "If you need anything, give me a call, and I will help you." A week went by, and the officer got a call from the woman. She started bringing the woman to meetings and eventually to detox. The woman is now five or eight years sober. Instead of leading with a threat, lead with an offer.

Allen P.

Addiction is a treatable and preventable condition. It's a lot cheaper to treat it and prevent it than correct it. We spend a lot of money on corrections and law enforcement by trying to build a structure that makes the use of toxic substances not okay. It's a lot cheaper to teach people how to feel enjoyment and correct their problems.

Amanda B.

Drug addiction starts young. Start working on prevention in preschool and teach social skills. Stop looking at what is politically correct and instill old fashioned ethics. Work is its own reward— base rehabs on abstinence and a good work ethic. I don't know anyone who stacks wood or weeds a garden who doesn't find it rewarding when they sit back and look at it. It is lovely to put them in class and have them do paperwork, but it's not the same as being out in nature and playing with dirt. Children need to play outside. They need to feel like there isn't a judgment, and that they do measure up.

Angela J.

Making the workforce proliferate by reducing qualification requirements is not part of the solution. I feel lucky to have been born in a place where lawmakers can hear my voice. I'm grateful to those lawmakers who listen to the stories of people in recovery and their families and translate those stories into solutions to help these systems work better.

Arvid D.

Put more money into treatment. Stop locking people up for stuff they can't control. I have a lot of charges because I was sick. I wouldn't normally do these things if I were sober. I know a lot of people who are suffering and are punished for it. Their disease isn't treated, and they're treated like a criminal. It's wrong. You can't fix this with jail time. Charging people with felonies and ruining their lives is only making the disease worse. It's only making the problem worse. By the time they do get help, they may be a multi-time felon. I have so many felonies; I can't get a good job. I can't make good money. It takes seven years after a felony charge to get a decent job. It's hard.

Barry T.

Addiction is a treatable disorder. We know how to treat it. We have the tools, but we don't have the financial resources. Prioritize addiction treatment and recovery.

Bonnie B.

There are a lot of unseen and unknown healers in the halls of Alcoholic Anonymous and other programs like it. There are a lot of healers out there who are not of a professional variety. Our jails need to be free of people who are addicted and are not criminals. Let AA and other programs into your prisons to help detect who is a criminal using the system, who is addicted, and who needs help.

Bonnie T.

A Band-Aid, a quick fix, is not going to fix addiction. No drug is going to help someone recover for the rest of their life. Maybe short term but not for life. People need treatment, education, therapy, and support meetings.

Bruce B.

Listen to the people who are now sober. Get the dealers. When we were moving drugs, the guys wore suits. We took all the risks. If you take down the head person, the others can't survive.

C.S.

Make recovery centers more accessible for more people and for longer duration. Twenty-eight days doesn't work. People need support throughout a year. It gives them a chance to get grounded with a life without alcohol or other drugs.

Cheryl K.

The country is a mess with addiction and poverty. You are not listening. I have a hard time believing you are on our side. People are reaching out for drugs because they don't know what direction they're going in. People aren't feeling safe anymore. You need to stop fighting against each other. There's just too much tension. Sensitive people feel this. You need to get along and have regular meetings, not all this back and forth. How can people grow up with no trust and bickering, especially if it happened in their own family? It seems to be happening everywhere. You need to get along and set an example for the state, the nation, and the world. You need help. Education is key. Have addiction classes in school. Kids have to know that there are resources out there. There are needles on the streets nowadays. Kids need to know about these things.

Dan L.

Listen to the people, not the deep pockets. A lot of legislation passed through because of financial backing, and people are dying. We can't Band-Aid this. It takes a village. The opposite of addiction is a connection. We need to create opportunities for this to happen.

Dana P.

Instead of investing money in legal drugs and keeping people walking around like zombies, invest that money in beds, rehabs, and programs that can help people reclaim their lives. My daughter is walking the street without anything because the shelter is full. She said to me, "I have nowhere to go. I have no clothes, no food, and no money." Without insurance, there's no help. People on the street have no options. Legal methadone and Suboxone clinics keep their minds mush, and they stay on the streets.

Daniel L.

The disease concept is real: mental, physical, and spiritual. When I was not drinking, I was thinking of it. Physical: once I put the substance in my body, nothing stops me from using it. Spiritual: I did things I never believed I would do under the influence of alcohol and drugs. The game was: how can I get high?

David L.

The drug addict is not necessarily a criminal. The drug addict is a drug addict first and a criminal second. The law isn't going to stop an addict from doing drugs. If you make it accessible and people can go and shoot up in certain places and ask for help, this is much safer. These are people that are mentally sick. Throwing them in jail isn't going to make it better. It's going to make the jails busier.

David W.

I was given a lot of psychotropic drugs in mental hospitals because my wife asked me to see if it would help. I've tried all of these. My disease is stronger than medication. Alcoholics manifest mental problems, but their real problem is pure alcoholism. Until the alcoholic deals with their addiction, they will act out like mental defectives. They have all the symptoms of a schizophrenic or someone with bipolar disorder. We manifest all of this, but it comes from alcoholism. Our solution is the connection with the life of the spirit. I'm a moral and sane person, but you give me drugs or alcohol, and I'll do anything. It's not because I'm immoral; it comes from my alcoholism. Leave us to help each other because we are the most qualified to do so. It's way more successful. There is nothing that comes close to the success of Alcoholics Anonymous. Not even close.

Donald M.

Suboxone is an addictive drug. It still alters your mind, so you are not able to receive proper emotional treatment.

Doug P.

They should become more aware of what opioids and narcotics do to the addicted person. They need to investigate this with a panel of doctors. The public needs to be involved. Find out, statistically, what effects are from doctors recommending opioids and narcotics. A forum on this has to happen. It's irresponsible for elected officials not to be realistic about this.

Dustin H.

Evaluate these medications. Focus on the source of the problem.

Ed G.

What got me in the AA program in the first place were the drunk driving laws, so these laws work.

Ed M.

They need to get educated because there are a lot of ideas and notions out there when it comes to sober housing. They're not talking to the experts when it comes to a lot of this stuff. Talk to people who have been sober a reasonable amount of time. If they want ideas on treatment, we have to bring in treatment professionals and experts. If you're going to talk about sober living and rules for that, then bring in the people that run those programs.

Ed P.

Educate our young people about addiction. We need more help in mental health treatment providers. In the '70s, we were one of the best states for mental health help, and then they took the funding away. Fund rapid response care for children, adults, and mobile crisis units. There are ways to fund this. Young people are dying at ridiculously high rates.

Elizabeth R.

I haven't seen anyone who is on Suboxone or methadone get off and stay off drugs. Don't punish someone with a jail sentence. It is not a deterrent to someone who suffers from this disease.

Eric M.

Instead of listening to people with lived experience, you are looking to people who have learned from a book. People who have lived through addiction and are now not using have more experience than someone who has not. You need to start listening to the right people.

Eric S.

Care about the American people more than you care about the dollars donated to your campaign by the pharmaceutical companies. Please reach out to people who are actually in recovery. One of the biggest problems is that we have an opioid epidemic that is killing more people than car accidents and more people than the entire Vietnam War, and there isn't one person with lived experience of recovery at the table. We got in this crisis by not being adequately represented.

Erin M.

Addiction is a big problem. We need support and not medical support. Addicted people aren't bad people, just sick people who need to get well. Some are people that need help because they have had struggles.

Gary F.

Understand the recovery program. Read the Big Book of Alcoholics Anonymous. It allows us to stay sober without a crutch.

Glenn M.

Heroin addicts have Narcan parties. An addict will overdose on purpose because they have Narcan as backup. When a person overdoses on the street, other addicts say, "Where did he get his stuff?" and they are off to purchase the stuff from the same dealer.

Grant O.

Incarceration isn't the answer. There needs to be a long-term treatment for people to get sober.

Thirty-day treatment isn't enough. Changing behaviors takes 10 to 15 years. We need at least nine-month programs and then transitional living. Incarceration teaches people how to be better criminals and puts a burden on taxpayers. There are still drugs and alcohol in jails and prisons. Legalizing marijuana is not going to lighten up the opioid epidemic.

Jack Q.

I don't know if they can orchestrate how to help people. Look at the people in AA. It works. The spiritual program works.

Jaimie D.

Protect inmates who are having Big Pharma pushed on them when they leave jail or prison. If people have fulfilling lives, they will stop using drugs on their own. Help people find fulfillment in their lives. They don't need another medication; they need jobs and housing.

Jane K.

Jail does not work. Addicts don't need jail time; they need treatment. Treatment is essential. Twelve-step support programs are free, and they work. It is a community of people who stay sober together day by day. We also need more opportunities for people to find sobriety.

Jane S.

The disease of alcoholism and addiction is a "real disease," and there are many pathways to recovery. As a country, we should recognize this fact and make opportunities available to those who seek treatment and make it affordable for those who are unable to afford it.

Janessa F.

You need to realize addiction to drugs is an epidemic. Start paying attention to the fact that people are dying every single day. It's not just one group of people. It's not just homeless people; it's everybody and from all walks of life. There needs to be more funding for treatment programs. Women need more programs, and programs need to be a lot longer than 30 days. If someone has been using for a significant amount of time, you can't take it away in 30 to 90 days; that's not going to help. Programs need to focus on what's going on inside the person. You can't just give them medication.

Janice H.

It starts with the pharmaceuticals. Pharmaceuticals are all about the money. They don't care about what it's doing. We need to stop putting money in their pockets and start cleaning up the mess they've made.

Jasmine L.

There is more than just a physical component. There are underlying causes that need treatment.

Jason S.

Suboxone is being sold on the black market in high quantities and smuggled into the jails in mass amounts. Incarcerations don't work as a deterrence. It creates more trauma and adverse effects on our psyche, which perpetuates a cycle of addiction even further. Jails are privatized. Their survival depends on inmate recidivism.

Jeff B.

Please support those who are fighting addiction and who want help recovering through more programs, facilities, etc.

Jennifer B.

They need to know addiction is not a character flaw; it's not a weakness, it's a disease. It's a public health crisis.

Jesse H.

People in recovery are the most resilient people on the planet. Put money into long-term recovery solutions, not just 28-day programs. Put money into ways to sustain long-term recovery, and it will change the world. A holistic approach is mandatory. Taking into account what we've learned from the positive aspects of meditation, yoga, whole food diets, ancient wisdom traditions, and more, a multi-disciplinary approach is needed. You need multiple disciplines in treatment, instead of just merely using a 12-step model with medication. Relapse today means death for a lot of people. We need to move money into actually studying recovery-based solutions that might not even be evidence-based. Go to the people in recovery, study them, and get into their communities. It's time for a global addiction summit.

Jill K.

Addiction has received a lot of medical attention in the last four years. It's not a new problem, and it's not specific to opiates. Methamphetamines, crack, cocaine, and prescription medications are still a problem. Prescription medication is overprescribed, and alcohol is still a big problem. People need education about alcohol and the dangers of benzodiazepines detox. They need to know what harm reduction is. Educate people about Narcan. You can overdose again without using again—they don't know that Narcan wears off faster than the opiates. People suffer from terrible endocarditis and abscesses because of being afraid to get medical treatment. They're using dirty needles and dirty water. We need needle exchange programs and safe injection sites. People in active addiction need help connecting to people.

Jim G.

Invest more in treatment and treatment providers rather than medical providers. Build infrastructure and treatment for not only substance abuse but also mental health. Stop going to mental health and substance abuse as the first budgets to cut.

Joe K.

Don't treat the symptom, treat the disease. Treat the core issues. Don't waste your time on people who don't want it. You're throwing bad money after bad money. We all carry baggage in different ways, and it needs to be addressed.

John B.

It's easier to use Suboxone or methadone as an answer and to fund these kinds of things because you can measure it. There are documented numbers of people and the drugs they're on at these clinics. I've never seen so many people succeed and ridiculously change their lives until I saw the 12-step program at work. My life didn't change, and I didn't contribute to society until I had the resources to try abstinence-based therapy. I had access to medication-assisted treatment but couldn't get my life together. We need to make this kind of treatment more available. It is much cheaper and easier.

John M.

Don't categorize people as losers, expendable, or worthless. Fund programs that give people opportunities, even though that person may have failed previously. People will have better lives and society would be better if you continue to fund programs that help them.

John P.

There needs to be a combination of discipline and a treatment plan. Someone who committed a crime to get money for heroin should get help instead of getting locked up. We need to implement programs for offenders to look within themselves and find spirituality. Do not remove them from being responsible for their actions and help them find the solution at the root of the problem.

John C.

Spend less money on the war on drugs and more money to long-term solutions. We need a full continuum of care.

Joseph K.

It's not a moral issue. It's a disease that affects our brains. More funding needs to go into treatment centers that are trying to help people. I understand some places manipulate the system. Check on centers and make sure they're doing the right thing. Each person with an alcohol or drug problem should receive treatment, regardless of whether they have insurance. Insurance should not be a barrier to treatment. People who don't have insurance, a lot of times, go without treatment. We need a level playing field. Give those who need treatment a fair chance to recover.

Joshua T.

Support churches and faith-based programs. Let them have the authority to do the treatment they know how to do. Let them teach what the Lord has to say about addiction. The more secular our country gets, the worse it gets. New England is the least churched area in the country and has some of the worst overdose rates.

Jules R.

Go after the pharmaceutical companies and the doctors that are causing this epidemic. They have to pass laws holding pharmaceutical companies responsible for passing out these opioids like they're candy.

Karin B.

If you put people on a maintenance plan with medication-assisted treatment, you're not helping them. They are still high. What does help are tools and life skills. People need to feel and process feelings. We need to work through our fears and anxiety. Rope skills are helpful for this.

Karen P.

Look at the bigger picture. Not all people with a SUD have underlying mental health issues, but some do. People self-medicate by drinking and using drugs. Fix our mental health system. It's not about sending someone to detox or rehab, and they're all better; instead they need support. There is no easy fix. Strengthen the mental health system by not allowing insurance companies to dictate reimbursements for mental health services. Mental health counselors make lower rates than other services. It's a disaster. Increase the amount of money mental health workers get paid. Provide more services for the homeless, housing, and outreach.

Katie N.

Addicts are dollar signs to corporations, like the legalization of marijuana. People want their cut and say things like they are going to use it anyway. I don't think so. Don't commercialize drug use. We need a tighter grip on what people are doing in sober houses too. We're dealing with people's lives.

Kelli K.

Medication is not necessary. It can be a substitute for using. Someone taking Suboxone is not free. Suboxone was the last thing I shot up.

Keith A.

We need more community re-entry services, and there's a lack of support for addicts in jail. When released and monitored, they should attend treatment. The court system needs to change some of the sentencing guidelines. If sentenced for possession, add treatment to their sentence.

K.H.

Addiction is not going to be legislated out. Money is not the answer. Freeing people to do the good work they're naturally drawn to do as people in recovery is a more effective answer. Spend money on recovery that lasts for the rest of people's lives.

Kim C.

There need to be more facilities for women and men. We have people dying on the streets and in cars. It is a disease like diabetes. If they don't get the help they need, they die. Why is it so easy to get drugs? It needs to be easy to get into a treatment center. People don't choose to be an alcoholic or drug addict. If you have diabetes and don't get medically treated, you can die. With addiction, if you don't get medically treated, you can die as well.

Larry G.

I'm not an expert on the drug situation or the ideology of it, but I know people do get better. At one time in New Hampshire, we had more than a dozen treatment centers back in the Beech Hills days. Almost all went out of business. Farnum stayed in by the skin of its teeth. Now they're springing up again. I hope they stay. Some people who are walking around using, with proper access to care, can get better. Some may need a push. Don't give up on people.

Leslie G.

I've had conversations with lobbyists and lawmakers. They know nothing about recovery. They are risking people's lives and don't understand the true nature of addiction. There is a lot of confusion about who an addict is and who is not. A lot of kids are dying. We have this giant situation that makes it look like lots of people are addicts. Lots of people are using these drugs, but not lots of people are addicts, so the real addict isn't getting help. Lawmakers' lack of knowledge is killing people. It's killing people who are addicts and people who are not addicts.

Lewis H.

Please fund education on family dynamics and why people start drinking and using drugs. Drug companies give free education about opiates to doctors as tools, but they're addictive, and the quantities that are out there are absurd. Put more restrictions on the distribution, methods, med seeking, and doctor-hopping.

Lou P

Local police need to know that people incarcerated for drunk and disorderly may need medical attention and not detention.

Mark B.

We need more resources in the northern part of New Hampshire. There are not enough detox facilities, and there is no place to dry out. They have to go to the hospital and can only stay there if they threaten to harm themselves.

Matt D.

Stop making it more and more difficult for people to get the treatment they need. Make insurance and funding work for people to get the help they need and for the length of time they need it. Insurance companies should not be able to cut people off their insurance in the middle of getting treatment. Homeless people don't have insurance, and funding isn't coming to them. They don't have a place to get mail. Life is challenging for them. Many people who are addicts are homeless. Give people a chance to get a life.

Maurine P.

Everyone deserves a chance. Throwing someone in jail is not the answer. Sometimes treatment needs to be mandated, and jail sometimes saves people's lives. Make treatment accessible.

Melissa C.

Non-clinical recovery support services work and are worthy of funding. There will NEVER be enough clinicians. It's messy and disorganized by design, and it's worked for millions of people for almost a hundred years.

Mike A.

Treatment without a plan to mainstream an addict is a waste of time. If we, as a society, don't offer career training and mentoring to folks coming out of jail or prison or who don't have a lot in life, we will see them fail again and again.

M.M.

There needs to be more protection for people in recovery. I've been sober for eight years and still have to be careful who finds out. Why justify making healthy, positive choices if this comes to light to an employer? I run into people at meetings who may tell my employer. Their personal feelings regarding that can personally impact my future. I would like to see a law that protects me. People shouldn't have to fight to make healthy, positive choices. New Hampshire has a skewed mental health system. Medication provided is a breeding ground for substance abuse. While I believe there was something wrong with me that caused my level of substance use, it is by no means helping to over-medicate.

Mona F.

Addiction is a rough road. The primary drug I've seen people die from is heroin.

Nick B.

I think that there need to be more programs for people who can't afford them. There are plenty of programs for people who have money.

Nick W.

Create laws with people who have been through it and know what works, not with people who are in an intellectual space and studying it from the outside. The people who have been through it know the answers.

Paul D.

Use the Shelter First Program. Get people off the streets and give them counseling. Staff apartments 24 hours a day to help people adjust to life and get sober.

Paul L.

There's a battle between insurance companies and the people suffering from addiction and their families. There is a revolving door, and patients are not getting enough treatment. Insurance companies need to pay for long-term treatment to solidify a client's new habits, before they are launched back into society, including high, medium, and low residential treatment and sober living. They put people on medication to avoid paying for residential treatment, which is not a panacea for recovery. Slow down the push toward relying on pills to treat drug addiction. Go back to the basics of changing behavior and addressing underlying causes, which works for people. Recovery via abstinence shows people a better way of living overall. It is the most effective way to help a person become the best version of themselves.

Peter A.

Take a good look at people in jail who are non-violent. They may have substance misuse or dependency issues. They may be productive people locked up who could be doing good and contributing to society. Have compassion. It doesn't get people out of the crimes they committed. Focus on rehabilitation and not locking them up. Addicts are not bad people. There's bad behavior but locking them up will not solve the problem.

Peter M.

People are sick and throwing them in jail or prison systems doesn't help. They don't have a model to adequately support someone who has a physical, mental, and spiritual condition. People need treatment. New models of treatment are emerging, and that's what is going to work. Pour dollars into creating laws that will help and not hurt the people that need help. Leading with education would be helpful as well. Support those who need medically-assisted treatment. People need help; putting them in a cell isn't helping.

Peter O.

AA and NA work. Recovery Centers are useful for helping people in crisis. Mainstreaming those individuals into AA and NA programs is a good practice and may lead to long term sobriety. AA and NA programs are self-supporting and do not tax the system. I'm a former military man. I find myself wondering if we went to war today, would we have enough sober military men and women to get the job done successfully?

Phil R.

The answer comes from people with SUDs who have succeeded in not using. Have them share their experience, strength and hope. You can't throw money at things.

Piers K.

Provide resources that equitably support forms of treatment other than medication-assisted treatment. Consumers need to choose what route they want to take, whether to go by way of medication if it's available or abstinence-based treatment if it's possible. Studies and endorsements by the National Institutes of Health identify yoga as a complementary form of medicine. Insurance needs to pay for alternative medicine and for practices that take you out of the stress response and address trauma. Take power away from Big Pharma so they don't run the show.

Rebecca S.

Have grace on the people suffering from addiction. Longer rehabs need to be the norm. Thirty-day rehabs are not sufficient. Long-term rehabs offer to heal what caused the addiction as opposed to short-term rehabs that just help people stop their use.

Regina B.

It behooves the system of healthcare to listen to those of us in long-term recovery. Those of us with addiction don't need another seat on the Titanic, if you will. MAT is highly abused and keeps the individual who is receiving MAT from meeting their internal challenges, trauma, mental, and emotional needs. Real sobriety is a well-lived life. You know, at the end of life, when you look over it, you will not have had quick attempts to fix problems—a pill for this, a pill for that—but you will have lived well. You will have lived a full life because you dared to live through all your forms of pain, experiencing compassion and trust of yourself and others. You will know exactly who you are. By having a spiritual and meaningful life, because of recovery, you will be prepared to leave this life and move on to the most critical form of the unknown, this thing we call death.

Ronnie O.

Support programs that offer behavioral modifications help build self-esteem and support networks to sustain individuals with sobriety. Help relieve the stressors for those suffering. Build community resources and financial support with basic needs, like sober housing!

Richard D.

Fire and police officers are reviving the same people all the time. They don't understand how they don't get it. People with this illness don't respond to reason. The disease responds to abstinence, that's it. It responds to not having anything in their system, and it takes time. It takes time for the brain to make new connections and reset the automatic thought process. Once somebody puts alcohol or drugs into their system, it becomes a problem. They end up with their drug of choice eventually. Marijuana maintenance might work for a little while, but it's not usually a good outcome. They're functioning, but they haven't changed themselves. They're on medication that's numbing them, numbing their feelings. Watch what happens when they try to come off it: they're trapped. People need to change spiritually.

Robert M.

Please understand that it is so much deeper than somebody putting something in their body simply because they like the way it feels. They're not a scumbag or any other stigma that we place upon addiction, they are suffering souls. If we pride ourselves on being a nation of treating all people equally and justly, make the laws accordingly. Increase the help for people who are addicted and alcoholic. Don't make it political, make it behavioral. The money you're spending on panels and round table discussions needs to go to the streets, the alleys, the parks, and the crack houses. Get people in recovery to show yourself and others the way.

Robert W.

Address addiction early in people's lives, in elementary school. There are a lot of parts to this, from drug manufacturing and advertising to institutions. A lot of different areas need work. Help treatment agencies succeed. Don't just throw money at them.

Russell B.

There is funding from the insurance agencies and the government for medication-assisted treatment. Get some real, measurable studies about the effectiveness of non-medication assisted therapy because it works.

Ruth C.

Lawmakers should step into the shoes of the addicted and try to make a connection with the reality that high functioning alcoholism and recreational drug use are very destructive. It is an unfortunate thing that a whole new and innocent generation is going to learn the hard way. A lot of people do not have the word "commitment" in their vocabulary. With addiction, if an addicted person can arrive at abstinence and learn to have a commitment to sobriety, one day at a time, one week, one month at a time, one year at a time, etc... then they can leave substance abuse and have a better life.

Ryan G.

National and statewide policies of prescribing don't work. We did the same thing with our mental health population. We no longer wanted to pay for treatment, so we put them on medications for diabetes and other treatable illnesses. Help people resolve the problem. When you're first sober, you're not in a normative state and can't make a rational decision. As providers, we need to help individuals make intelligent decisions because they are entirely irrational when initiating treatment. If we keep people on medication, we'll have a different problem a few years down the line when people are still on them.

Sandy H.

We need more sober housing. We need doctors and clinics that genuinely understand what addiction is. Help fund something like that, not pills. My therapy was the 12-step program and other addicts who helped me. Those were the people who went through hell to sober up and to help me. Fund places like this.

Shelley R.

I want them to throw the pharmaceutical companies who helped cause the crisis in jail for the rest of their lives. Take all their money and put it into early elementary prevention and treatment.

Steve I.

Don't overthink it. AA is a simple program. If you over-legislate recovery, you're going to screw it up. When I was a selectman, we had flexible personnel policies. The new selectman came in and put in new strategies. There's no flexibility in these new policies, and our hands are tied. Just because you get elected doesn't mean you're an expert on anything.

Susan B.

Addiction is a public health and social issue. Urgency is needed to help people struggling with active addiction. Emergency response funding is also required. Funding for recovery agencies and programs needs to happen now.

Taylor B.

Addiction doesn't discriminate. It doesn't matter who you are. Passing judgment on people is not acceptable. There needs to be less judgment and more compassion for addicts. There need to be more resources and education for something to change. I tried to get a girl in treatment, and each of the 20 places I called had a two- to three-week waiting list.

Thomas E.

You can't legislate morality. We have to teach people the goodness in life. Insurance companies need to reimburse a minimum of six months of treatment.

Tom G.

People are dying. Medication isn't necessarily the right route to take. Give people what they need.

Tracy S.

There are programs to help people without any medication. Medication use is so out of hand. It's scary to me. I didn't do heroin, but that's all the people I see here now. They're coming in, and they can't get off the medication. They're talking to me, and they're high as a kite saying they want to get off it, and they can't. They want to taper down, but their doctors tell them they're not ready. Some have been on it for years. It's scary, and it's sad.

Vanessa B.

In general, we know New Hampshire is in a crisis. Federal and state funds could ensure immediate access to treatment. I found that when a patient called, they were ready at that moment. If they waited too much longer, we might lose them back to the opiates. I also think private companies might need to be looked at as well because it feels funny that people's suffering makes someone a lot of money. I appreciate capitalism just fine, but that one feels a little strange.

Zachary B.

Utilizing long-term treatment as an alternative option to jail time or probation, for non-violent offenders, should be at the forefront of trying to prevent recidivism and relapse. We have 60 years of data telling us long-term treatment is the most effective, yet we are calling long-term programs "too long." It simply does not make sense.

Epilogue

After you reach a summit and enjoy the scenery, your journey doesn't end. You still have mountains to climb. Be a through-hiker and keep stepping forward. Enjoy the trail laid out in front of you and take time to heal yourself while bringing these stories and the participants with you in your mind. Remember, your recovery is a journey and not a destination.

It doesn't matter where you come from, what drug you used, or how much money you have, we can help you stop drinking or using drugs and stay stopped. It is possible. People in recovery care about you. We know the struggle and defeat and have learned to experience the serenity and peace that comes with recovery. Join us on this journey and feel the love and kindness of others who share this journey with you. We are connected to each other and grateful for the gifts that only sobriety can bring.

As I write to you today, in the middle of Manhattan, I am awestruck by the fact that my partner, who is also in sobriety, is hiking the Appalachian Trail. He is on his incredible journey, and I on mine. We are able to have these adventures because we don't use alcohol or other drugs. We have a connection to God, a bond with others in sobriety, and use the 12 Steps of recovery to heal. When we were in the throes of our addictions, neither of us ever thought we would amount to much. We had dreams and goals, but none were focused on God's plan. Today, I know God has a plan for us and for you. Mine is to bring this book to you. I hope you find it helpful and wish you only the best that life can offer. I also hope you feel empowered by the stories you read and find serenity and peace in your recovery journey.

Resources

Alcoholics Anonymous World Services
475 Riverside Drive, Floor 11
New York, NY. 10115
212-870-3400
http://www.aa.org

Alcoholics Anonymous Online Intergroup - Listing of online meetings from AA Intergroup.
http://aa-intergroup.org/directory.php

Celebrate Recovery
A Christ-centered 12-step program
https://www.celebraterecovery.com/

Narcotics Anonymous
PO Box 9999
Van Nuys, California 91409
818-773-9999
https://www.na.org

Narcotics Anonymous - Listing of online meetings provided by NA.
https://www.na.org/meetingsearch/

Refuge Recovery
https://refugerecovery.org/

Refuge Recovery Online Meetings - Listing of daily online meetings
https://refugerecovery.org/meetings?tsml-day=any&tsml-region=online-english

SMART Recovery International
7304 Mentor Avenue, Suite F
Mentor, OH. 44060
440-951-5357

https://www.smartrecovery.org/about-us/leadership/
Smart Recovery - Message board, chat room, online meetings, and online library.
https://www.smartrecovery.org/community/calendar.php
https://www.smartrecovery.org/smart-recovery-toolbox/smart-recovery-online/

ABOUT THE AUTHOR

Suzanne Thistle, MA, MLADC, began her non-chemical journey in sobriety in 1987, which then led her to become a licensed alcohol and drug counselor. Her professional addiction experience spans over 20 years, and she currently teaches about drug use and misuse at a local university. Her roles have included executive and clinical director of two agencies, manager, and therapist. While serving in these positions, she received the "Legislative Advocacy Award" for addiction professionals and the "Treatment Agency Provider of the Year" award, both from her peers. During time off, Suzanne enjoys being with family, traveling, bike riding, hiking, and relaxing at Newfound Lake.

For speaking, consulting & training requests:

Suzanne L. Thistle, MA, MLADC
PO Box 251, Bristol, NH. 03222
suethistle@hotmail.com

If you have stopped drinking or using drugs as a result of reading this book, please write or email to let me know.

Made in the USA
Monee, IL
05 May 2020